N. C. EDSALL
1984

D0875547

THE CHARITY COMMISSION
AND THE AGE OF REFORM

STUDIES IN SOCIAL HISTORY

Editor: HAROLD PERKIN

Professor of Social History, University of Lancaster

Assistant Editor: ERIC J. EVANS

Lecturer in History, University of Lancaster

For a list of books in the series see back endpaper

THE
CHARITY COMMISSION
AND THE
AGE OF REFORM

Richard Tompson

Professor of History
University of Utah

LONDON AND HENLEY: Routledge & Kegan Paul

TORONTO AND BUFFALO: University of Toronto Press

First published in 1979
in Great Britain
by Routledge & Kegan Paul Ltd
and in Canada and the United States of America by
University of Toronto Press
Toronto and Buffalo
Printed in Great Britain by
Redwood Burn Limited
Trowbridge & Esher

Copyright © Richard Tompson 1979
No part of this book may be reproduced in
any form without permission from the
publisher, except for the quotation of brief
passages in criticism

British Library Cataloguing in Publication Data

Tompson, Richard Stevens

The Charity Commission and the age of reform
– (Studies in social history).
1. Great Britain. Charity Commission – History
I. Title II. Series
361. 7'6'0942   HV248

RKP ISBN 0 7100 8984 8
UTP ISBN 0-8020-2342-8

Contents

Tables

Preface

Through extensive use of the Charity Commissioners' reports in an earlier study, I became aware of their wealth of information, and I became curious about the lack of a historical study of the Commission. In pursuit of the reasons behind this commission, the greater void in the whole area of Royal Commissions of Inquiry became evident, and that condition has governed the shape of the present work.

The focus here is the history of inquiry rather than the history of charity. The Charity Commission was an early and successful instance of the Commission of Inquiry, although it would be misleading to describe it as a prototype, due to the long and varied history of inquiry. However, the elongated career and very full record of the Charity Commission make it unusually apt for a close observation of an inquiry at work.

While the peculiarities of the Charity Commission plainly prohibit generalization of its experience, those same features also raise serious questions about how we have regarded (or disregarded) the operations of such inquiries. This work aims to call attention to the hitherto neglected area of commissions of inquiry as a means of deepening our understanding of the Age of Reform.

It is a pleasure to acknowledge the extremely generous assistance of the staff of the Charity Commission, particularly Miss Sheena Smith, Mr R.L. Till, Mr Alistair Campbell, and Mrs Linda Borthwick. I also wish to acknowledge the help of the University of Utah, both for the financial aid of the Research Committee, and the leave granted for completing this work. Finally, to my wife and children, a note of thanks for their support and encouragement, which made everything possible.

Abbreviations

CJ   Journals of the House of Commons.

LJ   Journals of the House of Lords.

Hansard 'Parliamentary Debates' - here cited under date concerned with volume and column numbers, e.g. 3 June 1818 (38 Hansard 1218). The series number is not cited, as date and volume suffice to locate the reference.

C2   Charity Commission MSS, designated 'Charity 2' (see 'Guide to the Contents of the Public Record Office,' vol. II, p. 50). Cited with box and bundle (or page) numbers, e.g. C2/439/1.

Sessional Papers follow the form of their own index references, with year, volume, and page, e.g. 1818.IV.1. Where the citation refers to papers in the House of Lords Series, the prefix (L) is used. Papers printed before 1801 follow Sheila Lambert (ed.), 'House of Commons Sessional Papers of the Eighteenth Century' (Wilmington, 1975), giving volume and page number, e.g. 46 Lambert 5.

Introduction: Historians
and the Age of Reform

The Age of Reform is one of those clichés which historians use while apologizing for using it. Surely it is sweeping and indefinite, yet that is exactly what it was intended to be. What else could characterize the period of English history which encompassed the fashioning of parliamentary democracy and a civil service, the industrialization of Britain, the decline of aristocratic society, and the rise of science, secularism, and free expression?

But while historians make apologies for the 'age,' it seems they have not shown enough concern for 'reform.' The conscious effort to make a significant alteration in government, either by restoration or by renovation, was the dominant feature of the so-called age. This dynamic process has been rather casually analysed, while great energy has been expended on distracting debates over the influence of individuals (e.g. Jeremy Bentham), the virtues of central vs. local administration, or concepts like *laissez-faire* and class warfare. Consequently, several loose assumptions persist in the historiography of reform. Authors are apt to see their subjects as progressive movements, powered by heroic reform leaders and riding a wave of righteous public opinion. Of course these phenomena (or their symptoms) were present in some reforms, but only rarely together, and certainly not as a matter of course.

One reason why the Charity Commission has never been studied is its thorough nonconformity with these assumptions. In 1818, a Royal Commission of Inquiry was created to examine the educational charities of England and Wales. Its origin was confused and decidedly nonpartisan. The Commission continued in various forms for nearly twenty years, and its work was by any measure a highly significant social reform. However, the apparent absence of agitation, the methodical proceeding of the inquiry, and

1

the undramatic conclusion of its work placed the Commission outside the conventional interpretation of reform.
What is more, the Commission's evolution and operation
failed to fit any other easy interpretation. This was
unfortunate, for it was the earliest and best-documented
body of its kind. Paradoxically, this timing probably
worked against the Charity Commission, for the earliest
histories of reform assumed that the general process began
with the Whig government of 1830, or possibly with the
religious reforms of 1828 and 1829. Of course, no inter-
preter today would accept such a chronology for the Age
of Reform. (1) The reform of Parliament was a principal
issue of politics from the 1770s, even though its discussion was muted from time to time. The great historian of
the 19th century, Elie Halévy, wrote in 1913 that

> historians are too much in the habit of regarding the
> *ancien régime* in England as a solid block which did
> not begin to crumble till about 1832. In reality a
> great reform movement began about 1780, and although
> this movement died down during the anti-Jacobin reac-
> tion, during the last years of the war it was once more
> in full swing. (2)

The achievement of the Great Reform Act of 1832 was the
culmination of a half-century of agitation. It was hardly
the beginning of an era of reform in its own field, while
it may be true that it gave inspiration or licence to
improvements in many other areas.

The Reform of 1832 was once thought to have shaken up
the social composition of the body politic, by causing or
allowing the entry of the middle class into active
political life. Later work has modified that conclusion
but not destroyed it. While the aristocracy remained in
control, it was not the control they had in 1815, not to
mention the 18th century. This underlying shift, whatever
its speed, was manifested in innumerable ways and in all
institutions in society after 1832. The greatest impact
was in government, where, again on the heels of a half-
century of discussion, offices of state were overhauled,
municipal corporations reformed, and even the established
church was probed by an exhilarating breeze of inquiry
and reform. Pressure for these changes had been building
for at least a generation; the year 1832 happened to be
when the main safety valve of reform released, and this
encouraged a brief acceleration in many parallel currents
of reform.

One of the major pressures which was operating, and
which had a history of at least a century before 1832, was
the transforming power of industry. This is not the place
to repeat the oft-told tale of technology and capital and

transport and markets which so fortuitously came together
in the late 18th century. That is still one of the most
dramatic chapters in British history, and historians have
done their best to maintain the drama by debating every
conceivable element of the 'industrial revolution.' One
fact rarely disputed was that industry had a radical power
to alter society. This power was in production for large
markets: profits made the industrialist a man of social
position; mass production brought a radically different
lifestyle to the worker, both in the workshop and as a
consumer. The latter touched all ranks in society - and
ranks were beginning to coalesce into social classes.
This socioeconomic activity was of course another kind of
'reform,' for it was innovation largely outside the control of existing institutions, a collection of alterations
which called forth a series of government acts (themselves
designated reforms) to accommodate new social and economic
conditions.

The shifting of social structure, or rather of the
power centres within it, depending as much as it did on
the impersonal impulse of industry, was a process which
created enormous anxiety on all sides. The defenders of
the old regime foresaw the collapse of hereditary, paternal, deference-based authority, and they feared that most
institutions might go along with it. On the other hand,
radicals planned for a new age when those institutions
would be replaced. Of course conservatives and radicals
both underestimated the durability of institutions. Moreover, while social reform seemed inevitable, there was
never a serious possibility for social revolution. Social
reform took the shape of a host of piecemeal and particular adjustments - outside government and in - and
inquiries and legislation dealt with a legion of 'abuses'
(prisons, workhouses, parish apprentices, etc.). From
about 1830 more attention was given to government-
sponsored supervision in such forms as the Factory Inspec-
tor, the Poor Law Commissioner, the elected borough
councillor and the 'revising barrister' charged with oversight of voter registration. This new government
initiative seemed to portend the demise of old county and
borough power structures but real power remained in the
old governing class until near the end of the 19th century.

In the realm of the intellect, the Age of Reform was
at least as vital as elsewhere. Science, secularism and
free expression were in league with radicalism against
the old order. The century between Priestley and Darwin
was of major importance to modern science, but probably
it was even more important for the relation of science to
society. For it was in the 19th century, with the

enshrining of 'progress' from at least 1851, that scientific inquiry became firmly established as a new orthodoxy.

Long before the Great Exhibition, scientific method was applied to social questions, a process we also call 'secularism.' The prime exponent of this was the great utilitarian, Jeremy Bentham. With his 'felicific calculus' Bentham was ready to calibrate pleasures and pains. This was the impractical end product of his central tenet: that policy was best which promoted the greatest good for the greatest number. If the calculus was impractical, Bentham convinced some contemporaries to examine legal, social and political institutions more critically, with an eye to their efficiency and utility.

An integral feature of scientific inquiry and social criticism was freedom of expression. By the early 19th century, freedom of the press – never the 'constitutional right' it was in the American sense – was beginning to be recognized and upheld in the common law. The crown had exercised its prerogative by licensing, stamping and otherwise regulating publication. This was done with the endorsement of parliament, but during the Age of Reform that endorsement had begun to weaken and disappear. The resulting 'freedom' of expression was vital to reform, for without the capacity to criticize, to publicize, and thus to influence legislators, many reforms might never have been proposed or passed.

The range of acts which fit under the umbrella of reform is too wide to define. In view of the main topic of this book, we will do well to look primarily at reforms of a loosely social and administrative nature. And since our subject is a royal commission which functioned in the 1820s and 1830s, we may focus our discussion of the nature of reform around the first decades of the 19th century.

I

The historiography of reform has seen considerable development since its beginnings about a century ago. All the while, several analytical problems have tested the individual historian, for they are inherent in the general idea of reform. In the first place, reformers sought and shared the appearance of attacking abuses in the interest of the general welfare, so they were assumed to have the support of 'public opinion.' Second, the advocates of reform assumed the stance of heroes struggling against an established opposition, which lent a partisan cast to their activity (or to their own version of events). Third, a reform assumed (at least for its advocates) the

place of a step on the road of 'progress,' and as such it
invited a Whig interpretation. Yet it is clear that the
assumed features did not exist in every reform, and over
the years, more and more students of the subject, having
probed their evidence deeply, have resisted the automatic
acceptance of these assumptions.

One of the most widespread assumptions about reform
was its popularity. The contemporary reformer and the
later historian both were prone to enlist 'public opinion'
in their support. The idea has been nourished by generations of progressive historiography and it has rarely
been suffered to stand critical examination. Yet there
are obvious limitations. In the first place, 'public
opinion' or 'opinion' has been used without a generally
accepted definition, and the 'public' whose opinion is
cited usually turns out to be an elite. Second, the
influence of opinion within elites (not to mention the
space between governors and governed) is extremely difficult to trace in any concrete manner. Third, opinion
was and is readily manufactured; indeed, the whole process
of expression via press, petition and public assembly
merely has the appearance of a democratic process. In
its early days of conflict with 'tyranny,' the process
had some claim to this description, but soon it began to
evolve into the vehicle for competing interest groups
which it remains today. Finally, there were internal
sources of reform which had nothing to do with and might
even contradict 'public opinion.' Most notable were cases
of an internal momentum in administration, reforming
itself for the sake of better operation or self-preserva-
tion.

It was no accident that the early 19th century
developed a concept such as the ruling power of 'public
opinion.' For the idea, which had intellectual roots in
the 17th and 18th centuries, was matured and manifested
in the numerous reforms of the 19th. At the same time
that governmental processes opened up (debates, blue
books) and inundated a hitherto uninformed public, the
active members of all classes took to political assemblies,
newspapers and journals multiplied, and there was a great
amount of talk about 'opinion out of doors' - about what
it was, what it was worth, and what it did or should mean
to the governing process. The consensus *c*. 1800 was
decidedly negative: the governing class should not be
swayed by the rabble, who were no doubt led by unscrupul-
ous agitators. By mid-century a new consensus was emerging which saw popular expression, lawfully and properly
made, as worthy of a hearing provided that it had sufficient sponsorship within doors. This may seem but a

mild step from our present vantage point, but it represented an important change. English liberty had included
the right of protest or petition as a legal custom, not
as a regular part of the political process. It was during
the Age of Reform that opinion went beyond general toler-
ation by the governing class to being a part of the orthodoxy (at least of Liberals). (3) By the end of the 19th
century, major steps had been taken toward popular
sovereignty and more open reception of opinion could be
expected. It was toward the end of that century that the
earliest works on the Age of Reform appeared.

One of the first in the field was Albert Venn Dicey's
'Lectures on the Relation between Law and Public Opinion
in England during the Nineteenth Century.' (4) Dicey had
lectured at Harvard in 1898, and the text of his lectures
was published in 1905 and again in 1914. He was a lawyer
who confessed no historical expertise and had only a
slight command of 19th century history. A Liberal in
politics, Dicey had broken with the party over Irish Home
Rule in 1886, and he was trying to explain in his lectures
what he saw as a dangerous drift away from Liberal
individualist orthodoxy (which he tagged Benthamism)
toward an ominous and undefined danger zone called
collectivism.

On the central matter of 'opinion' Dicey stressed the
uniqueness of England, being a country whose laws were
governed by public opinion, or the 'wishes and ideas ...
(of) the majority of those citizens who have at a given
moment taken an effective part in public life.' Dicey
conceded that 'public opinion itself is, after all, a mere
abstraction; it is not a power which has any independent
existence; it is simply the general term for the beliefs
held by a number of individual human beings.' However,
his lectures persistently ignored the implications of
that reasonable conclusion. Writing of the 'state of
opinion (1760-1830)' Dicey argued that 'legislative
quiescence' was the norm, and 'the changelessness of the
law is directly traceable to the condition of opinion.'
Yet his argument that there was an 'absence of changes in
the law' was plagued with internal contradictions. He
even included a section to discuss 'why considerable
(legal) changes took place during the period of Quiescence.' His answer was that two forces produced change
when there should have been none: on the one hand, 'panic-
stricken Toryism' and on the other, reform.induced by
humanitarianism or 'necessitated ... by the irresistible
requirements of the day.' In this category he considered
the Act of Union with Ireland and a collection of social
legislation. For some reason, laws such as these were
caused by 'the needs of the moment.' (5)

We can understand Dicey's reluctance to invoke opinion here when he moved on to explain the advent of Benthamism. Quiescence was to vanish in 1832, after the English people adopted 'Benthamite Liberalism,' a process which 'had developed slowly and gradually during a period of more than thirty years.' The speed of eventual changes (1832) 'was due to the fact that a slowly developed revolution in public opinion had been held in check for years, and had, even when it became general, not been allowed to produce its proper effect on legislation.' Where does this leave the power of opinion? And who held it in check?

Dicey has had many critics, and the attention he has received has kept his work in a place of prominence far above what it deserves. (6)   Although many have analysed this work, their main interest has been in the presumed antipathy between 'Benthamism' and 'collectivism.' His concept of public opinion, however imperfectly developed, has not been challenged. Instead, many authors have accepted the importance of opinion and in some cases have made the concept more sophisticated. At the same time, renegade opinions of opinion have begun to surface.

A few examples will illustrate the prevalence of the phantom of opinion. G.S. Veitch was one of the early historians of parliamentary reform, and in 1913 his study of the years 1760-1800 assumed the place of a standard work. (7) Speaking of the third quarter of the 18th century, Veitch said 'it was not until public opinion began to be more definitely formulated ... that there was any hope of a serious measure of parliamentary reform.' In the early years of the 19th century 'public opinion was being influenced and educated by virile journalists' and in 1832 reform 'was carried because public opinion demanded it.' (8)

With a much different tone, Simon Maccoby described the force of opinion when he wrote in 1935:

Whigs and Tories alike now (1830s) being subjected almost without intermission to 'a constant and active pressure from without': alike they were moved by it to adopt measures of reform. It is that very 'pressure from without' which calls for definition and for due recognition among the constructive historical forces of the period. But any full picture of Whig and Tory 'reforming' activity recalls other and complementary circumstances. When 'pressure from without' had become highly inconvenient and even positively danger- ous, a modicum of sedative legislative compromise was prepared in which all 'the settled institutions of the country' were most carefully safeguarded ...
'Public opinion,' finally, in the shape of 'The Times'

newspaper and the like, hastened to congratulate an
often dubious, jeering or actively hostile populace on
living in the liberal and progressive era which permitted 'great changes' to take place peacefully almost
every year. (9)

Despite his sneering view of liberalism and his naive con-
spiratorial theory, Maccoby seemed to hold on to a belief
in some sort of valid public opinion ('pressure from
without') which was being cleverly undermined by the
masked villains of 'The Times.'

The stock citation of 'opinion' still crops up. In a
landmark study of reform within the Anglican church,
Geoffrey Best has given us what may be the finest work on
the 18th/19th century church since Norman Sykes. (10)   In
one section on 19th century reform, Best wrote that 'it
was the force of public opinion that more than anything
else precipitated the crisis in church reform.' Indeed,
he found that

Sometime between the end of the French wars and the
formation of Canning's ministry, this new kind of
public opinion became too strong, too vigorous, too
determined, and too largely respectable, to be safely
or even in good conscience ignored. Each man is
entitled to date the pivot of change as he will: it
can only be an impressionistic judgment: 1820 seems
about right. Before that date a conservative might
still think of suppressing or ignoring it without
forfeiting his title to political rationality. Thereafter he had to work with it somehow or other. And
the established church felt this rough cold gale
rising no less than did the government.

The impressionistic judgment applied to more than the
dating involved. There was supposed to be in this case a
qualitative shift in the power of opinion - from a stage
where it could be ignored to a stage where it demanded
attention. Of course the argument is circular: opinion
got attention in the 1830s as never before, hence we are
to assume that the demand was more powerful.

A number of points have been raised over the years as
to the defects in the nature and significance of 'opinion.'
Contemporaries knew it existed, but were unsure of its
merit. In a memorable comment in 1820, Robert Peel
referred to 'that great compound of folly, weakness, pre-
judice, wrong feeling, right feeling, obstinacy and
newspaper paragraphs, which is called public opinion. (11)
Peel stumbled, perhaps intentionally, on a problem which
has refused to go away, namely, how does one define
'opinion'? Historians have been reluctant or unable to do
it. Sheltering behind expressions like 'the needs of the

moment' and 'the mood of the nation' many narrators of the
Age of Reform willingly evaded the responsibility to
explain events and abdicated their function to some cosmic
historical process. This is the more unfortunate, for
their case is plausible. Important contributions were
made to English social and political thought between 1780
and 1830, and Wilberforce, Bentham, Shaftesbury and
Chadwick are names which echo with deep resonance in the
history of 19th century reform. To catalogue and correlate
their contributions, and to assess their impact on the
public mind (or more to the point, on leaders of society)
is an estimable albeit challenging task. But it is more
often the case that authors reconstruct a reform or 'movement' from Acts back to their antecedents; and the latter
often include a presumptive definition of 'opinion.'
When referring to the statute book, Dicey used the nice
lawyer's construction of 'legislative opinion.' Presumably this was the opinion of a majority in Parliament
(or the Commons?) at the time of a given vote. This was
easily, and not accidentally, confused with opinion in
general, from which it was often quite distinct. Indeed,
others have used 'public opinion' as the obverse of
'parliamentary opinion.' The critical point which needs
exploration is the intersection of these two opinions.
Indeed, there can be no better definition of public
opinion than an occasional one, as Dicey seemed to recognize. Another scholar, Joseph Hamburger, recently
explained:

> 'Public opinion' remains amorphous, with no fixed
> relationship to the political process until it is
> articulated so as to give it shape and substance.
> Until this happens, it remains a varied aggregation of
> sentiments, aspirations and dissatisfactions, which,
> with regard to any topic, are held with differing
> degrees of salience, varying degrees of intensity,
> and are justified with varying amounts and kinds of
> information. These 'opinions' are given shape by
> self-appointed spokesmen who formulate the grievances
> and demands of the people on behalf of whom they speak.
> And the plausibility of the claims made by these
> spokesmen is roughly established by their organizing
> large numbers of followers in public meetings and
> associations who apparently endorse and clearly do not
> challenge the formulation of grievances and demands
> uttered on behalf of their chosen 'constituents.' (12)

When forced to define opinion, most historians would con-
cede that they are dealing with a few 'spokesmen' and not
a general 'public.' These individuals more often than
not were members of an elite: churchmen, philosophers,

journalists, and/or politicians. Thus, they may speak for
a public, but its size and scope should be estimated and
the effectiveness of the spokesmen ought to be verified
by some independent evidence.

In the same vein, the opinion of an individual needs
to be accepted by others before it can be called 'public
opinion.' This touches one of the more challenging
problems the historian faces - the definition and attribution of ideas. In general histories this is a problem
frequently avoided. In intellectual history, where it
cannot be avoided, it is seldom solved. No miracle for
its solution can be offered here, but we need to note
the effect of this problem on accounts of reform. For
example, Dicey freely cited 'Benthamism' without a serious
attempt to prove its nature and its limits and its
specific adherents. (13) The rationale for so doing was
his discovery in the statute book of a long list of
'Benthamite legislation.' But in fact this was merely
shifting the ground of the question rather than answering
it.

What influence did Bentham have on contemporaries, and
how are we to locate and measure it? David Roberts looked
for traces of Benthamite influence in the administrative
structure of the 1830s and 1840s. In comparing the
'Constitutional Code' with the several reformed agencies
of government, he found many discrepancies in specific
items. Roberts concluded that:

> The ideas of Bentham had, to be sure, an influence on
> the growth of the central administration. His per-
> ceptive and telling attacks on old institutions pleased
> men anxious for reform, and the coherence and complete-
> ness of the 'Code' excited those few of similar ideas
> who laboriously waded through its formidable detail.
> Above all, it excited those able to see the needs of
> the future. But to foresee future developments, to
> inspire veneration, and to lay down principles that
> justify change, is not always to cause those develop-
> ments nor to govern the actions of those men. The
> Victorian administrative state was a practical con-
> trivance shaped by men of various persuasions, all of
> whom were disturbed at the existence of ignorance,
> disease and misery in their changing society. It was
> a very confused and disjointed state, and in all
> probability Bentham himself, the passionate lover of
> logic and efficiency, would have vigorously disclaimed
> its authorship. (14)

One way we can illustrate the difficulty is with a
specific situation where transmission failed. In his
history of the Treasury, Henry Roseveare pointed out such
a case in 1831.

Lord Althorp's appointment as Chancellor of the
Exchequer had been approved by his mother - 'Jack was
always skilful at figures' - but became an embarrassment to his party, for his budget - ambitious and ill-
considered - was badly mauled and had to be reconstructed. Yet he had been at pains to take the best
advice. He had dined and wined all the experts,
including Hume, Poulett Thomson, Parnell and other
members of the Political Economy Club, and the result
was a poor advertisement for political economy.
Indeed, the Whigs were never able to extract the full
political advantage from their contacts with advanced
opinion. (15)

In short, we may find evidence of communication to highly-
receptive audiences, and still not be able to show
successful intellectual transmission. However, this is
not the end of the perils of opinion.

On the attribution of influence, it is easily forgotten
that 'good' and 'bad' (or positive and negative) influence
can be transmitted with equal facility. We recognize
that good and bad may be ambiguous or arbitrary. Yet if
opinion had one consistent feature, it was that it was
divided. A Bentham, a Cobbett, or an Oastler surely
triggered as many negative as positive responses from
their contemporaries. The ideas which they advocated
(rational penal laws, a cheap press, or regulated working
hours) may now be seen as good. However, that is not to
say that the opposite impression was not transmitted in
the early 19th century. The picture which reform historiography conveys is usually one in which the efforts or
influences endorsed by later generations are studied to
the exclusion of others. As a fair rendition of a state
of opinion this construction is hardly accurate.

Another aspect of attribution arises when we admit
that some 'opinion' was cultivated or manufactured.
Indeed, it is likely that some degree of this feature
came into every case where an individual presumed to
state 'public opinion.' The extreme cases were those
where individuals and groups engineered expressions of
opinion to create or augment an impression of widespread
discontent. In the repeal of the Combination Acts in
1824, for example, it is commonly assumed that the work
of Joseph Hume and Francis Place in arranging testimony
for a Select Committee was instrumental in the subsequent
action of Parliament. A similar experience on a much
wider scale has been detected in the campaign for the
Great Reform Bill. Hamburger has suggested that Francis
Place and Joseph Parkes went beyond publicity and public
speaking. They aspired to influence the general public

and 'were also concerned to shape the beliefs of the
governing class as to what the opinions and feelings of
the populace were ... to create a convincing image of
the populace as being unanimous in its demands and
threatening in its attitude.' (16)   This the radicals
presumably did by speaking to ministers and by publicizing
their assessment of opinion.   This sort of influence is
harder to assess than any other, yet its presence in any
degree demonstrates another pitfall in the general problem
of establishing 'public opinion.'   If it was in some ways
moulded by its spokesmen, the more creative they became,
the less likely we are to find a true 'public opinion.'

One final illusion of opinion underlies all the rest.
That is the notion that opinion had to impinge upon
government from the outside to produce reform.   This
perception prevents adequate recognition of what we might
call public servants' opinion, a phenomenon not common,
but certainly not unknown before the 19th century. (17)
In order to have a reform of government policy or procedure, it was always possible for officials to take the
initiative to achieve those ends.   In our context, that
they did so infrequently is less important than their
power to do so.   While we are on this point, we should
allow for a negative side of internal inspiration.
Roseveare described such a situation in the 1820s under
the heading 'demoralization and reform.'   His point was
that civil service type recruitment 'became a matter of
urgency when demoralization made itself felt in resignations, absenteeism, and flagrant acts of indiscipline.'
This was the paradoxical result of earlier reform:'Spas-
modic and sometimes intensive reforms had been going on
in the Treasury since the late 18th century.   Indeed, that
was the whole trouble, the Treasury was demoralized by
reform.'   Thus, in more than one way, government had the
ability and the incentive to reform itself, which action
was not necessarily connected to any public opinion. (18)

What we have seen suggests that in its conventional
form the invocation of opinion is simplistic and misleading.   There was certainly one way in which the force of
public attitudes was effective in politics, and that was
through the perceptions of opinion by politicians.   Peel's
remarks in which he defined opinion were in a letter to
Croker which dealt with the shaping of policy in the
ministry in 1820.   Although it seems like a reactionary
idea, we may best guess at the force of opinion by
weighing the available evidence of contemporary assessments.   If one is interested in measuring the effect of
opinion on, say, the Ten Hours Bill, it is better to con-
sult the evidence of ministers and MP's, and not the

speeches of Shaftesbury and Oastler. Our best route to
what opinion meant is not through the rhetoric of reform
spokesmen. It is through the reflections and ruminations
of men in politics. It was their task to gauge the attitude of the public, and of course to enact or endorse a
measure of reform. (19)

II

The second danger area in the historiography of reform is
the image of partisanship. There is no doubt of the
existence of political battles for various causes in the
early 19th century. Indeed, they help to explain why the
old-style imagery of reform somewhat resembled that of
warfare (the ultimate in partisan activity). Reformers
'attacked' abuses, and those attacks became a part of
'crusades' and 'campaigns,' which predictably ended in
'victory' when the 'ramparts' of the establishment were
'stormed.' But several flaws prevent us from generalizing
this heroic picture of reform. First, there were often
no clear political party lines on which to arrange
reformers. Next, reform movements were usually less
organized and distinct entities than their names implied.
Further, reformers have generally been the best and sometimes the only source of evidence about a given movement,
creating a biased foundation for our study. Finally, in
a constitutional regime, a reform at some point had to
become the view of a majority. That point might be
reached early or late in the process of reform, but it
had to come. If the majority was a relatively early
development, then there was a very different sort of partisan situation - bi-partisan or non-partisan - but at
least one in which the reform heroes were not underdogs.
    The misperception on the first point is in our expect-
ation that party groups will unite on reform questions.
In the disoriented party atmosphere of 1800-30, positions
for and against the slave trade, corn laws, currency
reform, the poor law, Catholic Emancipation, and parliamentary reform - the biggest issues of the period -
were not clearly drawn on party lines. Nevertheless, the
partisan assumption shows through in writers like Halévy,
whose pioneering work on the early 19th century had to
rely heavily on political sources.
    The Tories were undoubtedly right in insisting that
    the system owed its origin and character to the Whigs,
    and had been constructed to reduce to a minimum the
    authority of the head of the executive over the agents
    of the executive. Sometimes indeed, for instance,

during the early years of William Pitt's ministry, the
Tories had even played the part of reformers. But by
1815 they were pledged to the defence of all the abuses
employed by the 18th century Whigs to secure their
power; for that power was now in Tory hands. It was
the leaders of the Whig opposition who, to storm the
citadel occupied by the Regent's advisers, were batter-
ing to pieces the old edifice of Whig aristocracy. (20)
Of course Halévy simply classified governments, as would
most observers, by what they called themselves. So,
except for 1806-7, there was a Tory ascendancy from 1784
to 1830. But as with the Whig ascendancy from 1714 to
1760, the dominant party could not maintain real discipline. Several factions were more accurate indicators of
real political sympathies. One of the factions contained
the perennial 'men of business' who placed governing ahead
of principles. Lord Liverpool did this task well and was
able to balance and hold together Tory factions. Canning,
Peel and Wellington were unwilling or unable to do so,
and from the late twenties more vigorous partisanship
surfaced within the Tory ranks. Political organization
was in fact fluid, and usually insignificant in the reform
context, even though rhetoric endowed a speaker's opponents with either entrenched power or revolutionary plans.
This phenomenon was detected by Cecil Driver:

> There was nothing inherently unrealistic in the idea of
> a fusion between Toryism and radicalism at that time
> (1832). Shrewd contemporary publicists in the Whig
> camp showed plainly enough by their comments that they
> were far from regarding such a move as beyond the
> bounds of possibility. It is only when considered in
> terms of preconceptions and alignments derived from a
> later age that the suggestions seem at all anomalous.
> Political energies were in an extremely fluid condition
> and there was no certainty about the molds in which the
> they would finally become set. (21)

After the crisis of 1831-2 and until the Second Reform
Act there were still unclear party lines. Outspoken Tory
reformers (Cobbett, Oastler, Shaftesbury) were as much in
evidence as aristocratic Whigs (Grey, Melbourne, Palmer-
ston). The works of reform have thus been treated more
often as the product of 'movements' - e.g. the anti-
slavery movement, the Catholic Emancipation movement, the
Anti-Corn Law League or the Ten Hours' movement. Beside
these well-defined issue-based activities were broader
efforts: parliamentary reform, poor law abolition/reform,
financial reform and legal reform. Factions or individual
members of either party combined, sometimes with radicals,
to press for or against particular measures. (22)

The historian of reform has sometimes been led into difficulty by the partisan assumption's demand for a 'reform movement.' It was the logical manifestation of the outcry which was supposed to precede reform, or perhaps the movement or its leaders generated the moral indignation; in either case, it was implied that the movement was the agency of reform. That this was true for some reforms may be argued, but certainly not for all. The generalized usage may derive from the prevalence of organized bodies in the later 19th century, but clearly such was not the case with the first half of the century.

A movement may be defined as a collection of individuals whose actions are more or less coordinated in support of a policy objective. Movements may have widely varied shape and size, but they share an ability to remain obscure under the treatment of historians. The obscurity of movements is less a function of historical evidence than one of historical conception. One rarely encounters a discussion of what constitutes evidence of a movement; yet there is widespread (implicit) agreement that movements cause historical events, particularly reforms. The action (speeches, pamphlets, meetings, petitions) does not have to be directly connected to the later reform. It need only bear a resemblance in tone, in terminology, or in objectives to acts of contemporaries and to a later 'final' measure. There are several problems connected with this formula.

First, the loosely-described movement may or may not contain elements of formal organization; there seems to be no consensus as to what amount of organized activity constituted a movement, and a slight account of whatever organization existed generally is considered sufficient.

Second, the contributors to a movement were often the same characters whom we met in trying to define public opinion. In this context, however, there are added dimensions to the problem: we must establish relations between members of a movement, show connections between concurrent movements, and also try to assess the ability of the members to communicate with and to influence a larger audience.

Third, the significance of what a movement did, regardless of its degree of organization and its ability to communicate, presents a separate problem. That is the problem of attribution or accountability. To what extent can a particular movement be given credit for certain events?

Many movements pose inordinate problems for the historian describing their organization. Since the activity which they purported to control was so diverse, and since

it resembled sedition (if not treason) in the early stages,
we can understand some reluctance on the part of contemporaries to publicize all aspects of their relationships. It is harder to sympathize with a complementary
factor: historians are wont to see movements wherever
there were reforms. The absence of clear evidence and a
convincing record of activity is only a mild deterrent.

Even the best recent scholarship has had limited
success on this point. E.P. Thompson gave us a masterful
analysis of the roots and development of radical (political) movements. (23) His treatment of the period (1812-16)
and the phenomenon of the Hampden Clubs showed in vivid
detail the 'problems of leadership.' Thompson was led to
conclude that 'at the national level, Radicalism never
knew the self-discipline of political organisation.'
This he attributed to rivalry between the leaders. Nevertheless, he cited a widespread pattern of local organization, and he implied that this had grown into an effective
organ of working class opinion and action by the 1830s.

Harold Perkin discarded Thompson's view of a heroic
group of working class radical leaders. Those who were
rebellious he classified as 'a few cranks and extremists.'
(24) But he also found a wave of protest 'organized on a
national scale for a non-violent purpose' which he identified with 'the birth of class.' Perkin saw the 'working-
class Reform movement' as a significant departure in its
non-revolutionary approach. But he only listed a few
short-lived endeavours (The Philanthropic Society, the
'Philanthropic Hercules,' and some tracts by Robert Owen)
as signs of this development, c. 1818-19 Such organization as he cited was hardly impressive, and without the
character of later national efforts (NUWC, GNCTU, and
Chartists). In fact, it is hard to credit the work of
the period down to 1820 with anything like the organized
significance which Perkin wants to assign.

Indeed, the advent of organization may even have been
counterproductive. T.M. Parssinen has written recently
on the curious fate of the idea of 'association.' (25)
He concluded that the concept and its corollary of an
anti-parliament were strong symbols so long as neither
was implemented. In this interpretation, the Chartist
convention of 1839 becomes a demonstration of the weakness
of practical association. For the larger context of
reform movements, this view raises a serious question:
even if we can demonstrate its presence, how much does
organization really contribute to reform? The success of
agitation must always nourish the seeds of its own opposition. The repressive policies of the 1790s and of the
years 1816-19 were surely a mark of reaction to 'success-

ful' agitation. In this light, our image of the effect
of movements may need some elaboration.

Of course it can be argued that overt structural forms
are not the best yardstick for assessing a reform movement.
If the phenomenon was more or less effective by virtue of
communicating ideas to a significant audience, then it
should be possible to identify and evaluate the contributions of important individuals and to make some judgment
on their reception. Here the ground is as unsure as in
the formation of public opinion, and for the same reasons.
The question is whether or how far the work of leading
reformers generated a distinct following and helped to
concert action toward a mutual goal.

The discussion of movements on the level of communication is not much more effective than that on the structural level. There are problems in describing and measuring the major themes of a movement, and there are usually
a few counter-forces generated by any significant movement: internal and external obstacles and complications.

In dealing with the intellectual or psycho-social
transmissions which we identify with a reform movement, we
seldom find a rigorous analysis of ideas and their dis-
semination. More typically, we settle for a notation of
several individuals or groups, a sampling of their slogans,
and a sketch of their objectives. This kind of description is not confined to general surveys of reform, but may
be found in much of the monographic literature.

One example of a general account with these features
was David Roberts' study of the 'Victorian Origins of the
British Welfare State.' As a background to his subject,
Roberts treated the movement broadly denominated 'humanitarian':

> The Evangelicals and the Utilitarians had no monopoly
> on the spirit of philanthropy, nor did this wave of
> humanitarianism stem from any one school; its intel-
> lectual tributaries were many, ranging from the logical
> reflections of Scottish moral philosophers to the
> generous sentiments of the Lake Poets, from Broad
> Church sensibility to the piety of the Quakers. It was
> Dugald Stewart who impressed upon the leading Whigs
> a moral earnestness about reform, and it was the
> Quakers who mitigated the hardships of prison life and
> helped to found the Prison Discipline Society, typical
> of dozens of other philanthropic associations, whose
> extent suggests that the desire for reform lay in the
> very social processes of the age, above all in the
> increase of wealth, growth of cities, and advance of
> knowledge. (26)

Here the roots of reform have been effectively planted in

'the social processes of the age,' i.e. economic and cultural expansion. Yet those were not the necessary concomitants of reform, nor was reform their only likely result. The narrator needed to describe humanitarian impulses and their origins, and the statement does succeed in a limited way. It may describe a mood, yet it does not describe a movement.

A narrower example of the same problem might be taken from S.E. Finer's study of the life of Edwin Chadwick. Here the story is one of an individual who was reputed to be the chief disciple of the chief Utilitarian. While Chadwick did not have the personality to command a movement of his own, he might have been expected to be a major exemplar and elaborator of Bentham's theories. It is arguable that much of his later career did represent the influence which Chadwick absorbed from the master, but it is also made quite clear that he pointedly refused to accept Bentham's wish that he be a sort of 'official continuator' of utilitarian projects. (27) Finer explains this by alluding to Chadwick's independent temperament, but the episode raises the interesting question: if this sort of major relationship was subject to the frailty of human passion for independence, what right have we to assume the larger and more sweeping forms of 'influence' which historians readily invoke?

There is a further difficulty in the rhetorical analysis of movements. In several ways, the ideas generated by a movement (or its members) may have been subverted or stymied, thus they may survive in print far better than they ever did in practice. Fights within movements and opposition from governments provided the major counterforces. When Thompson discussed the postwar radicals of 1815-20, he headed one chapter 'Demagogues and Martyrs.' In it he gave a sizeable catalogue of leadership squabbles, concluding that 'the greatest cause of Radical disagreement was sheer vanity' of the leaders. (28) Finer's description of the followers of David Ricardo identified two hostile camps of economic theory. (29) The list could be extended, but the point is clear enough. A movement, even when considered as the exchange of ideas, moved with all the predictability of a tornado.

Of course the friendship of the establishment was not to be counted upon. Spies, informers and the regular judicial apparatus were used for the diversion and toward the suppression of some movements; the inertia of traditional sociopolitical values blunted the impact of others. The patterns of interaction between reform and continuity, though sometimes simplified for partisan rendering, were also more diverse and complex than such treatment suggests.

There were several types of interaction, and each had complications. To take the conventional obstructionist first: the history of reform has been beholden to stories such as that of Oliver the Spy for some time. In the best recent analysis of the subject, E.P. Thompson makes the seemingly paradoxical observations that

> evidence presented by the authorities as to a con-
> spiratorial underground between 1798 and 1820 is
> dubious and sometimes worthless.... So far from being
> led a dance by a series of imposters, one is impressed
> by the extraordinary skill with which Government,
> between 1792 and 1820, succeeded in forestalling
> serious revolutionary developments, and in maintaining
> a steady flow of reliable information as to insurrec-
> tionary conspiracies.... Notions as to the traditional
> stupidity of the British ruling class are dispelled by
> an acquaintance with the Home Office papers. (30)

The paradox is resolved by the parallel talents of government to filter out contrived or inflated reports, and to
use the same on occasion for political purposes.

Of course the subversion of reform did not require
that many spies. In some instances reform was easily
outflanked. The famous 'war of the unstamped' newspapers
(1830-6) ended with a reduction of the stamp duty from
4d to 1d. But this actually benefited the major papers
more than the small, radical press which had fought for
repeal. (31)

By the same token, reform might not be bluntly opposed
or even subtly subverted. It could often be exhausted
by traditional and customary inertia. The Elizabethan
Poor Law was tinkered with so extensively in the 18th
century, and came close to abolition in the early 19th
century. By 1834, the famous amendment Act was truly
anticlimactic.

The paramount difficulty in explaining reform movements arises when the historian attempts to demonstrate
their relation to eventual reform(s). For the classic
picture of a movement 'leading' to a legislative victory
is but one possible pattern. It was possible to have a
movement and no reform; similarly, it was possible to
have a reform and no movement. In the former case, the
Spencean Philanthropists, the Luddites, or the Chartists
produced no reforms (on a national scale). However,
these movements have been taken as antecedents of later
democratic reform. Their immediate impact is played
down, and their inspirational value is extolled. Thus,
Veitch tells us of the early 19th century parliamentary
reformers:

> In their shining moments, no doubt, political societies

like the Reform Union and the Hampden Club helped to
sustain the spirits of the reformers during a period
of discouragement and apparent failure. They also did
much more; for though their record of directly effective work was not magnificent they were great exemplars.
Up and down the country, especially in the industrial
towns and manufacturing villages, there sprang up
political clubs which took their names, imitated and
developed their machinery and employed their methods.
(32)

Yet whatever value the clubs may have had as 'exemplars,'
Veitch did not prove what he implied: that their experience was somehow directly connected to parliamentary
reform, which finally came in 1832.

On the other hand, there were two basic ways in which
reforms were made without (or independently of) reform
movements. Either the government made internal changes
without apparent outside influence, or the cause of a
particular reform was accepted (pre-empted?) before a
sizeable and hostile movement could be generated. Both
of these instances run against the grain of the partisan
assumption, and they have been given little account in
reform historiography. Yet it seems fair to say that a
significant portion of reform activity was generated
without movements. (33)

The third point of weakness in partisan accounts stems
from the sources. When using the contemporary accounts
of reformers and their movements, more than ordinary
caution may be required. Writing of the historian of the
19th century, George Kitson Clark found that he

often worked on his central figures and events very
carefully, but he filled in their background more
easily, accepting generalizations about it without
paying much critical attention to them. Those generalizations had sometimes actually been inherited from
contemporaries of the events themselves, who might have
been strong partisans of one side or other in the con-
flicts of the period.

Clark went on to detail the effects of this liability in
the actual workings of 'central figures and events' in
the case of the Anti-Corn Law League, pointing out that
historians had relied on the League's version of events,
to the serious distortion of the facts. (34) Clark's
verdict on this practice is a worthy caution to any
historian:

When historians accept the statement of a partisan as
a truth of history they often put themselves at the
mercy of a bias which is not their own.

Alternatively, they may identify with the contemporary

bias. In either case, the clear danger is that a partisan
statement logically cannot serve as historical truth.
There are in fact a number of cases in reform historiography where a partisan account has escaped elementary
critical evaluation. (35) When such an evaluation is
made, the effect on interpretation can be impressive.

For example, the thrust of Norman McCord's history of
the Anti-Corn Law League is to probe the account of that
body's work through and beyond its own evidence. McCord
reached the conclusion that

> The repeal of the Corn Laws in 1846 had not been the
> direct result of the League's agitation; certainly the
> League had made a great deal of noise during its life,
> had kept the question of the Corn Laws in the forefront
> of public attention, and had produced a considerable
> effect by its propaganda, but the final repeal was
> implemented by other hands and in the last crisis the
> whole settlement of the question was taken out of the
> League's hands. The League had certainly not yet
> succeeded in its aim of building up its own independent
> strength to a point at which repeal could have been
> carried in the face of the influence of the united
> landed interest.... Nevertheless the League was gener-
> ally credited with the responsibility for the repeal of
> the Corn Laws. This was so because of the growth of
> the legend of the League. The Leaguers claimed to have
> been the main agents of the repeal and carefully
> fostered the idea that it was the work of the League
> which culminated in the Act of 1846, although this
> story does not coincide with the political facts of
> the situation, and does not take account of the
> decisive part played by Peel and his followers, who
> could scarcely be called Leaguers. (36)

McCord arrived at his conclusion by close examination of
the claims of the League, and by a careful comparison of
those claims with other evidence. That is, he rejected
the self-description of the reformers on the ground that
it was a biased and incomplete version of historical truth.

The most challenging problem in handling partisan
activity seems to come with the last stage of reform.
Every reform received majority support at some point, if
it was to succeed. At that point, reformers ceased to
be an embattled minority - or any other kind of minority.
This sometimes occurred late in the process, giving the
minority role a prevailing image, and making the final
'victory' (which was the attainment of majority support)
more dramatic. However, a majority sometimes occurred
early in the process, which could seriously undermine an
explanation based upon partisan conflict; indeed, there

is some ground to suspect that cases in this category
have been bypassed because they did not conform to the
partisan hypothesis.

Late majorities occurred in some of the better-known
reforms. In the Reform Act of 1832, for example, the
forming of a majority for parliamentary reform occurred
between 1829 and 1831 out of a complex mixture of dis-
contents within the unreformed Parliament. Yet a majority
was found, containing a fair number of those who, on a
simple party or interest analysis, should have opposed
the measure. (37) The repeal of the Corn Laws, a long-
standing topic of debate, was passed by the unusual alliance of Peel and Russell in 1846. The 'apostasy' of the
Prime Minister owed something to the Irish famine. But
the reform was, as always, the act of a majority in
Parliament.

The less-noticed early majorities did deprive the
historian of parliamentary rhetoric, newspaper paragraphs,
indignant treatises, and angry public meetings. But
because historians have been drawn to the best-publicized,
most delayed, and most apparently partisan encounters -
these have taken the limelight and have subsequently been
treated as the norm of reform. It was unlikely, in such
circumstances, that other historians would bother to
describe undramatic, nonpartisan reform activity. We need
to examine a selection of reforms in which majorities
were early. Some developments from the half-century
before 1830 may be taken which are not normally accorded
places of importance in the annals of reform. Our object
is simple: we will try to establish whether or not these
events should be regarded as reforms, and if they should,
did they owe their majority to a reform movement? For
simplicity, what follows is a discussion of several
legislative acts. This is not to say that a history of
reform should begin with statutes - that is one reason
for some of the problems discussed here. Yet for convenience in making this point on nonpartisan reforms, it
seems fair to continue the sins of our historical fathers.

As a first example let us examine the Friendly
Societies Act of 1793. (38) This measure was proposed by
George Rose, the Secretary to the Treasury, and it conferred legal rights on those societies which were duly
registered. Thus those groups could sue and protect
their funds. Many hoped that the societies would help to
solve the problem of rising poor rates by drawing workers
into mutual benefit associations. Apparently, very many
workers found the societies attractive, for by 1803 a poor
law return showed there were nearly 10,000 friendly
societies which had registered, and these bodies claimed

a membership of over 700,000. (39)

Was this a reform? The recent historian of the societies points out that:

> In the earlier part of the nineteenth century the societies were regarded as useful organizations for lowering the poor rate but potentially dangerous in a political sense. The efforts made directly by the governing classes to run societies were aimed principally at reducing the poor rate and such societies attracted comparatively little support. The friendly society movement, as it developed between 1815 and 1875, sprang from the efforts of those who became members and it owed comparatively little to outsiders. In this respect it might be compared with the trade unions or the co-operatives, both of which grew as a result of the energy and determination shown by the members they served. These three movements represent, in a sense, the ways in which those without political power sought to protect themselves in an increasingly industrialized society. (40)

It is noteworthy that the legal protection afforded the friendly society was about thirty years ahead of unions, and forty years ahead of cooperatives. (41) But our basic question is whether legalizing such societies constituted a reform. It seems clear that the drafters of the Act thought that it would reform the conditions affecting the level of the poor rates. It is also likely that such a step to organize workers was regarded as risky, but as a lesser evil. However much paternal social control might be seen in these societies, there was also the element of 'concerted action' and 'group consciousness' which Asa Briggs wisely noted. This was part of a new 'pattern of relationships (which) did more to break down the traditional view of the social order than the writings of any single theorist or the precepts of any reformer.' (42) The Friendly Societies Act was surely a measure intended to reform a social activity of great importance.

If the Act was a reform, how then did it obtain a majority? Where was its massive movement? The measure seems to have been inspired by discussion of several poor law reform ideas, in particular Rev. John Acland's plan to nationalize the societies. (43) According to the recent analysis by J.R. Poynter, Acland's plan was 'too ambitious and too speculative in its claims to win much support from cautious legislators, though the principle continued to gain in popularity.' (44) All the same, Poynter saw the discussion of this scheme as the origin of the Act of 1793. Of course that Act did not provide nationalization of friendly societies; more important

from our standpoint, there was no sign of a movement con-
necting the Acland scheme and the eventual Act.

As a second example, we may look at the first of the
famous 'Factory Acts' which was passed in 1802. (45)
While later legislation, especially the Acts of 1833 and
1847, is of good reform standing, the same cannot be said
of the first Act. Indeed, its early historians called it
'an extension of the old (Elizabethan) poor law,'
more than ' a conscious assumption of control over
industry.' (46) The authors put the bill's introduction
in the context of scandals in the hiring of parish apprentices:

> It was no doubt in consequence of these and other
> revelations that Sir Robert Peel, in 1802, brought in
> a Bill known as the 'Health and Morals of Apprentices
> Act' which passed with little or no opposition....
>
> Peel said later on that he had no difficulty in
> getting this Bill passed, the House being quite con-
> vinced of its necessity, and it does not appear that
> the Act was received in at all a controversial spirit.
> It was in reality not a Factory Act properly speaking,
> but merely an extension of the Elizabethan Poor Law
> relating to parish apprentices. (47)

In order to be a 'Factory Act properly speaking' the
measure should have had a proper movement and it should
have come from a certified reformer and not an extremely
wealthy owner of factories. But for our purposes, it is
not important to decide the classification question:
whether the focus was the factory or the apprentice, the
Act of 1802 was meant to be a reform.

We have the opinion of Hutchins and Harrison that there
was 'little or no opposition' to the Act, leaving only
the question of whether or not this harmony was the
product of a movement for the legislation. The authors
gave full (if tainted) credit to Peel for the measure:

> The Government, having taken upon itself the responsi-
> bility of bringing up and placing out these children,
> found itself compelled, when need was shown, to attempt
> to regulate their conditions of work. Peel rather
> naively gave as a reason for bringing in the Bill that
> he was convinced of the existence of gross mismanage-
> ment in his own factories, and having no time to set
> them in order himself, got an Act of Parliament passed
> to do it for him. (48)

Thus there was little trace of organized effort on behalf
of the Act.

In 1808 Parliament created a royal commission to
inquire into the 'administration of justice in Scotland.'
This Scotch Judicature Act, as it was called, was an

omnibus measure to reform the Court of Session and the
appellate procedures to the House of Lords. The commission of inquiry was tacked on after an address from the
House of Lords. (49)

The early decades of legal reform have not attracted
much attention from historians. Yet all of the high
courts in the British Isles were the subject of formal
inquiry between 1808 and 1825. The most recent study of
the legal system calls the years 1750-1825 'barren years'
and suggests 'the main campaign for reform of the courts
began in 1828.' (50) A glance at the statute book belies
this summary judgment. Between 1750 and 1830 there were
137 statutes on the courts of law in all parts of the
British Isles. (51) Perhaps there was no 'reform movement' with the traditional features; but movement there
was on the part of legislators.

The problem for the judiciary, which was somewhat
aggravated in the case of Scotland, was basically one of
a growing volume of business. None of the medieval
courts had been effectively modernized before 1800 and by
then industrial and demographic change brought radical
increases in litigation. This growth of business was the
chief object of the measure which Bentham called 'Lord
Eldon's Bill' in a series of letters in 1808. (52)

The Bill was designed to reform the arrangement of
Scotland's highest court, the Court of Session. It also
regulated appeals to the House of Lords, and most notable
of all, it established a commission of inquiry to carry on
further study of the Scottish legal system. That commission produced three reports and it contributed to several
more reforms. (53) From all appearances there was no
typical reform movement here, or at least if one existed,
it was not known to Bentham. He criticized the motions
in the House of Lords which preceded the legislation on
the ground that they were clumsily and mistakenly composed; but his criticism was too little and too late, as
the bulk of the resolutions were embodied in the Act as
passed.

Elsewhere in the legal system, the better-known issue
of mitigation of the criminal law and its penalties was
under discussion by 1808. (54) This sector of reform saw
a measure for official inquiry carried against the government in 1819; most of the statutory recommendations which
resulted were not followed at the time, but some were
adopted and executed by the younger Robert Peel in 1823.
At that time, significant and substantial reforms were
made by Peel, and Norman Gash says

The uneventful passage through the legislature of such
controversial and pioneer measures was only made

possible by careful preparation beforehand.... What the Whig legal reform movement had lacked was organization; it was that which Peel made it his primary business to supply. (55)

Of course, as Home Secretary, Peel was somewhat better placed to afford this element of 'organization.' But it is also likely that what we are seeing here is a good example of bipartisan reform. And the story did not end in 1823. Peel went on to make more major contributions to criminal law reform.

To take but one of Peel's great measures, jury reform in 1825, (56) we may get some idea of the measure and the movement, if any, which accompanied it. Gash says the Bill 'represented the first calculated attack on the general state of the law.' Peel hoped to consolidate some eighty-five existing laws and to introduce several reforms. 'These changes were generally welcomed by the House. The ease with which the Bill passed through both Houses' prompted Peel to pursue further reform measures. (57)

As for an accompanying movement, it does not seem to have extended much beyond the Home Office. Peel did attest the 'assistance of eminent members of the legal profession' when he introduced the Bill. Another speaker, James Scarlett, a barrister and later Attorney-General, observed that it would have been 'very difficult for a private individual to carry a Bill of this importance through the House.' And Henry Brougham could not let the occasion pass without commending the measure and adding that 'the passing of this bill would be a useful lesson to those who were so wedded to things as they were as to be alarmed at the mention of any change.' (58) With congratulations all round, including those of Joseph Hume, Peel eased his Bill through without the aid of a movement.

These examples of reforms without a pitched battle between an organized group of reformers and an entrenched government are not supposed to be any more typical of the process of reform than their opposite numbers. The examples add a final dimension to the point which is made here, namely that a partisan assumption is often erroneous or inadequate. In the first place, the political party offers little or no help in aligning the forces for or against a measure. The surrogate agency of the 'reform movement' raises different and difficult questions (organization, communication, and effectiveness). Not the least of these questions is the historical reliability of the records kept by partisans themselves. So when we finally turn to a number of reforms which were made without a well-defined movement and with bipartisan support, it

seems evident that no easy general assumption on the partisan question can be sustained. Perhaps the concentration on clearly partisan reform efforts over the years
has made it very hard for us to give adequate notice to
the variations which logic would suggest. We have come
to expect partisan behaviour; to see leaders whom we
identify with particular parties or causes behaving in a
nonpartisan manner may be unexciting. It is not unimpor-
tant.

III

The third major area of weak interpretation in reform
historiography derives from what may be called the
presentist assumption. This disability is known to all
areas and periods of historical writing. It occurs when
the historian transports the perceptions of his own time
into that of his subject, and allows present views and
values to colour his interpretation of the past. It is
doubtful that the historian of 19th century reform has
been more prone to this failing than others; it is certain
that many have succumbed.
    Indeed something of a historiographical tradition
developed around this aberration. Herbert Butterfield
called our attention to the phenomenon many years ago
in his analysis of 'whig' political interpretation. (59)
But the tendency goes beyond the narratives of Macaulay,
Lecky and Trevelyan. From the beginning of the present
century, the rising school of social history also had
clear marks of presentism. Sidney and Beatrice Webb's
magisterial work on English local government grew out of
their current political desire for an understanding of
the intricacies of local administration, and scholars
will forever be grateful for whatever motive urged the
Webbs on with their monumental labors. Still that should
not keep us from recognizing the sometimes patronizing
condescension with which they approached the quaint
government of earlier days. They once called it 'the
anarchy of local autonomy,' for to them, centralization
was the only creed, and their mission as historians was
to tell the saga of its achievement. (60)
    The work of the Webbs was paralleled by another couple,
John and Barbara Hammond. Their goal was a description of
the evil consequences of the industrial revolution, a
present fact on which they harboured no doubt. They wanted
to expose the origins of the pernicious system, and
through their accounts of 'The Town Labourer,' 'Village
Labourer,' and 'Skilled Labourer,' they made some fine

reconstructions of the period 1760-1830, all of which were subservient to a larger plan: the tale of the tragic evolution of industrial society.

In studies of reform and reform movements in the early 19th century, a category of work has emerged since the 1940s which is now dubbed the 'administrative revolution.' This body of scholarship is aimed at the explanation of reform in government processes at the national level, and it too displays presentist features. One of the early works in this field was a study of the evolution of royal commissions of inquiry. (61) Hugh Clokie and J. William Robinson said their work, 'concerns the significance and present status of Royal Commissions of Inquiry in relation to British politics.' Given this orientation, the authors did a fair job tracing the early history of commissions. Coming to the 19th century, which was christened 'the great era of commissions,' we learn that 'the guardians of the state became increasingly interested in investigating every phase of social life with a view to remedying the evils which were apparent.' While the authors struggled to reconcile this generalization with notions of *laissez-faire*, they explained that commissions of inquiry were established units, that they outperformed select committees, and they had special qualities making them attractive to political leaders. (62) The development convinced the authors that from the 1820s MPs 'were awakening to the desirability and indeed to the necessity of the investigative function as a prelude to public legislative determination of policy.' In other words, the untutored lawmakers of that earlier day were realizing what good 20th century legislators took for granted. Unfortunately for the authors, they have to explain later in their book why there was a marked decline in the number of commissions after 1930. (63)

More recently, David Roberts has written about the 'Victorian Origins of the British Welfare State.' As its title implied, the book was an effort to locate the inception of the administrative development which became 20th century welfare bureaucracy. Such an approach invited a present-oriented analysis, and Roberts was aware of the difficulty. 'Scarcely an Englishman in 1833 either foresaw or desired that profound growth in the role of the central government which marked the beginning of a welfare state.' However, Roberts went on to say that, by the 1850s, 'England, the historic home of Anglo-Saxon local government and the economic doctrines of Adam Smith, had begun to construct a welfare state.' (64)

A presentist bias undermined Roberts' study. First the assumption that reform began in 1832 or with the Great

Reform Bill pervaded the work. The theme of the growth
of central government was very much tied to the future
destination of that growth. The small size of departments
in 1833 was detailed, with the implication that government was equipped to do very little. Much was left to
local authorities, and Roberts did not see the main alteration in a sudden shift of that balance; rather the
granting of regulatory power over 'private enterprise for
the public welfare' seemed to him to be the primary fact.
Yet this was an old power of government, unless he meant
it to be taken in the context of mid-20th century government power.

   A major contribution in recent administrative history
has been made by Oliver MacDonagh. He too found reformers
working toward the goal of present-day conditions. After
developing a 'model' of what he called the 'administrative
revolution,' MacDonagh proceeded to study the Passenger
Acts (1800-60) as a 'pattern of government growth.' (65)
Commenting on the early phase of this legislation (1800-
27), he criticized the 'failing' he felt was characteristic of early reforms: 'reliance upon the existing arms
of government to carry out the new measure.' Surely this
was only a failing when measured against later bureaucratic patterns; and MacDonagh might have noted that
modern agencies have something less than a perfect record
of law enforcement.

   The presentist approach encourages two basic types of
error. Unless presentism is consciously resisted, the
perceptions of reformers may be misinterpreted, and the
contemporary significance of reforms may be overlooked.
On the first point, the modern observer is apt to see
reformers as foresighted and progressive. Yet reform
(or reformation) has more than one meaning. (66) Asa
Briggs said that in the 1780s 'even radical reformers,
for the most part, spoke of restoring old rights rather
than creating new ones.' (67) E.L. Woodward made a
similar observation for the period around 1815:

   ... even the most active reformers tended to think in
   terms of past issues, or, at all events, of reform
   within the limits of society as it was known to their
   ancestors. Demands for reform were more for the
   redress of grievances, or for the improvement of the
   conditions of life. (68)

   A mark of the 17th century was the historical-minded-
ness of reformers (and of rebels). The correction of
abuses was regularly presented as a path on which to
return to a traditional ideal. Until the late 18th
century, there was little respect for innovation. The
ideal of progress, enunciated in 18th century philosophy

and then vividly adduced in 18th century technology, was
to convert the prevailing view by the middle of the 19th
century. At that point, accumulating reforms and the
cult of progress helped to fix the image of reform in
the pattern of renovation. Around 1800, this transition
was still underway. There were still reforms which were
perceived essentially as acts of restoration. There
were of course acts containing a mixture of restoration
and renovation. The works of evangelical reformers,
for instance, were very much concerned with restoration.
The abolition of the slave trade, often taken as the
most significant Act inspired by evangelicals, has
normally been studied in the progressive perspective.
The presentist view saw abolition as part of the progressive advocacy of civil and human rights, the natural
product of Enlightenment. Yet it owed as much or more
to the Judeo-Christian natural law tradition, and surely
was perceived that way by its proponents. Wilberforce,
after all, said he took up abolition as 'a sacred
charge.' (69) Whether it has historically advanced the
more modern tradition is beside the point. In this
case, one must agree with Asa Briggs that the reformers
'sought not political regeneration but the opportunity
to save souls through the medium of political action,'
or what he called 'introducing into the world a new leaven
of righteousness.' (70)

The actual story of the abolition of the slave
trade was replete with ironic twists, and according to
one of its recent historians, it was an 'essentially
fortuitous achievement.' (71) While the trade had been
attacked as inhumane, it was banned only when the West
Indies could no longer prove its economic dependence on
the trade. And that condition altered during and because
of the Napoleonic wars. In other words, a full understanding of this reform requires a very extensive
reconstruction of current perceptions, current conditions,
and the debate on rival views of those elements. The
easier route of hindsight will fail to reach historical
truth.

The second major error of presentism concerns contemporary significance. Here there are two related
difficulties. Sometimes acts which are significant in
their own day will fail and not be heard from further.
On the other hand, acts may fail at one point, or in
one form, and then be revived in another, only to succeed.
The later success then appears to endow the earlier act
with a kind of presentist sanction as a 'forerunner.'
Both of these tendencies are plainly cases which invite
serious distortion.

The first area encompasses many kinds of 'failure' and a considerable effort is required to overcome our built-in bias against the study of failure. Yet on closer inspection, all acts which did not get a majority, or those which did and were not implemented (or were unenforceable) or those which were terminal measures (i.e. repeals, reversals, or isolated local acts) should not be arbitrarily assigned to the outer darkness.

In an era such as the early phase of the Age of Reform, there logically should have been more defeats than victories. We may have little help from historians in locating these apparently insignificant acts, but the statute book, the press, and other records bear their traces. This is not a suggestion that a new field in the history of failure lies ready for the ambitious student; it does suggest that the prudent historian will unravel unsuccessful acts with as much care as any others, for their record will tell him a great deal about his subject.

Above all, a careful study of failures will alert the historian to the 'forerunner fallacy.' Here is where the irony of presentism's influence is clearest. When a measure has been defeated, and then a reasonable likeness later prevails, the later success instantly (and often unwarrantably) endows early failure with some measure of precocious or premature wisdom. This is transposed presentism; the later generation knew better, but at least the earlier one was trying to move in the direction of progress. One of the greatest forerunners in the Age of Reform was the Chartist movement. Textbooks are often more interested in how five of the six points of the People's Charter were later enacted, than in the tremendous significance of the first organized workers' political movement. That effort, and its dogged pursuit of the traditional grievance procedure of petitioning, are critical factors in the success of the Age of Reform; there one will find its true significance for its own time.

The presentist treatment of reforms tends to compound the confusion of populist and partisan assumptions. Together the three are being addressed by some historians, and there is little reason to regard the history of reform as in serious jeopardy from their continued influence. However, much more might be done to improve the historiography of reform. Several directions stand out as avenues for new research.

There is a great deal more to be done with larger developments in the society of the reformers. To take but one example, a profoundly important point for the understanding of the subject is the full meaning of what Harold Perkin (following Carlyle) has called 'the Abdication on

the Part of the Governors.' (72)   The anomalous role of
paternal aristocracy in the early 19th century, wherein
the governors ceased to shoulder many traditional duties
but continued to exercise traditional privileges deserves
much more study.   Perkin concentrated on the power of
this abdication to precipitate 'the birth of class,' yet
it seems clear that if the thesis is valid, it has major
implications for the genesis and achievement of numerous
reforms.   For instance, a change of such magnitude would
be a more credible basis for widespread 'opinion' on
issues than reliance on radical spokesmen, especially
since in higher circles at the time, 'opinion' was thought
to be best expressed through the voice of the independent
country gentlemen.

Another point of reassessment should emerge from the
area of local history.   What will emerge is uncertain,
for no area of promised illumination has been more
frequently cited and less efficiently explored.   If we
follow the impressions of E.P. Thompson, we may expect
to find widespread evidence of local cells of working
class reformers:

> By 1832 - and on into Chartist times - there is a
> Radical nucleus to be found in every county, in the
> smallest market towns and even in the larger rural
> villages, and in nearly every case it is based on the
> local artisans.... this autodidact culture has never
> been adequately analysed. (73)

On the other hand, we may uncover a multitude of local
actions by governing bodies, as J.R. Poynter found in the
realm of the poor law:

> Despite the failure to achieve any major amendment in
> the Poor Law there is evidence that the system was
> changing in practice, in many parishes if not in all.
> In the 1820s, as in earlier decades, local innovation
> was the harbinger of national legislation, though the
> outcome in this case was to be more drastic than the
> merely permissive enactments of the eighteenth century.
> Some, perhaps most, of the Royal Commissioners of
> 1832-4 were deeply influenced by examples of successful
> local experiment, and George Nicholls, the dominant
> figure on the Poor Law Commission established in 1832,
> always claimed that the origin of the new system lay in
> local reforms rather than in abstract doctrine. (74)

Whatever else results from a broad effort to amplify the
story of reform at the local level, there should be a
stronger basis for characterization of reforms and
reformers.

A third area for further study is in legal and administrative history in the early 19th century.   For all the

concentration on politics and constitutional questions, massive areas in the process of government have barely been touched. Some promising work has already been done on the personnel and the major institutions of the period. (75) Yet there are great gaps in legal and social areas of administrative history. One such is the area discussed below, namely the history of royal commissions of inquiry. Another is the story of the multitude of societies spawned in the 19th century. Yet another area is the more traditional but still vital business of explaining the inner working of government offices with the subtle skill that Henry Roseveare has brought to his work on 'The Treasury.'

Finally, to return to the area where the story of reform, and its ailing assumptions, had their origin - the world of politics - there are recent signs of new directions which will add to the better perception of reform generally. John Cannon has surveyed the franchise question and its pedigree. (76)   John Brewer has revisited the worn territory around 1760, and he shows with convincing detail and sound argument how the period contained roots of popular political activity. (77)   These works are indicative of the room for reconsideration which exists in the central theme of the Age of Reform.

The foregoing discussion indicates that public opinion, partisan organization, and the march of progress have not been the most effective aids to our understanding of the Age of Reform.   In fact, it may be more accurate to say that the historian of reform has felt obliged to put the great changes of the early 19th century into a formulated pattern which has the apparent virtue of being intelligible to the 20th century reader.   However understandable, this recurrent presentism has done more to distort than to explain the vital events of reform.   For on some occasions, instead of genuine public opinion being an active agency, there was a mixture of elitist agitation and radical deception, artificially identified with 'the people.'   Instead of heroic reformers and movements, there were relatively few crusades and many more cases where the governors chose what seemed to them a sound policy. Instead of 'progress,' reform ought to be seen in the variegated image of its own time: an attempt to renovate or restore, an 'abdication,' or a compound of a thousand local events.   The Age of Reform was at the same time the product of a remarkable generation of progressive thinkers, opportunist politicians, and aggressive entrepreneurs - but to focus on them alone will always show us but one part of the larger and more fascinating spectacle of English reform.

IV

The Charity Commission has had no historian.(78)   It has
been generally ignored in spite of (or because of) a
massive collection of documents and an impressive set of
printed reports. The Commission has also languished in
this obscurity because of its inconclusive and undramatic
history from 1818 to 1837. It was plainly not aligned
with the conventional assumptions of popularity, partisanship and progress. Yet it has a great deal to tell us
about the second generation of the Age of Reform. In fact
the Commission's work is an excellent example of the
potential of new areas of research in the process of
reform.

   In obedience to its terms of establishment, the Charity
Commission reported semi-annually from 1819 to 1836 with
only short periods of inactivity. In its last phase, six
volumes were compiled, bringing the total number of
reports to thirty-eight folio volumes. Nearly 29,000
charities had been surveyed, and the attendant correspondence, minutes, draft reports and miscellaneous records now
fill 469 boxes deposited under the cryptic heading
'Charity 2' in the Public Record Office repository in
Hayes, Middlesex. What may have been filed under 'Charity
1' is unknown, but what remains is surely an ample record.
In addition, the present offices of the Commission in
Ryder Street maintain the original general minute books
(5 volumes) which are an invaluable source.

   The Commission began its career in an era and under
conditions in which such inquiries were only known within
the walls of government offices. It functioned throughout
the country for two decades, in which time the process of
inquiry grew and extended to many other parts of English
society. But the inquiry which began as an investigation
of charitable endowments by trained lawyers did not change
in any fundamental way. And because it was in the form of
a legal inquiry, the Commission had limited potential for
enlisting an emotional political following during its
career.

   When the fourth and last issue of the Royal Commission
expired in 1837, there was an unsuccessful attempt to
establish the body on a permanent footing. Failure in
this effort was the final reason why the Commission did
not attract the notice of historians. It had not achieved
that essential link to the march of progress which would
have admitted it to the ranks of significant reforms.
When this gap is coupled to the absence of a partisan
movement and the nonprogressive sort of popular support
for charity reform, it is clear why the Commission has
waited so long for historical attention.

The Charity Commission will offer some excellent
evidence in the new directions already suggested for the
history of reform.   Certainly the weakening of charity
administration which was the occasion for the inquiry was
an example of the 'abdication of the governors,' although
the defects were by no means simple or easy to attribute.
The history of charities is in the main local history.
The inquiry was appropriately a tour through England and
Wales.   That it spanned twenty years suggests the magnitude of the task.   The achievement was to compile local
records from thousands of parishes on the current state
and past history of endowments.   The visits of Commissioners were often the occasion for some kind of reform, and
thus we have an interesting collection of records of local
activity, more or less dependent upon a central stimulus.

The Royal Commission of Inquiry is also a useful topic
for analysis.   As one of the myriad developments in
government and administration in the first half of the
19th century, these inquiries have been surprisingly
neglected.   There is no way they can be easily summarized,
and surely this book is not an attempt to provide a prototype.   In many ways, the Charity Commission was quite
unlike the 160 Royal Commissions of Inquiry which were
founded between 1800 and 1850.   Yet it and its counter-
parts demand further study as instruments of legal and
administrative developments in the period.

A thorough study of a body such as the Charity Commission suggests many possible strategies to the historian.
From a simple narrative account through a sophisticated
quantitative analysis, there appear to be unlimited
opportunities.   The method chosen here will doubtless
disappoint some, for it is neither a narrative nor a
computer study.   Instead, the analysis is mainly functional and institutional.   It seeks to explain what lay behind
the inquiry, both in general and in the particular field
of charitable trusts.   It attempts to show how the inquiry
was created, how it was conducted, and what it accomplished.   As an afterword, the study of this commission
is used as the basis for suggestions on the value of
further study of Royal Commissions of Inquiry.

The Charity Commission was a direct product of some
highly improbable political moves, although we can see
ample justification for inquiry over a long period of
charitable trust history.   In the half-century before
1816, there was a fair amount of government and private
inquiry; at the same time there was a growing legal
vacuum as a result of the ineffectiveness of Chancery and
the abandonment of older procedures for charity cases.

Yet in the years 1816-19 some strange manipulations

set the inquiry in place, with the support of ministers.
It continued, relatively unmolested, until 1837.   The
total cost came to about £291,000.   At the same time,
the Commission probably recovered £800,000 in endangered
charity property; surely its studies preserved or stabil-
ized a large additional (if unmeasurable) amount.   Thus,
on the most basic calculation, there was a sizeable and
significant reform.

   The story of the Charity Commission is only a small
piece of one larger sector of the history of reform.
It and other commissions of inquiry have been taken for
granted as agencies of reform, yet it is safe to say that
they are poorly understood.   This book is offered as a
small beginning toward a better understanding of this
aspect of the Age of Reform.

1

The State of Inquiry:
Empiricism and Politics

For centuries Englishmen tolerated a wide range of government inquiries. Law and administration demanded them, and the occasional stability of society seemed worth the price. In the 19th century there was a dramatic alteration. Inquiry was turned upon the agents of law and administration in the name of reform. Of course inquiry only became a vital tool of reform after, and because it was reformed.

In the late 17th century, the long-standing tradition of judicial inquiry was joined by a new brand of empiricism known as 'political arithmetic.' In the 18th century, the strategy of inquiry was exploited successfully by a number of philanthropists. The newer modes of inquiry were instrumental in changing the focus of investigations toward social problems. At the same time, there was a further development which altered the political base of inquiry. The crisis of the American war triggered serious reform efforts, and part of the government's response was experimentation with the Royal Commission of Inquiry. This ancient and once-ominous agency of prerogative was meant to offer the appearance of empirical study of government while allowing the essential continuity of its basic form. In a sense it did the job. However, this form of inquiry also was linked to the social objects which were being raised at the turn of the century. The repeated use of that configuration would bring unpredictable results. The first clear example of the fusion of social inquiry and the Royal Commission was to come in 1818.

I

Acts of inquiry were an integral and indispensable part of
the English legal tradition. Royal justice and administration were built upon legal inquiry, both in the
formal system of courts, and in the ad hoc agencies of
prerogative, whence the courts themselves originally came.
Moreover, the government's ability to inquire extended
beyond the judicial sphere early and often. So pervasive
was the influence of legal inquiry that by the 17th
century we may speak with assurance of an ingrained 'habit
of inquiry.'

Courts of law in their original form were anything but
agencies of empirical inquiry. Ancient folk moots and
royal courts appeared to base judgments on the validity
of oaths, which value was assayed by human or divine
intuition. With the fundamental changes which brought
the beginnings of the common law, the judicial process
began to move in an empirical direction. The Frankish
Inquest was brought by the Normans, and this method of
taking evidence in and from a sworn body of men was made
a part of the judicial system by the later 12th century.
(1) At first, juries were considered as sources of
evidence. Their competence to judge issues of fact was
a much later development, well underway by the 15th
century.

While this evolution of fact-finding procedure was
going on, the functions of the courts were changing in
other ways. Meetings of courts were being formalized
and their records becoming more secure. This regularity
and record-keeping were essential to the emergence of
the common law. There was no innovation in the idea of
judicial precedent (which may only be a latter-day form
of the 'legal memory' of other customary systems). The
important addition in medieval England was a mass of
records, which were available for future citation. To
this mass were added the accumulating judicial decisions,
which served as guideposts to the courts.

By the 15th century this process of judicial growth was
complete for the common law courts. In other jurisdictions, ecclesiastical and mercantile, feudal and
manorial courts, there were similar developments. The
provision of courts would surely be regarded as adequate
by any measure, nevertheless, there always seemed to be
more areas in need of royal justice than there were
courts to serve them; and the prerogative power was
always ready to supply more judges and procure more
revenues. In such cases, two modes of change were possible: either a royal judge was in such demand that a new

court or commissioned judge was permanently established, or royal justice was dispensed ad hoc by specially commissioned judges.

Common to both modes was of course the exercise of the royal prerogative. With the 16th century, there was a flourishing of prerogative justice. The new courts and commissions were established in much the same way that the courts of common law had been. But their numbers and their novelty, to say nothing of their clear intent to bypass the older courts, were cause for judicial conflict. When a high level of effectiveness in collecting evidence was added to a high degree of efficiency in rendering judgments, prerogative justice was sure to be intolerable.

The new courts of the Tudors have quite naturally attracted the historian. They were novel establishments, and as such, they were apt to develop new procedures. Both contemporaries and historians came to see the courts as instruments of absolutism, but later scholarship has modified that impression. What is quite clear is that the judicial rivalry which fed into the 17th century revolution brought with it significant questioning of methods of inquiry and strict limitation on the prerogative power to create new courts (in the realm of common law). These consequences served to direct, but not to diminish, the habit of inquiry.

Our concentration on the new courts of the 16th century has distracted us from the equally significant use of special commissions. This device, which granted powers to named individuals for specified tasks, was a prerogative exercise of very long standing. We see one kind of precedent in special inquests from the Domesday survey, through the Inquest of Sheriffs, to the *valor ecclesiasticus* of Thomas Cromwell and Henry VIII. There were numerous examples of narrower inquiries which were commissioned directly, either because courts were unable to deal with certain matters, or because the crown wanted to deal with them directly. The Acts of the Privy Council are littered with these commissions, and their range of use was remarkable.

The impact of prerogative justice on the habit of inquiry had two contradictory elements. The prolific institution of these agencies showed a remarkable strength and flexibility in royal administration. That same power evoked a strong conservative reaction from the established (common law) agents of inquiry. Neither element questioned the need for inquiry; each found support in the community for rival modes of inquiring. The idea of the power to inquire was not under attack - the forms and agents used to inquire were.

In 1700 the ingrained habit of inquiry was evident in several aspects of the enduring network of the judicial system. At the most elementary level was the proof of the system's entrenchment in its continuity between 1642 and 1660. The courts of common law continued to function through the Commonwealth period, and their acts were later upheld, making them unique among all institutions in the 17th century. (2) That experience reinforced the already strong judicial habit of inquiry, and we can detect several directions in which the strength of empiricism was enhanced.

First, from the 16th century onward, the increase in written testimony and evidence intruded far enough into the normal process of the courts so as to require development of the law of evidence. In Holdsworth's opinion, 'we begin, at the end of the seventeenth century to see in outline, some of the main principles of our modern law of evidence.' (3)

Second, the records of the courts' decisions were being more carefully preserved and self-consciously edited and published. From Plowden in the 16th century to Coke in the 17th, there was a vital development of the law's own sources, and a corresponding vitality added to the concept of common law precedent. (4)

Third, the legal profession and the study of law were at the centre of emerging modern historiography. (5) There was a paradox here, for the common law mentality was ahistorical. Custom was timeless, but the shock of revolution and the formal ending of feudalism emphasized the mutability of custom. Sir Matthew Hale's 'History of the Common Law' stressed this theme:

> It is very evident to every Day's experience, that Laws, the further they go from their original institution, grow the larger, and the more numerous.... But whatsoever be done touching their *Old* laws, there must of necessity be a provision of *New*, and other Laws successively, answering to the multitude of successive exigencies and emergencies, that in a long tract of time will offer themselves. (6)

The law, in spite of inherent conservatism, had fostered opposition to absolutism. If it was no friend to democracy in the 17th century, it did coincidentally help to develop a more empirical study of its past, and this was a precedent of the greatest significance.

During the long term of judicial inquiry, many quasi-judicial (we would say administrative) forms of inquisition and record-keeping were evolved. Their precise origins and particular development are less important to us than the evidence which they provide for the pene-

tration of the habit of inquiry into most areas of social
life. Nor is there any attempt to suggest that such acts
of government were popular or efficient. They were omni-
present, and the population was conditioned to expect and
endure. The most prevalent kinds of inquiry were ancient
visitations and more modern inquisitions into vital
records, property records, and taxation.

The church had used visitations from the earliest
times as a means of governance. (7)   Archbishops, bishops
and archdeacons periodically conducted these inspections,
which by the 16th century had become triennial events.
Until the 18th century, records suggest that the practice
was widely followed as a means of general regulation as
well as a basis for disciplinary action. On the secular
side, the visitation of heralds was begun in the 15th
century, and the College of Arms was incorporated in 1484.
The busiest period of these visitations was in the 16th
and 17th centuries, and they have left a large body of
documentation. Ironically, the pedigrees of that period
must be treated with some suspicion, even though the
visitations were designed to root out imposters. Inquiry
in this instance was more susceptible to subversion, for
the penalties were less severe than those attending other
inquisitions. (8)

Vital records existed in various forms before the well-
known institution of parish registration by Thomas
Cromwell. That action was however most significant in
standardizing and implementing the basic process of
keeping such records. Cromwell's plan was carried on by
the Church, and it only received statutory authorization
in the 19th century. (9)

On another footing, records of property ownership and
transactions in property were kept, both for the legal and
social security of the owners. While there was only
limited mandatory registration in this area, (10) there
was vast documentation held in private hands (deeds, conveyances, and leases). The document(s) would attest to
the tenure in one's lifetime and that of one's heirs
(with a valid will and testament) after death. The
essential purpose of these documents was as proof, if
need be in a court of law, of one's property rights.

A final area of accountability for most of English
history has been the perennial nemesis of taxation.
Whether in the shape of feudal dues, tithes, customs
duties, subsidies, poll taxes, or forced loans, the
inquiring power of the tax collector was well-known. The
17th century saw unique and extensive opposition to tax
collecting, but hardly any reduction in taxes. If anything, the resistance to Ship Money and other archaic

levies forced administrators - beginning with the rebels themselves - to be more innovative and more effective.

The net effect of centuries of legal inquiry and adjuncts of administrative inquiry was a society totally conditioned to and interested in the process of inquiry. We do not suggest that this made the ordinary Englishman an empiricist, nor that the practice of inquiring by itself was motivated by empiricism, or indeed by any other philosophical orientation. The actions which were comprised in these practices may surely be seen as a sort of exercise which trained large segments of the society in habits that would later be subtly and just as casually redirected.

II

The inquiry discussed thus far was a government enterprise, oriented to specific cases, governed by elaborate rules, and rarely taking in the population at large. From the later 17th century, a different breed of inquiry was generated. Social inquiry was originally, if marginally, unofficial. It measured the contours of society, assessed its wealth, probed some of its nastier problems and suggested policy directions. In essence it was not new, in methodology it was nothing less than revolutionary. The pioneers of 'political arithmetic' had various and sometimes selfish motives. But their methods could also be used by the most altruistic inquirers. In the 18th century several philanthropists achieved remarkable results in social policy-making by their energetic coupling of old moral injunctions and new empirical analysis. The demonstrated power of this method was so impressive that by the end of that cnetury it was becoming a fixture in the political process.

The creation of political arithmetic was the prime social application of the scientific revolution. The empirical analysis of social and political data was in clear imitation of new methods in the study of nature. That it was sometimes flawed is less significant to our study than that it appeared to achieve and hold considerable support, mainly because there was practically no sustained methodological opposition. Political arithmetic slowly evolved toward statistics, the original name disappearing by 1800. In its first century, the study of social data advanced from crude estimates to passing accuracy. At the same time, its influence improved accordingly. (11)

The earliest example of political arithmetic was the

work of John Graunt, a prosperous London merchant. (12)
He studied the London bills of mortality and his was the
first attempt at a systematic analysis of this data.
Graunt's work was a curious catalogue of demographic,
medical and political conclusions, based upon the mortality figures of the metropolis. He concluded that this
type of work meant a new departure in the study of
politics:

> whereas the art of governing, and the true *politiques*,
> is how to preserve the subject in Peace and Plenty,
> that men study only that part of it, which teacheth
> how to supplant, and overreach one another.... the
> foundation, or elements of this honest harmless
> Policy is to understand the land, and the hands of the
> territory to be governed, according to all their
> intrinsick, and accidental differences.

The study of population, trade, and social activity was
advocated by Graunt, for, he said

> I conclude, that a clear knowledge of all these par-
> ticulars, and many more, whereat I have shot but at
> rovers, is necessary in order to good, certain, and
> easie government, and even to balance parties, and
> factions both in Church and State. But whether the
> knowledge thereof be necessary to many, or fit for
> others, then the Sovereign, and his chief ministers,
> I leave to consideration. (13)

Perhaps Graunt's nervous conclusion was justified; he of
course was breaking new ground by merely venturing on
this kind of study.

Graunt soon had company. His friend and associate
William Petty, the anatomist and the renowned surveyor
of conquered Ireland, was keenly interested in this type
of inquiry. Indeed, he considered himself the inventor of
the method. Petty seems to have begun his well-known work,
'Political Arithmetick,' in 1671. In it he discussed the
strategic economic and political position of England. He
proposed to do so in a manner

> not yet very usual; for instead of only using com-
> parative and superlative words, and intellectual argu-
> ments, I have taken the course (as a specimen of the
> Political Arithmetick I have long aimed at) to express
> myself in terms of Number, Weight, or Measure; to use
> only arguments of sense, and to consider only such
> causes, as have visible foundation in nature ... (14)

In 1682, Petty supervised a survey of the Dublin Bills of
Mortality. He did a number of other quantitative studies,
many unpublished, some published posthumously. His energy
was remarkable, his devotion to empirical study unquestion-
able. Petty may have done for applied 'statistical'

inquiries what Francis Bacon did for the intellectual
concept of inductive method.

In the initial phase of social statistics, Gregory
King was another important figure. King's father was a
mathematician and a surveyor, but Gregory had become an
engraver, a genealogist, and a herald. In 1662, he
became clerk to Sir William Dugdale, and he assisted with
a number of heraldic visitations. In 1695, King became
secretary to the Commissioners for Taking and Stating the
Public Accounts; he also served as secretary to Control-
lers of the Accounts for the Army. In these official
positions, King was to have access to records, and to
apply his professional curiosity to a new type of document.
His 'Natural and Political Observations and Conclusions
upon the State and Condition of England, 1696,' was not
published until 1804. (15) Yet it has been carefully
analysed by modern demographers, one of whom concluded
that

> having regard to the nature and limitations of the
> basic material with which he worked, it is evident
> that King's estimate was a remarkable effort, and it
> is likely that in general terms it is not far from
> the truth. (16)

Rounding out the cast of early enumerators was Charles
Davenant the economist. After a classical education at
Cheam School and Balliol College, Davenant studied for a
law degree at Cambridge and was admitted to Doctors
Commons in 1675. He left the law for politics and government service, taking an Excise Commission post in 1679 and
sitting as an MP in 1685, and again in 1698 and 1700. (17)
While Davenant's work had a clearer political orientation
than his colleagues in political arithmetic, this may
have been the inevitable result of his choice of subject.
In his 'Discourses on the Public Revenue and on Trade'
(1698), he defined political arithmetic as 'the art of
reasoning by figures, upon things relating to government.'
He acknowledged Petty as the founder of the school and
suggested that his mentor lacked sufficient data. But
Davenant asserted that recent years and new taxes had
changed that picture. All the same, Davenant did not
advance far beyond Petty's basic method, which was essentially a series of educated guesses.

Indeed, the first generation of political arithmetic
had little to offer in its specific conclusions. The
reason may well have been as Davenant suggested: an
absence of reliable data. What was vital, however, was
the new method. As Petty said:

> Now the observations or positions expressed by number,
> weight, and measure, upon which I bottom the ensuing

> discourses, are either true or not apparently false....
> And if they are false, not so false as to destroy the
> argument they are brought for; but at worst are suf-
> ficient as suppositions to show the way to that know-
> ledge I aim at. (18)

The main achievement Petty made, and his early colleagues
could do little more, was to offer numerical evidence for
purposes of illustrating a point or an argument - not as
incontrovertible empirical evidence. Hence early political arithmetic was as much rhetoric as it was science.
All the same, it established a vital milestone of method.
The data and its manipulation were placed in open view,
accessible and easy to evaluate.

In the course of the 18th century, the technique of
political arithmetic made significant advances as the
number and variety of records improved, public availa-
bility was increased, and interest in the calculations
grew among the commercial, financial and legal sectors
of society. Needless to say, we are speaking in relative
terms, and in the century before the census, few if any
record series existed which would satisfy the modern
statistician. But that may be all the more reason to take
note of the work of those political arithmeticians whose
labour led to the better collection of data in the 19th
century.

Arthur Young, the peripatetic agrarian essayist, was
conscious of a need for observed data. Not much was
available - or at any rate collected - when he published
his first famous 'tour' in 1768. Nor indeed would there
be an extensive and consistent body of material until the
Board of Agriculture's county surveys and their respective critiques were completed (c. 1817). While Young's
'Political Arithmetic' (1774) was hardly numerically
oriented, its reasonings were based on exhaustive observation. The method was clearly empirical:

> The observations I made in my journies through the
> kingdom, fixed my opinions concerning population -
> the inclosure and division of landed property - the
> prices of the earth's products &c. I found the
> language of plain facts so clear, that I could not but
> listen and be convinced, and I laid the facts before
> the world on which I founded my opinions. (19)

In this particular work, Young concentrated on the arguments for a variety of fiscal and economic policies, with
relatively little quantitative evidence. Paradoxically,
his detailed local observations probably had given Young
a healthy disrespect for available national figures,
while they had not been sufficient to provide him with an
alternative supply.

George Chalmers was a Scottish lawyer and antiquarian. He had lived in the American colonies, returning to England in 1775. After the rebellion, Chalmers took the post of Chief Clerk to the Committee of the Privy Council for Trade and Plantations (1786). Prior to that, and perhaps to show his qualifications, he had written an extended survey of economic conditions at the close of the rebellion. (20) Chalmers offered documentation of what he called 'authentic intelligence' on the nation's resources and its temporary trade losses.

> The inferences which result from facts are irresistible, when they are themselves authenticated. He was induced therefore to mention, secondly, the sources whence the documents before-mentioned were drawn, in order to enable the Reader to judge of their authenticity, and, by examining his reasonings, to add the authority of experience to the decisions of judgment.

Chalmers accounted for perennial pessimism in histories of trade ('A twelve-month has scarcely passed away, in which a treatise has not been published ... bewailing the loss of our commerce, and the ruin of the state') by lengthy tabulations which showed wide fluctuations in imports and exports. He suggested averaging as a surer means of estimating: 'it is from the averages of given years at given epochs, that we can only form a decided opinion with regard to the real prosperity or decay of commerce, or of navigation.' (21)

Chalmers went from the discussion of trade to join the debate on population. He accepted the enumerations of houses made by Rev. John Howlett which were used to show the unreliability of official surveyors' returns to the tax office. (22) Chalmers estimated that the errors in house-counting caused an underestimate of close to one-third in the work of such theorists as Richard Price. The work of Chalmers showed signs of a maturing skill in statistical work; it is probably our loss that he turned to antiquarian research for the remainder of his career.

In the last decades of the 18th century, still others in government service tried to introduce empirical evidence into their official and quasi-official work. Patrick Colquhoun was the son of a registrar of records in Dumbartonshire, and after a brief career in trade, Patrick became Lord Provost of Glasgow in 1782-3. Later he came to London and became a police magistrate. Committed to a number of social causes, Colquhoun wrote and organized on behalf of several reform efforts. In 1795, he published his major work, 'A Treatise on the Police of the Metropolis.' This book went through seven editions in the next eleven years, and Colquhoun's testimony was often called for by committees of Parliament.

While the bulk of Colquhoun's 'Treatise' dealt with a survey of crime and punishment in the capital, his most compelling section was an empirical review of social institutions in general and law enforcement in particular (Chapter XIX). He demonstrated effectively, by a sketch of small debt cases in 1793, that the cost of the judicial apparatus might be several times greater than the sum recoverable claims. (23)

Sir John Sinclair was a barrister who became one of the first statisticians - or at least one of the first persons to devote his career to rendering national accounts. (24) In 1790 he sent out circular letters to the parochial clergy throughout Scotland, and asked them to return a description of their parishes. These descriptions were collected and published in the 21-volume 'Statistical Account of Scotland' (1791-9). There was not much novelty in the use of clergy for questionnaire-type inquiry; indeed, we can see the history of visitations behind it. The idea of collection and publication was more novel, and unquestionably a step in the direction of further use of empirical data. Sinclair himself made a much more important personal contribution in his 'History of the Public Revenue of the British Empire' (1785-). This was a detailed analysis of government expenditures, which appeared in three editions and demonstrated further advances in the genre.

John Rickman was a career statistician, perhaps the first in English government. In 1796 he wrote an essay on 'the Utility and Facility of a General Enumeration of the People of the British Empire.' This was apparently the catalyst for the Bill which was introduced in 1800. When the Census was enacted, Rickman was given the supervision of the Census returns, which came in from the parish officers around the kingdom. (25) Rickman continued to supervise the census through 1831, meanwhile becoming Clerk to the House of Commons in 1814, in which position he was also the superintendent of a broad range of inquiry-related material. Modern scholars have numerous reservations as to the data gathered in Rickman's tenure with the census; nevertheless, he deserves credit from later generations for a highly significant pioneering effort.

On its own, political arithmetic might well have been joined to the judicial mode of inquiry, and its powers turned exclusively to the service of the establishment. While each of our examples had some concern for social reform, they were government servants. They were not radicals of any sort, and they were not likely to perceive their methods as means of change. Fortunately,

there were some significant adaptations of empirical
inquiry by leading philanthropists. Their extra-govern-
mental enterprise was to have a telling impact on a body
politic which was feeling new sensitivity to humanitarian
arguments in the later 18th century. And part of the
success of these arguments had to be due to the influence
of empirical data.

Jonas Hanway was the son of a naval agent. After
apprenticeship to a merchant, he entered the Levant trade
and earned a fortune. He returned to London and plunged
into a series of philanthropic efforts, the most notable
being the Foundling Hospital and the Marine Society. In
the former case, Hanway joined other philanthropists in
working to reduce the toll of infant mortality in London.
He investigated all of the parish workhouses in the metropolis and collected data on poor infants. This evidence
assisted the passage in 1762 of the first act for registration of parish poor children (2 Geo. III c. 22).
Further efforts brought a committee of inquiry in 1766
and a new law in 1767 (7 Geo. III c. 39). By this law,
parish children under six were required to be removed
from the city, to be maintained at parish expense in
healthier surroundings. Unquestionably, Hanway's efforts
were bolstered by the collection and publication of
detailed figures on the parish children. (26)

The work of John Howard was as impressive as Hanway's,
if somewhat slower in its fulfilment.   The son of a
craftsman and a grocer's apprentice, Howard was England's
first great prison reformer. He was deeply affected by
a term of imprisonment in France in 1755-6. Later, as
a landowner in Bedford, he became High Sheriff. In this
position, he began an inspection tour of prisons, and the
appalling conditions he found induced him to continue
that work. He published 'The State of the Prisons in
England and Wales' in 1777, and he continued surveying
penal institutions for most of his remaining years. (27)
The core of his work was a census of prisoners by different categories, and elaboration of the physical conditions
of places of confinement. Even before the publication of
his first work, Howard had testified before a committee of
the House of Commons, and he was instrumental in some
early reform legislation. (28) For several generations,
Howard's work was a model for prison reformers. His long
and arduous tours of inspection were a demanding example
for other social reformers, applying the social equivalent
of scientific observation.

Thomas Clarkson was the son of a clergyman and a gradu-
ate of St Johns College, Cambridge. In 1786 he wrote a
prize essay on the slave trade. (29) His timely com-

position brought him membership in a group of reformers who established an anti-slavery committee in 1787. The following year, the group managed to gain Pitt's support for the formation of a committee of the Privy Council to inquire into 'the present state of the African trade.' In Clarkson's opinion, the inquiry was a necessary first step:

> To abolish the trade, replete as it was with misery, was desirable also; but it was so connected with the interest of individuals, and so interwoven with the commerce and revenue of the country, that an hasty abolition of it without a previous inquiry appeared to (the authorities) to be likely to be productive of as much misery as good. (30)

After collection of evidence by this committee, opponents of abolition joined the struggle, more evidence was presented to a Committee of the Whole House (1789) and then to a Select Committee (1790, 1791). The abundance of evidence gathered was a sign of the intensity of the dispute if not the accuracy of information. The role of inquiry at this stage was as dubious as the material it collected, for a minor regulatory act passed before all the evidence was in; (31) the abolition of the trade had to wait almost twenty years longer. One conclusion was inescapable: from this period, a major political issue with significant social ramifications such as this one was unlikely to escape the process of legislative inquiry.

The later 18th century saw considerable use of the inquiry procedure by the legislature. To both sides of the slavery question it had appeared that inquiry would bring justification. (32) Of course the reality of politically oriented inquiry was that it followed the influence of whatever forces were directing political acts at the time. There was and is no way that a completely disinterested investigation could be conducted by political men. (33) That said, there remained plenty of room for the improvement of political discussion and decision by way of added objective data. One of the easiest means to this end was the use of the Select Committee of the House of Commons. It is arguable that the mere existence of the Select Committee was the vital fact: it could be used to present a body of evidence to the whole House. Lacking the kind of powerful resistance which could be mounted by the resourceful defenders of the slave trade, such presentations often meant an easy victory in the legislature.

The Select Committee's importance to reform in general is that it was available for occasional use in the early stages of social inquiry. It became less important in the

heyday of reform in the 19th century, and it was super-
seded by the Royal Commission. Yet its value in the
earlier years should not be overlooked. Examining the
subject-matter of Select Committees in the House of
Commons (1760-1800), there were some clear instances of
social inquiry in the modern sense, that is, studies of
social problems. They were not numerous, nor always
consciously styled as inquiries, and surely in some cases
they were less than objective. In these four decades,
Sheila Lambert's list contains 580 select committees'
reports. She excluded a number of routine committees,
and if we also eliminate those whose task was procedural
(preparing the reply to the Address), political (contested
elections), fiscal (militia estimates), and judicial
(impeachment and fraud) - there remain 353 which were in
the broadest sense social. Of those some 49 were more
clearly inquiries related to social reform, though others
may well have been so motivated. No satisfactory classification is really possible: was pavement in Westminster,
or an inquiry into gold coinage, or into the transport of
felons in the full sense a social question? In any case,
the Select Committee was important, whatever its inherent
limitations. And at the same time, the ingenuity of
inquiry was finding further application, under Parliament's
direction but outside its immediate structure.

III

In the political crisis of 1780-4 there were serious
reform impulses and severe criticism of the King's government. They help to explain the early experiments with
non-judicial reformatory Royal Commissions of Inquiry.
Yet the course of their development, to the point in 1818
when the Commission was linked to a member of the broad
family of social inquiry, was neither a planned nor a
precise movement. Rather it seems that the venerable
prerogative exercise of a special commission where regular
jurisdiction failed was brought to bear on some of the
archaic agencies of government. The method gradually
proved its effectiveness (1780-1830) and went on to
become a centrepiece of Victorian reform. Naturally, the
Royal Commission of Inquiry simultaneously underwent
changes of its own, and one of the most important was its
junction with the currents of political arithmetic and
social inquiry.
     The basic urge in the 1780s was for more responsible
government through more careful and honest financial
dealings - 'economical reform.' One of the first steps

TABLE I Commissions of Inquiry 1780-1818 (a)

Title	Origin (b)	Term	Pay (c)	Initial Report
Public Accounts	P	1780-87	S	41 Lambert 1
Fees and Gratuities	P	1785-87	O	1806.VII (reprint)
Woods and Forests	P	1786-93	S	76 Lambert 5
Customs Fees	P	1789-90	S	1821.XIV.65
Public Records (d)	AR	1800-	S	1812.XII.1
Naval Fraud	P	1802-06	S	1802-03.IV.163
Fees, etc. (I)	P	1804-14	S	1806.VIII.1
Military Expenditure	P	1805-12	S	1806.VI.1
Education (I)	P	1806-12	S	1813-14.V.1
Administration of Justice(S)	P	1808-	S	1809.IV.381
Saleable Offices	W	1810	O	1810.IX.125
Duties, etc., Courts	W (e)	1815-24	S	1816.VIII.91
Customs Excise	W	1818	S	1820.VI.559
Charities	P	1818-37	MS	1819.X (A-B)

Source: Parliamentary Papers as listed, and Returns on Commissions 1826-27.XX.499

(a) The list excludes commissions for claims, specific cases of fraud, and specific uses such as improvements. These near relatives in the judicial family were not involved in shaping public policy, as the commissions listed above generally were.

(b) P-Act of Parliament; A-Address of the Commons; R-Report of a parliamentary committee; W-Royal Warrant.

(c) S-Staff salaried; C-Commissioners (all) salaried; M-Mixture of paid and unpaid Commissioners; O-No salaried employees.

(d) First for England and Wales later extended to Scotland (1808), and Ireland (1812).

(e) Separate warrants issued for England, Scotland, and Ireland.

to this end was the establishment by Lord North of a Commission of Inquiry into Public Accounts. There had been
other Commissions for Accounts in the past, especially
in the period 1691-1713. But those were notoriously
political enterprises. The novelty in 1780 was that the
Commission would be composed of financial experts instead
of politicians. The novelty did not end there.

> Spread over seven years, the Commission's fourteen
> Reports laid down principles which, in their outrageous
> simplicity - 'every office should have a useful duty
> annexed to it' - revolutionized British government. (34)

The Commissioners themselves were well aware of their
innovative condition:

> A Commission of Accounts, to the extent and for the
> purposes expressed in the Act, is not an ordinary
> institution; and we have been obliged to content our-
> selves with the suggestions of our own understandings,
> unassisted either by the lights of our ancestors or
> the experience of contemporaries. (35)

The Commissioners, in breaking new ground, dealt with
numerous official functions. In fact, their mandate had
been 'to take an account of the public money in the hands
of the several accountants.' They recommended a number
of reforms, such as the end of sinecures, the substitution
of salaries for fees and gratuities, and the institution
of effective auditing.

Many of the ideas of the Public Accounts Commission
were widely shared already and easily given some legislative embodiment. Equally important, in the course of
the 1780s, several more reformatory commissions were
established. A Commission on Fees and Gratuities was
established in 1785; a study of crown woods, forests and
land revenues was commissioned in 1786; and inquiry into
the fees of customs officials was instituted in 1789. (36)

The 1790s were barren of similar inquiry commissions.
Most energy of the governing class was devoted to the war
with France and the unrest of domestic radicals. The
combination was unhealthy for further reform inquiry.
Yet an important Committee of Accounts picked up the work
of the earlier Commission in 1796, and with the turn of
the century, a new and broader kind of inquiry appeared.
In 1800, a Commission was formed to inquire into 'the
State of the Public Records of the Kingdom.' Irish
education was the focus of another commission in 1806, and
the administration of justice was targeted by the first
of a series of inquiries in 1808. (37) Here there was a
significant variation. Inquiries were starting to look
at activities without direct political purposes - that is,
at the social impact of government. The shift was subtle,

and there is no evidence of planning.   Rather, the circumstances in each case, severe problems of governance and a
will to remedy them, were responsible for turning the
inquiry commission toward a social objective.   All the
while, inquiries of a judicial or political nature - navy,
army, customs, fees and gratuities - were continuing the
more traditional pursuits.

It may surprise us that contemporary reaction to the
resurgence and extension of commissions of inquiry varied
from slight to non-existent.   But executive commissioners
were ubiquitous in the 18th century, they were not easily
distinguished from commissioners of inquiry, and the work
of the latter only aroused mild constitutional opposition.
(38)   From the commission of the peace to the commissions
for the land tax, sewers, lunatics, bankrupts, customs
and excise, enclosures, and so on, the overwhelming form
of delegated power was the royal commission.   This condition must have meant a degree of familiarity which, if
not assuring a welcome for more commissioners, would
nevertheless mean they could not become highly visible
targets in such a setting.   And contemporaries were
probably no surer of the difference between the executive
commission and the commission of inquiry than we are.
The distinction was real and vital: the holder of a royal
commission was in a permanent post as a servant *pro
tempore* of the crown.   A member of a royal commission of
inquiry was in a temporary position, although the position
might become permanent.   The temporary nature of inquiries
probably added to the constitutional significance of
these bodies for ministerial power.   Ironically, historians have been more interested in those inquiries which
became permanent.   The latter are associated with the
notion of 'administrative revolution' even though they
were clearly in the tradition of offices 'going out of
court' and establishing their own bailiwick.   The real
revolution, if the word must be used, was in the capacity
for repeated use and discard of inquiries on an unlimited
range of subjects.   Some were promoted to permanence,
others were stalled, others were rejected.   This technique
of using prerogative in disposable containers was of
obvious significance for ministerial power; at the same
time, it provided what can be regarded as a temporary,
piece-work, and inexpensive transitional civil service.

Finally resistance was minimized because the Royal
Commission of Inquiry was introduced slowly and carefully,
due to the unhappy reputation of commissions, and because
of the natural circumspection of ministers.   That circumspection was increased by the probability that no minister
saw the use of such commissions as a broad policy, but

rather took each one up in its own context. In any event,
a series of inquiries from 1780 to 1816 had given
ministers a better grip on the reins of power, and it had
increased their confidence in the management of commissions.

This initial phase of modern commissions was vital in
several ways. The first was that it showed that ministers
could undertake meaningful reviews of funding and staffing
and could initiate reforms. In turn, that fact meant that
ministers had become more powerful vis-à-vis the crown:
they were following the dictum that 'the influence of
the crown ... ought to be diminished' and were assuming
it themselves. But finally, the process of commissions
of inquiry kept matters under the nominal control of the
crown - and at the same time made affairs public, and gave
them the sanction of empirical analysis. This stroke of
accidental brilliance was vital to the peaceful constitutional evolution of the English monarchy. The
success of that evolution rested on the ancient tradition
of judicial inquiry and the modern uses of empirical
analysis - and these were neatly brought together by the
Royal Commission of Inquiry.

The State of Charity:
Autonomy or Anarchy?

The English charitable trust was a body with considerable
legal autonomy. The trustees managed the gift property on
behalf of the beneficiaries. The trusts were rooted in
a special field of property law, judicial oversight lay
with the Lord Chancellor, and of course the ultimate
legal fate rested with Parliament. But from day to day,
trustees were virtually independent. The exercise of the
so-called central authorities was a remote and rare occur-
rence.

The course of the 18th century saw this autonomy drift-
ing toward a state of anarchy. The intervention of Parliament erratically increased without plan or principle;
the control of Chancery was diminished and brought into
disrepute; the nature of charity itself was drastically
changed by benevolent societies to the disadvantage of
charitable trusts; finally, the government of trusts
became impossible in many instances unless trustees
defied the law. As trustees did choose in growing numbers
to evade or violate the law for the sake of their trusts,
their disregard for authority seriously blurred the line
between autonomy and anarchy.

I

The law of charitable trusts was confused by the Parlia-
ments of the 18th century. The general law of trusts
was tied up in an ambiguous application of the law of
mortmain. The particular lawmaking on trusts was extensive and unorganized. Although charitable trusts were
subjected to numerous interferences, there were no clear
principles applied. Thus the legislative acts of the 18th
century contributed to a drift toward anarchy among
charitable trusts.

The heart of private law was the regulation of the disposition of land. In this area, there were two types of regulation which were old and well-established in English law: the limitation of grants to corporate bodies (the law of mortmain); and the confinement of inheritance to the immediate heir (entail). Both objectives were frequent themes of statute law, both were breached constantly and cleverly, both were problems for the charitable trust, and when they were combined in one Act in the 18th century, serious confusion was the result.

The law of mortmain had been a principle (of the crown at least) since Magna Carta: no lands were to be alienated to or by the clergy, as the said property then passed to an undying owner. Mortmain was not fully enforced, but rather the royal right to enter and seize such lands was waived for a fee (or license). The mortmain principle was extended to civil corporations in the late 14th century (15 Ric. II c. 5).

Of equal concern to the crown was the facility with which private donors found means of evading feudal control. As early as the 13th century, grants of land outside the natural line were limited to gifts before death (*De donis conditionalibus,* 1285). With the simultaneous ending of subinfeudation, the more modern concept of estates emerged in the place of fees and tenures, and the brisk business in making and breaking entails was soon underway. One of the major devices in this contest was the 'use,' an ancient legal trick of giving property to feofees or trustees, 'to the use of' oneself or others. The legal property vaporized while very real ownership was retained. The use was superficially similar to the legal corporation, but gifts to uses were not proscribed by mortmain: trustees were not as such a legal corporation, though a corporation might be vested with a trust. Thus the law of mortmain did not apply directly to charitable trusts.

The crown opposed the apparent abuse of 'uses,' and Henry VIII's Statute of Uses (1535) took the simple but effective step of declaring the legal ownership of a use to be in the beneficiary (the *Cestui que use*). But this manoeuvre backfired; it was easily evaded by new strategies, such as the lease and release. The Statute also had the effect of abolishing the devise of lands by will. That unpleasant consequence was corrected by the Statute of Wills (1540) which allowed such devices on the condition that the heir assumed the old feudal dues.

Meanwhile 'charitable uses' had appeared at least as early as the 15th century. They were tended by the Lord Chancellor, as common law had no way of handling the use. The Chancellor's power to control charitable uses was

fortified and codified by the Statute of Charitable Uses
in 1601 (43 Eliz. c. 4). This Act empowered the Lord
Chancellor to issue a commission to bishops and others,
who were to conduct hearings and decree findings in cases
of mismanagement and abuse of charitable trusts. The
statute recognized charitable uses, defined their objects,
and set up the judicial authority to correct abuses, more
accurately to correct those under its jurisdiction. For
the Statute of Charitable Uses exempted a category of
superior or immune trusts: the Universities and Colleges
of Oxford and Cambridge, the foundations of Eton,
Winchester, and Westminster, collegiate and cathedral
foundations, and any charities with special visitors.
The immunity was based on the legal existence of royal or
special powers of supervision, with which the Chancellor
was forbidden to interfere.

The law of charitable uses was not seriously altered
until the end of the 17th century. After the Glorious
Revolution, the law of mortmain was reformed, and in the
18th century it was awkwardly amplified. In 1696 the
mortmain licenses were authorized by Act (7 & 8 Will. III
c. 37) as it appeared that the long-accepted practice of
royal waiver might then be interpreted as an improper use
of the dispensing power. Dispensing did become the order
of the day in the 18th century, but it was dispensing
with the licenses themselves. Beginning with the waiver
on gifts to Queen Anne's Bounty (2 & 3 Anne c. 20, S.4),
a growing number of statutes renounced the crown's claim
in particular cases.

It was therefore strange that an apparently restrictive
Act, commonly referred to afterward as the 'Statute of
Mortmain,' was passed in 1735 (9 Geo. II c. 36). The Act
was not about mortmain, but was a new attempt to restrict
devises of land, especially to charitable trusts. It provided that no devise of land, or money for the purchase
of land, could be made to any charitable trust after
24 June, 1736. Such gifts as were made had to be concluded at least twelve months before the donor's death,
and the deed of gift had to be enrolled in Chancery within
six months of the making of the gift. The Act had a preamble which echoed Henry VIII's Statute of Uses, to prevent 'ill-considered dispositions by persons near death.'
This object was accompanied by a desire to keep land on
the market. But it appeared to the public - indeed to
legal authorities - that the Statute was against charity,
or at best was meant to stiffen the terms on which gifts
were made to charitable uses. (1) The wake of the statute
saw both a sharp reduction in devises of land to charitable trusts, and an increase in devises of money or stock,

TABLE 2   Trust Deeds enrolled in Chancery, 1737-1865
          under 9 Geo. II c. 36

1737-46	307
1747-56	307
1757-66	324
1767-76	300
1777-86	303
1787-96	345
1797-06	606
1807-16	1743
1817-26	2151
1827-36	3429
1837-46	6710
1847-56	6875
1857-65	10272
Total	33672

Source: PRO, 'Deputy Keeper's Report,' XXXII, Appendix II, 1871

and an increase in gifts of all kinds (see Table 2).   In addition, we know there was also a rising tide of gifts to unendowed charity.   In other words, the mortmain Act was not about mortmain, nor did its apparent rigour mean a fatal decline in charitable giving.   Even where the act was potentially harmful to intended trusts, it was often ignored, easily evaded and occasionally overridden by heirs of would-be founders.

Mortmain was not the true concern of the statute of 9 Geo. II.   That concern was rather a compound of the classic fears surrounding bequests of land: disinheritance and gifts to superstitious uses.   In fact, the statute in operation was quite beneficial in undermining mortmain and providing a cheap and effective equivalent of licensing, via the Chancery enrolment.   Therefore the 18th century was, in spite of appearances, seeing the end of mortmain and not a late revival. (2)   The full and formal demise was only to come after prolonged hearings and discussion in the second half of the 19th century.

In local and general legislation in the 18th century, a wide variety of charity administration questions were dealt with by Parliament in its patchwork efforts to accommodate the transition from manorial to manufacturing society.   There was no consistent policy evident in all of this activity, but there was a fairly clear pattern of increasing intervention and legislative regulation.   The pattern was clear in each of the areas of legislation relevant to charitable trusts (poor laws, enclosures, local improvements, and taxation), and the motive seemed consistent: to integrate the resources of charitable trusts more effectively with the social budget. Within the general pattern, there were two distinct modes: first, treating charitable gifts as a form of public welfare (and here the relation to legislation on poor relief was paramount); the second mode was treating charity as a form of property, and involved the various incidental adjustments which the law made affecting property (particularly enclosures, improvements, and taxes).

There were several attempts in the early 18th century to assign a clearer role to charitable trusts as a form of poor relief. By the second half of the century, this tendency had reached the statute book in a number of local acts for the relief of the poor, where local authorities were given specific powers in relation to charitable trusts. And as poor relief was recognized as a critical national problem in the last quarter of the century, joint national surveys of poor rates and charitable donations were authorized by Parliament.

The earliest notices of parliamentary concern in the poor relief-trust relationship were fragmentary and uncertain. In 1705 an order of the Commons directed 'That it be an instruction to the Committee of the Whole House to whom the Bill for the better relief, employment, and settlement of the poor is committed, that they have power to receive clauses, for the better application of charities, given to the use of the poor.' (3) The clauses in question remain unknown, the Bill in question was unprinted and unpassed. Another Bill was proposed in 1747 'for the better relief of the poor by voluntary charities,' and while this passed the Commons, it failed in the Lords and was also unprinted. (4)

The first full account of a general measure was from 1765. This Bill provided district commissioners for the poor, which commissioners were to be incorporated, and enabled to receive 'all voluntary gifts and contributions, which well disposed and charitable persons shall think proper to make.' The Commissioners would apply such gifts 'as the Donor or Donors and Contributor or Contributors shall direct and appoint; and if no such direction or appointment shall be given or made touching the application of such gifts and contributions, the same shall be made part of the common stock, and applied for the general purposes of this Act.' (5) The Bill failed, but its objectives were already being attained via local Acts for relief of the poor.

In 1755 one of a new breed of local Acts incorporated

the guardians of the poor in Dunheved (alias Launceston),
Cornwall. Among their powers, they could 'without license
in mortmain, purchase, take, or receive, any lands,
tenements, or hereditaments, of the gift, alienation, or
devize of any person or persons whomsoever having a right
and not being otherwise disabled to grant, alien, or
devize the same, who are hereby without further license
enabled to give, transfer, grant, or devize any such
lands, tenements, or hereditaments unto or for the use and
benefit of the said corporation.' (6) It was further
enacted that any 'charitable gifts' which were thereafter
made 'in general terms' for the use of the poor 'shall be
paid to, and be had, received, and enjoyed by, the corporation hereby erected, to and for the use of the poor
aforesaid.' In other words, the guardians were empowered
to receive and use property given as charitable gifts,
whether to them specifically or to the poor generally.

We find a similar intent in the Act of 1771 'for the
better regulating the poor within the city of Oxford.'
(7) This Act created a corporation of guardians, gave
them a mortmain waiver, but stipulated that the churchwardens and overseers of the poor in each parish would
receive gifts 'now payable or which shall hereafter become
payable for and to the use of the poor.' The provision
was aimed at general gifts, and clear exceptions were
made: 'this Act, or anything herein contained shall not
in anywise extend to give the said guardians any power or
authority over any alms-house, or hospital, or any other
charitable building, or other special donation whatsoever,
within the said City, already or hereafter to be given.'
While varying in detail, this type of legislation was not
uncommon in the second half of the 18th century. (8)

The general tendency of these local acts was to link
the administration of charitable trusts and poor relief.
As far as it succeeded, so far did the trusts become
public corporations, and hence more a local relief agency
than an independent, autonomous trust. Without prejudging
the issue between parochial authorities and independent
trustees, it is clear that an important trend was present,
and was being impelled by the growing concern on the
issue of poor relief. That issue became even more heated
in the last quarter of the century, and so did its impact
on charitable trusts, when in the 1770s and 80s there
were demands for assessments of relief and charity. As
we shall see below, the surveys into these subjects in
the 1780s were harbingers of a new era in public policy.

When the legislature dealt with charitable trusts as
private property, there was no apparent steady motive
through the maze of incidental acts. While trusts were

treated fairly in most matters, it was easy for Parliament
to intervene, but impossible to manage a completely harm-
less relationship where the lawmakers were acting on
matters of charity law from so many different perspectives.

In enclosure acts, the 18th century parliament was
attempting to dismantle an ancient feature of landholding
- the common land, and secondarily, to create legal
machinery for redistribution (Commissioners, surveyors,
etc). Charitable trusts might be involved in enclosures
either as owners of private land or as common law beneficiaries of common land. In the latter case, enclosure
awards often contained an allotment for the poor. In that
situation, the process of enclosure was actually creating
a charitable trust, ordinarily one vested in the churchwardens or overseers of the poor. In the case of land
already owned by a trust, the enclosure act, or the
subsequent award, provided for a reallocation, and thus
nearly always indicated an exchange of land. Since the
expenses of enclosure were borne by all the landowners in
proportion, steps were necessary to enable trustees to
dispose of land or other property in order to meet the
expenses of enclosure. This had to be specially provided
in each act until Parliament passed the consolidating
act on Enclosures in 1801, and the sale of 'charity lands
or school lands' was systematized (41 Geo. III c. 109).

The growing mass of local improvements enacted in the
18th century were also often related to charitable trust
affairs. The proliferation of commissioners for sewers,
turnpike trusts, roads, bridges, etc. were in many
instances taking over functions which had depended on
charitable funds, though by the 18th century municipal
trusts were a relatively insignificant part of trust
activity as a whole. But more important were the instances where local improvement schemes comprehended the
property of charitable trusts. The improvements might
mean several different kinds of alteration in charitable
trusts: increased property values, forced disposition of
property, or some other intervention.

For example, in 1773 the trustees of a municipal
charity and an almshouse in Newark (Notts) were authorized
to sell or exchange property for the rebuilding of the
town centre and the erection of a town hall (Private Act,
13 Geo. III c. 96). The surplus of the more than £13,000
realized by this transaction was paid over to the corporation of Nottingham under yet another improvement act
(38 Geo. III c. 26, Local). Again, in Liverpool in 1786,
owners and trustees of property were authorized to sell
to the Mayor et al. for the purpose of building and
widening streets (26 Geo. III c. 12). The improvement

acts could bring complications. For example, in Allhallows
Lombard Street, one Ralph Carter had left property for
bread, coal, and prisoners' relief. When this property
was sold under an Act of 1812 (52 Geo. III c. 149, Local)
the amount of sale went to a jury trial, followed by a
Chancery order, and payment (in 1817) into the fund of
the Accountant-General of Chancery. (9)

But in some cases, improvement legislation did not, or
could not, stop at the simple authorization to sell or
exchange property. An excellent example occurred in the
case of Lord Scudamore's Charity, Hereford. The improvement act (14 Geo. III, c. 38) was aimed at 'paving repairing cleansing and lighting the streets and lanes in
the city of Hereford and the suburbs thereof, and for the
better application of charity money for setting the poor
people thereof to work.' In this case, a trust fund
affected by the legislation had never in fact been properly established. The Bishop of Hereford had held £400
since about 1670; that increased to £1320 by 1763, when
a Chancery decree (unsuccessfully) demanded the activation
of the trust. The Act of 1774 set up commissioners to
manage the trust, whose value had increased fourfold by
the time of inquiry in 1836. (10)

Yet another subject of 18th century legislation which
impinged on charitable trusts as property was taxation.
The trusts were eligible for land tax, house duty, stamp
duty, and legacy duty (and sometimes tithes or local
rates). Generally the tax picture for charitable trusts
was becoming brighter - more exemptions and less taxes
overall were the general tendencies.

The land tax was made perpetual at the current rate in
1798, with an option to redeem the tax. Trusts were
required to sell property in order to meet this cost, and
for small trusts it was a hardship. Thus in 1806 a waiver
was granted to trusts with an income of £150 or less. (11)
Ordinary property duties were assessed on charity estates,
but there were attempts to remit the burden of these.
For example, a proposal was made (and defeated) to exempt
the houses of masters of charity schools from duty in
1798. (12) There were several measures which relieved
trusts of stamp duty. The legacy duty, which varied but
was normally about 10 per cent, was a form of tax on
charity, though often assessed before a trust was in fact
in operation, and always a single instance tax. (13)

On all tax matters, charitable trusts suffered the same
state supervision that private owners did, but with
occasional special treatment. There was no policy, and
indeed we have no detailed information on the administration of the tax laws, except for land tax exemptions.

In addition to mortmain and the several varieties of local legislation, Parliament was active in one other way with respect to charitable trusts. Private Acts could be and were used for almost any kind of trust amendment. Theoretically this course was open to all, but only the well-heeled and well-connected among the trusts enjoyed easy access. The cost of a private act and the necessary connections precluded the vast majority from even making the attempt. Indeed, the record suggests that private legislation was used sparingly and probably did not exceed two statutes per year on an average. (14)

More important in our context was what these acts did, or tried to do, rather than their mere numbers. For the most part, private acts were used to authorize sales or exchanges of land, or to make other property arrangements. These uses accounted for fully two thirds of the acts tabulated by Bramwell. Otherwise, acts were used to establish or ratify trusts or variations therein. In all of these measures there was a special attraction in using the legislative method: there was no risk of the rigorous examination and the narrow application of precedents which would be expected in Chancery.

In general, private legislation was no indication of a policy or of a legislative trend. Parliament in this capacity was simply rendering a service to wealthy or influential clients, rewriting the law for these 'deserving' individual cases.

The net result of legislative action was an irregular but dramatic increase in lawmakers' interference in charitable trust affairs. But for good or ill there was no systematic policy or plan behind this increase - or for that matter behind the several interferences. In the one instance of general legislation there was monumental confusion, and in the innumerable individual acts on trusts and their property, there was concentration on particular needs. In neither case was there any sign of fundamental evaluation of or attention to the general condition of the charitable trust.

II

The Court of Chancery in 1800 had changed little since the time of the Glorious Revolution. (15) The Lord Chancellor's office was still a great power centre and the court was a massive bureaucracy by 18th century standards. These facts were by no means promising for the interests of suitors. The Lord Chancellor had been the premier royal official before the 16th century evolution of the

secretaries of state and the later rise of parliamentary
leadership through the Treasury. The Chancellor remained
a key figure in the cabinet, though in the 19th century
the strength of that position began to depend more on
the personality and political skills of the office holder.
In an interesting paradox of modern government, the Lord
Chancellor was simultaneously the head of the House of
Lords and exercised the greatest individual store of
patronage, while he was also the leading judge and titular
head of the legal profession and as such the highest-
placed meritocrat in government.

The Lord Chancellor sat during the four law terms in
Westminster Hall or in chambers in Lincoln's Inn Hall,
where he heard arguments and appeals, and whence he
delivered (or delayed) judgments. The court offices were
housed in several buildings in Chancery Lane. The principal officers assisting the Lord Chancellor were the Master
of the Rolls and the eleven Masters in Chancery. These
assistant judges were responsible for conducting preliminary hearings, making investigations and reports, drafting
decrees, and taxing costs. To assist the Masters, the
Six Clerks Office was in charge of the actual drafting of
reports and decrees, and the clerical management of cases.
The Six Clerks' places were virtual sinecures by 1800,
with the work passing to the ten Sworn Clerks who worked
under each of the Six. The Sworn Clerks in their turn
presided over a staff of assistants. Besides this
clerical core, there were important accessory judicial
offices such as those of the Examiners, the Register of
Affadavits, the Subpoena Office, and the Accountant
General. Finally, there were a number of offices whose
functions were tied to the older, non-judicial duties of
the Chancellor: the Cursitors, the Clerks of the Petty
Bag, the Clerk of the Hanaper, the Clerk of the Chapel
of the Rolls, and the Clerk of the Crown in Chancery.

The Court of Chancery was the centre of English equity
jurisdiction. The Lord Chancellor was the chief guardian
of trusts, but his jurisdiction over them was much broader
than his real power. Founders of trusts could specify
visitors, whose supervisory authority could not be super-
seded by the Lord Chancellor. In the case of charities
without special visitors, even though the visitor's role
passed to the Chancellor, he could only act on an appeal
made to his court; he could not initiate proceedings.
Finally, in the course of the 17th and 18th centuries,
powers of intervention and alteration in trust cases were
further limited by the court's own decisions. There were
**three areas where the court was likely to assume the power
to intervene: routine trust maintenance (renewal of**

trustees or deeds of trust); trust alteration (sale of property, change of beneficiary, clarification of objects of trust); or trust violation (adjudication of charges of abuse or mismanagement brought by or against trustees).

Until the late 18th century there were two different processes for bringing a charitable trust into Chancery - a commission of charitable uses or a bill of information (or 'English bill'). The special form of the commission had been created by Elizabethan statute, but it had ceased to be used by the end of the 18th century. When the Lord Chancellor was petitioned on behalf of a charity, he could issue a commission to the Bishop of the diocese and others, empowering them to take testimony (with a jury if necessary), and directing them to make a decree which would be forwarded to and enrolled in Chancery. Then the parties could file 'exceptions' (i.e. appeals) with the Lord Chancellor. While the commissions may have once been effective, by the 18th century they were expensive, laborious, and inefficient. Since most cases were appealed to the Chancellor, the commission of charitable uses became just another method of making the equity process more exhausting. At Burford (Oxfordshire) the school was the subject of three commissions (1628, 1702, and 1739), and 'the latter commission was strongly contested; there were forty three exceptions taken to the decree, which were argued and decided before Lord Hardwick in 1743, and the greater part of the exceptions were allowed.' (16) The last commission of charitable uses was issued in 1787. The decree in that case was made in 1803, and the argument on the decree was still continuing in 1818. (17)

The standard method for bringing suit in Chancery was the so-called 'English bill' (named by its early adoption of the vernacular). Persons who prayed relief or who sought a judgment on alleged violations were to petition or inform the Attorney-General, and with his clearance, proceedings would be brought in his name on behalf of the charity. The defects of this normal proceeding were high costs and long delays, to such an extent that, for charitable trusts, justice was effectively being sold, delayed, or denied. Bentham's caustic and exaggerated description of the procedure was based on a foundation of unpleasant fact.

Under the name of a bill, a volume of notorious lies delivered in, with three or four months' time for a first answer, and after exceptions taken of course, two or three months for a second - then amendments made to the bill with more such delays, and more succeeding answers - then a cross bill filed on the other side,

and a second such cause mounted on the shoulders of
the first - then volumes heaped upon volumes of depositions - then after years thus employed, a decree
obtained by which nothing is decided - then the whole
matter, and everything that has been made to grow out
of it, sent to be investigated in the hermetically
sealed room of a sort of under judge called a Master -
with days of attendance separated from each other by
days or weeks - length of attendance each day nominally
an hour really half or a quarter of the time.... The
judge paid for three attendances and bestowing one....
The party whose interest or purpose is served by delay,
attending or not attending, according as by attendance
or non-attendance that interest and that purpose are
best served - then in the course of a few more years
thus employed, out of a dozen or two of parties, one
carried off by death and then another - and upon each
death another bill to be filed, and the same or a
similar course of retardation to be run. (18)
Allowing for exaggeration, this description of the court,
with its antiquated and cumbersome proceedings, clearly
showed the dimensions of intimidating delay.

What is more, delays were caused or compounded in
several ways: by the inherent complexity of the case, by
the disobedience of court orders, and by the disinterest
of suitors. Many cases which went to Chancery were
extremely complex. The most difficult invariably faced
at least one prolonged referral to a Master for detailed
investigation and report. The filing of that report might
be expected to draw criticism (in the forms of exceptions,
appeals, rejoinders), possibly from both sides. Less
difficult cases often met with active or passive disobedience by the parties. In 1730 a decree was not obeyed,
and the receiver of the rents 'afterwards became a lunatic
and died insolvent.' (19) Presumably Chancery was not
responsible. Again, suitors might simply desist. In a
case involving Camberwell grammar school, both sides put
in papers in 1810-11, but eight years later it was
reported that 'no progress has been made in the suit, but
we are informed, that it is intended now to proceed in it
without delay.' (20) The point to be taken is that while
delay was a serious problem, and a prevalent one, its
causes were varied.

The cost of Chancery proceedings was an even greater
obstacle. The fees to be taken by officers and clerks of
the Court had been regulated in 1743. The scale was a
set of maxima, which may have encouraged that level of
fees as an actual minimum; surely it stimulated the
ingenuity of clerks, solicitors, and others to find ways

of augmenting income. At specified stages of process
(the issue, registration, or enrolment of affadavits,
pleas, orders, decrees, or reports) the official fees
were imposed. The suitor also retained a solicitor and
a barrister, who charged for each appearance or other
service to the client. The actual payment was finally
determined by the 'taxing of costs' - a determination
of shares by a Master in Chancery, as between plaintiff
and defendant (for both court costs and attorney-client
fees). Available evidence on costs cannot be easily
summarized, but contemporary estimates put the cost of
uncontested cases at about £50 in the early 19th century,
with contested cases easily three or four times as
high (21)

A few short examples will illustrate the problem. In
the parish of St Saviour, Southwark, Edward Speak left
the residue of his estate to charitable uses in 1766.
A suit was necessary to establish his gift, and in the
course of it the value of the residue was set at £445.
In 1782, after final costs were assessed, there remained
'£235 7s. for the use of the charity.' (22) An information was brought in 1783 on the property of Knowles's
Charity in Sowerby, Lancashire - costs on both sides
totalled £641, and the total property value was probably
less than £2000. (23) In another case, a 99-year lease
had been given on land owned by Samuel Whitney's Charity
(Bradninch, Devon) in 1796. The lease was set aside in
1817 after a six-year trial. The former rental of £4 15s.
was raised handsomely to £17. But this improvement cost
the charity £225 3s. 6d. (24)

To charitable trusts the danger of high court costs
were doubly serious, for the funds of the trust were
usually liable for payment. This condition arose from
the fact that costs could not be assessed against the
Crown; and only rarely were they directly assessable
against trustees. Thus the charity fund itself was left
to pay the bill. Indeed, the only case where funds not
belonging to the trust were sure to be taxed, was the
case where a friend to the beneficiaries brought suit
against (allegedly) misbehaving trustees, and lost.
Almost invariably, trusts paid and paid dearly for the
'protection' of Chancery.

But the economic injustice of Chancery did not end
there. From 1726, the court had a Suitors' Fund in the
custody of an official known as the Accountant General.
(25) This fund consisted of monies paid into court during
or after suits, and it was supposed to be invested on
government securities, and kept from any other uses by
the Accountant General. But Parliament soon conspired to

abuse that trust, and from 1739 various charges were laid
on the Suitors' Fund to support chancery building and
operating costs. (26) Thus ironically, charity funds
went to build and pay for the establishment of Chancery
'justice' which so few charitable trusts ever received.

Of course Chancery did from time to time serve trusts
and save them. However, we can safely estimate that only
a fraction of those trusts which needed help received it,
and only a portion of those were aided in a reasonable
manner in terms of cost and time. What was wrong with
Chancery? While the organization of the court was cumbersome to begin with, the problem of Chancery's inefficiency
deepened in the last quarter of the 18th century. Though
reformers were convinced that the defects they observed
were the work of Lord Eldon, it is clear that a complex
condition existed before he became Lord Chancellor, and
the worst that can be said of his reign is that he failed
to act decisively and radically, preferring instead to
hold by traditional methods and ideas. In the late 18th
century, a wave of novel jurisdiction and responsibility
reached Chancery, and with the court's archaic structure,
this created massive problems. The only major change made
before 1828 was the addition of the post of Vice Chancellor in 1812: this showed recognition of a caseload problem,
even if it simultaneously failed to provide the solution.
Chancery had been modernized by circumstances: it undertook a whole range of partnership, contract, and other
business cases. It remained for procedure and personnel
to be brought into line with the 'modernized' jurisdiction.
Meanwhile trusts were being poorly served, as the court's
records show. In 1813 it was reported that the general
caseload in Chancery had shot up to about 1900 per year,
and the total of cases was still rising. (27) Yet it was
reported in 1818 that the whole number of cases filed in
the name of the Attorney-General since 1785 was only 569.
Clearly the court was getting busier, and equally clearly,
charitable trusts were not among the principal customers.
(28)

III

A further inducement to anarchy in charity came from the
massive change in the nature of philanthropy in the 18th
century. Endowed trusts ceased to be the dominant form
of giving, either in number or in value of gifts. (29)
By 1800 the most popular mode of giving was in organized
donor-groups, which we may designate benevolent societies.

There were three basic variations of the benevolent

society: the self-help group, the functional or institutional association, and the general aid or improvement society. In the first of these, we have the only true innovation of 18th century philanthropy. Akin to insurance or social security, the Box Club, Friendly Society, and the Savings Bank undertook, without the paternal features of ancient charity, to aid the poor and near-poor by mobilizing their resources for their own support.

The functional-institutional society was the closest parallel to old trusts, in both its shape and its objects. But here too there were fundamental differences. These organizations managed hospitals, charity schools, and specific enterprises or agencies (e.g. the Society for the Maintenance and Education of Poor Orphans of the Clergy; missionary, bible, and visiting societies). (30)

The third form of benevolent society was that type which was set up with a self-imposed mandate for general social and moral improvement: the Society of Universal Good Will (1784), the Society for Bettering the Condition and Increasing the Comforts of the Labouring Poor (1796), or the Philanthropic Society (1788). (31) These societies, with their varied careers, were extremely influential as a group. They were organizations with national influence and impact, in many cases with numerous local chapters. The adaptation of this feature of sophisticated central-local organization was important. Societies were leaders in this, taking their first guide from the Society for the Promotion of Christian Knowledge and the Society for the Propagation of the Gospel.

Assuming that all societies were promoting 'benevolence,' why would they be a challenge to charitable trusts? How did benevolent societies make the old-fashioned trusts appear even less useful and more inflexible than they actually were? To answer these questions we need to examine closely the relative features of the two forms of philanthropy.

The outstanding feature of the of the benevolent society was its public nature: community participation, public interest, and publicity. In these, the societies were the antithesis of most charitable endowments. The aspect of community participation was the most radical feature of benevolent societies, regardless of type. The basic idea of a society was of course a membership - as subscribers, shareholders and/or directors of a co-operative social enterprise. In order for this to be realized, there had to be some form of public approval of the charitable object in question. But participation meant moreover a continuing check by subscribers, patrons, and other participants, since their support might be

withdrawn. This implied continuing authorization beyond
the original approval, perhaps even the approval of a
change in direction for the charity. For the benevolent
society operated well outside the limits of trust law
(saving only that property which some societies held in
trust). In some instances there were special statutory
provisions for societies, but for the majority there were
few legal concerns.

The publicity attending benevolent societies was a
basic part of their structure and was essential to their
success. As they depended upon public support, so the
public had to be made aware of the society's existence,
and it had to be encouraged to support the particular
efforts of each group. Here the contrast with an endowment was considerable. Trustees were ordinarily a closed
body, one which rarely had to make accounts, and then
hardly ever to the public. The public face of the charitable trust was of course shown in its service to the community, and it is safe to say that so long as that function was performed to general satisfaction, little anxiety
would be created by the hidden proceedings of trustees.
However, the other side of this coin was ominous: when a
slight suspicion arose, the very secrecy or privacy of
trust operation invited two mutually reinforcing pressures
against it: pressure for publicity and pressure for
purification. These pressures tended to grow exponential-
ly as they fed on one another. This phenomenon appears to
have occurred nationally in the early years of the 19th
century; the growth of it may be linked to the benevolent
societies, for as they multiplied and flourished in the
glare of publicity, so the mystique (or the mask) of
charity propriety was thrown off. There was now little
or no excuse for withholding trust information, except
the legalistic contention that no publication was required.
It took no great sophistication on either side to see that
without operating data, no charity could be evaluated
properly, in terms of its foundation or any other standard
of measurement.

But what standard did apply to charity operation?
Here too a change was in process. The simplest way to
look at this question is to consider what interests were
served by benevolent societies and what interests were
served by charitable trusts. The interests served by the
benevolent societies were those of the public at large,
and as already described, a mechanism existed in those
societies (however imperfectly it may have operated) to
make the link between service and interest effective. It

is true that 'public' and 'public interest' were and are
notoriously loose terms. But whereas they imply those
persons contemporary with a benevolent society, the only
'public' which was appealed to by a trust was that which
was contemporary with the donor. The passage of time
altered and sometimes eliminated the public served by a
trust. But more often, the interest represented in the
trust became more closely identified with the trustees
and less with the public at large.

An awkward truth about both kinds of charity was that
the interests of the recipients were rarely considered on
their own terms. The good of the poor - or the deserving
poor - was determined by donors and subscribers, or by
trustees and directors. Thus the administrators of any
charity translated the interests of the poor, but the
benevolent societies were apt to develop a more responsive
system of translation.

That system had to affect some charitable trusts, for
there was a fair amount of blending of the two forms in
the 18th century, and an unknown amount of exemplary
influence. From an early period, there were combinations.
For instance, in Buxton (Derby) a subscription was taken
for a school which produced a fund of £300 in 1674. The
fund was invested, and although the school decayed in the
18th century, it was reestablished as a result of a suit
begun in 1792. (32) A similar school was found in Cirencester. 'We collect from the documents in the parish,
that a school, called the Blue Coat school, from the dress
of the boys, was instituted in the year 1714, with monies
raised by donations and collections made in the town of
Cirencester.' The fund was invested in turnpike securities,
but as often happened, an endowment was added in 1717. (33)

The compound funds might be from several sources. For
example, the English school of Ormskirk (Lancs) was
originally endowed in the early 18th century, but it was
brought into the National System in 1819 in union with a
Sunday School. It had an endowment income of £32. 'Annual
expenses are about £90, the difference being supplied by
subscriptions and contributions and the whole concerns
of the charity are managed by a committee of trustees and
subscribers.' (34) In 1820, the widow of a curate in
South Cerney (Glos) left £1500 to the vicar to establish
a National School. Other donors gave £67 10s. 'by subscription, another gave a piece of land, and 'the National
Society granted £70 and the Gloucester Diocesan Society
£23.' (35)

There were also situations where endowment and sub-

scription became virtually indistinguishable. In West
Derby (Lancs) a Free School needed a new building.
Although a £700 subscription was collected for the project, a donor meanwhile gave a school building. So the
fund was invested in stock, in the name of the school,
and it became an endowment income. (36) Or in the reverse
direction, we may take the case of Reynold's Charity in
Bristol. By an indenture in 1809, Richard Reynolds gave
a number of properties to carefully-selected trustees.
(37) They were to meet annually and distribute the
revenue to any or all of seven charities 'as should be
supported by voluntary contributions.' Thus an endowment
was established to make regular contributions to benevolent societies, in this case the Bristol Infirmary, the
Bristol Samaritan Society, the Stranger's Friend Society,
the Asylum for Poor Orphan Girls, the Society for the
Discharge of Persons Confined for Small Debts, the Bristol
Dispensary, and the Bristol Female Misericordia.

In some cases, the combined charities must have
achieved a useful blend of the security of endowment
income, plus the freedom and public involvement of the
benevolent society. Surely in these direct cases of
influence, and in an untold number of indirect cases, the
trustees of endowed funds must have learned how differently - and how much more freely - the societies were able
to act, with respect to the law. Such knowledge in turn
must have given trustees added confidence in dealing with
their manifold problems, problems which it had become
impossible to settle easily or cheaply through the proper
channels.

IV

If anarchy means the absence of government, then there was
never any pure anarchy in charity. At least judges, lawmakers, philanthropists and trustees had not despaired of
charity government. However there were very serious
problems in the working of charitable trusts which problems were not readily soluble by the duly appointed higher
authorities. The maintenance of the trust itself, the
preservation of trust property, and the management of
trust income were chief among the problems. What often
occurred in each of these areas in the 18th century
charitable trust was a form of self-help. As trustees
were unable to meet the cost of legal action on behalf of
their trust, and as they were convinced by new laws and
new societies that the old trusts were being left behind,
they authorized or tolerated certain kinds of extra-legal

ad hoc measures. Occurring in growing frequency in the late 18th century, these measures may be seen as symptoms of a slide toward anarchy.

The most vexing trust problem was the matter of trusteeship itself. With few exceptions, trustees were unpaid volunteers. Often the post of trustee was for life. It was conferred by the founder, or by other trustees, or in rare cases by a Court or a local assembly. The job was not difficult, and though certain risks attached to it, there were few heavy liabilities. These were usually outweighed by the local prestige which could be attained, but there were very few instances where more tangible value came with the job.

Trustees were therefore not overstrained as a rule by their official duties. Those normally consisted of an annual meeting and possibly a term as treasurer or in some office. But being mortal, trustees were continually being replaced - that is, they were supposed to be. Death, decline and disappearance were of course expected, and provided for in most trust deeds. Yet the failing trust was a common and serious problem. The failure to renew a trust properly was usually connected to the legal effort and expense involved, or its proportional size next to the revenue of the trust. When trustees co-opted new members, it was necessary to validate the trust deed by a conveyance from old to new trustees. Often the expense of this was the obstacle, (38) sometimes the trustees were impeded by other problems (disputes, loss of documents, etc.). Whenever a proper conveyance was put off, a train of events was begun which frequently led to a fundamental trust alteration. Commonly, a continuing non-conveyance meant a reversion of the trust, after the last trustee died, either to private hands or to public control. It is difficult to know which was more common, and it is not easy to say which was more harmful to the trust. The evidence of private reversions is slight (though not perhaps because there were so few), and the evidence of public takeovers is quite extensive. It is safe to say that the trusts, as distinct from the property thereof, survived much better in public hands. But here there was another problem. A parish, town, or other authority found itself in possession of charity property, with all of its responsibilities. It would be apt to assume those as an official duty, for many local authorities already managed trusts specifically put under their supervision by donors and we have seen that the legislature was aiding the trend in some local poor relief acts. As the accession of trusts might occur several times, the effect was to produce a 'united fund,' or a

pooled trust. This merger was likely to obscure or sub-
merge the precise purpose or object of several small
trusts, and it opened the possibility that trusts would
be treated like ordinary local revenue. So, for example,
in Gateshead (Durham) a fund had accumulated from the
17th century, amounting by 1747 to £300. This sum was
lent by the local authorities on security of road tolls;
in 1755 a meeting of inhabitants voted to invest the money
in the construction of a poor house. With the £100 left
over from that project, a loan was made to the rector, and
in 1762 another meeting called in the loan, and invested
the sum in a gallery in the church, rents from which were
to go to the poor. But meanwhile the interest on the
£200 workhouse investment was overlooked. This sort of
freewheeling investment and reinvestment of charity funds
frequently led, through oversight alone, to serious dis-
placement of revenues. (39)

Not all such 'united funds' were dangerous, for in fact
the same act which merged the funds also provided secure
(if illegitimate) succession of trustees. And in some
cases there were signs of careful management. At Honiton,
Devon in 1760 ten funds were combined, placed under the
eye of a steward, and the accounts produced for 1816-19
suggest careful management. (40) In the parish of St John,
Hackney, a £20 annuity given in 1771 was combined with
three separate later gifts, but the provisions of all were
satisfactorily maintained. (41) And in the parish of St
Dunstan in the East, when a group of bequests was jointly
administered, the parish compiled a book of wills and
benefactions, thus apparently enabling the retention of
trust identity. (42)

Yet it seemed more common for merged trusts to find
their resources being pooled, either to supplement the
poor rates or to go to some use not specifically allowed
in the several deeds. There are cases on record where
such submersion occurred, and was later corrected at the
local level. In the parish of St Peter, Bristol, a vestry
meeting decided in 1797 to buy government securities from
the parish fund, representing several sums of money given
'for the use of the poor,' to vest these stocks in trustees and to give the annual disposal to the rector and
churchwardens. This clearly was a case of rescuing
charities from a united fund. (43) A like event occured
at Oxford in 1802. There a number of accounts of charitable trusts had been

blended with the general account of the corporation.
In the year 1802 the Town Clerk was directed to make
extracts from all the wills and deeds relating to the
several charities, and a committee was appointed, con-

sisting of the mayor, four aldermen, and eight assistants, with the town clerk, and other members of the
council chamber, to compare and examine the extracts.
The report of this committee led to 'separate and distinct
entry being made of the receipts and payments of each'
charitable trust. (44) The 'united fund' was a natural,
logical, and generally tolerated method of supplying
trustees. However, its dangers were real.

The second major area of trust 'self-help'was in the
handling of property. This property was not simply something to be conveyed from one set of trustees to another.
In most cases there were two features to the property
problem: securing the ownership and obtaining the income.
The cases of united funds were but one type of problem
of security, one out of a long list. As property owners,
the trustees' first concern was with their legal title.
In conveying property carefully from one set of trustees
to another, they could insure the trust's validity. They
also had to retain and preserve a record of the original
deeds, wills, or other relevant documents. In this they
received some assistance from the registers of wills, the
register of the Stamp Office, and in more prosaic manner,
the traditional parish chest or the stone tablet in the
parish church. From 1736, an enrolment of deeds of gift
in Chancery was a further record. But proof of ownership
was only one aspect of the property problem. Trustees
had to behave as owners, and from time to time they faced
decisions about sales, exchanges, and improvements; often
these were decisions which should have been made by the
Court, for only a few trusts had specific directions
enabling disposition of trust property. Further, as
owners, the trustees were responsible for the income of
the trust. They had to see that assessments were properly
made, that leases, loans, and other agreements were fairly
drawn. There was a large class of trusts where there was
no flexibility here - those which had a fixed annuity or
rent-charge; the responsibility in those cases was little
more than a book-keeping one.

The third area of trustee concern, and hence 'self-
help,' was in the management or application of the revenues. This involved spending, hiring and firing, and
record-keeping. Trustees were legally competent to do
most things necessary in these matters; but when income
had altered or when other circumstances had changed, the
trustees were obliged to obtain directions from the court
for management of property.

Needless to say, it was usually unthinkable to resort
to a court of equity for the alteration of some operating
rule, even when trust income had increased. The limits of

trustee authority were open to question, and could lead
to prolonged court involvement and even the limits of
spending for simple court orders were dangerously
uncertain.   It was safer to make alterations ad hoc, and
to hope that no one would challenge them, especially in
court.

One seemingly safe way of alteration was under cover
of legal transfer.   A case of this kind occurred in
Daniel's Charity (Broughton, Lancashire).   A twenty
shilling annuity for a school or church was augmented in
the 17th century.   When the fund was conveyed in 1734, the
document cited clothing, apprenticeship, and bible
charities in addition to the original objects. (45)   In
Blagdon (Somerset) Thomas Baynard had left land for support of a schoolmaster in 1687.   Baynard stipulated that
the master should have only eight pupils 'because I would
not have such teacher burthened more than is needful ...
and that the teaching of the number of eight children of
the poorer sort at a time may be sufficient for the needs
of the place.' (46)   By the time of inquiry in 1825, the
master had taken seventeen pupils, expanded the curriculum,
and his 'Methodist persuasion' was also against the
original terms.   However, the trust could never have
undertaken the expense of legal variation of these terms.
In another case, Thomas Knight had left a twenty-five
shilling annuity for two students, for bible-reading and
book purchases in 1722.   But the Charity Commissioners
reported that

This sum of 25s. had been regularly received by the
former rectors of the parish (Cucklington, Somerset)
... and applied as near as possible according to the
directions of the testator, until 1806, when Mr Martin
became rector, who, finding it was impracticable,
from the smallness of the gift, to carry the will of
the testator into effect as directed, it seemed to him
to be better to pay for the instruction of four children, and to discontinue the gift of the books.   This
plan is now adopted by the present rector, and is considered the best mode of employing this small sum. (47)
The common thread in all the instances of ad hoc decisions
was that for a majority of trusts there was no appeal to
higher authority which the funds of the trust could afford.
It was therefore necessary to work outside the law.
Whether this caused serious trauma or anxiety is doubtful,
but that it must have caused further loss of respect for
Chancery and further desire for more effective and sens-
ible charitable trust administration seems certain.
Anarchy was no one's idea of a solution for philanthropy.

By 1800, the experience in managing the charitable

trusts of England had proven that existing central machinery was incompetent and disruptive. It had also shown that trusts were valued more highly than legal traditions - put crudely, real social equity was sought in spite of and outside of the equity court. While parliament legislated willy-nilly on charity problems and specific local cases, the trusts were left to solve most of their own difficulties. As they saw benevolent societies on every hand independently dealing with poverty and ignorance and disease and immorality, no doubt charity trustees took courage from the example.

Something like benign anarchy prevailed in charitable trust administration at the close of the 18th century. It was not a situation of crisis, but neither was it one of stable order. The anarchy imminent in trusts was a symptom of breakdown in legal machinery, coupled with a bonanza of unsynchronized legislation. But in this same period, other signs were pointing toward new empirical approaches and new government strategies.

3

Charity and Inquiry

The state of charitable trusts in the 18th century
undoubtedly reinforced the suspicion or curiosity which
they seemed destined to attract. The result can be seen
in a number of investigations of trusts during the century.
At the outset, most inquiries were made through the medium
of the Commission of Charitable Uses. As that device
atrophied, others were employed. There were numerous
local inquiries without official legal status, and toward
the end of the century some inquiries were mounted at
the national level. Few of these efforts offered any
remedial design, and most were content with the enumeration of 'abuses' and simple registration of the trusts'
existence. Thus the consequences were limited and widespread problems in trust administration remained unsolved.
The closing years of war with France saw increasing
economic distress in the country and more determined
reformist activity in the legislature. Amid a variety of
other social inquiries and activities, a spurt of charity
reform legislation appeared between 1810 and 1815. The
failure of these early measures set the stage for the
appearance of the charity commission inquiry in 1818.

I

Local charity inquiries followed different styles but
shared a common motive. Publicizing the terms of an
endowment was thought to offer an implicit guarantee of
better performance or at least protection against the
trust's disappearance. In 1713, George Ritschel published
a history of the charities of Tyndale Ward (Northumberland). He presented a catalogue of donations (with texts
of documents) together with a history of the parish of
Hexham which he and his father had served as Vicar. His

work concluded with a plea for local support to petition
the Lord Chancellor for a commission to investigate the
charities, because some trustees had obstructed his work,
and none of the school governors 'can or will tell' who
gave lands to the school. Ritschel wanted all present
and future donations to 'be engrossed in a register to
provide for that purpose, and kept by the Minister of
Hexham ... till such time as there shall be occasion to
make it publick.' (1)

A vigorous attack on charity administration in Coventry
was published in 1733. Describing abuses of money left
for low-interest loans, the account aimed at 'rectifying
any past misconduct, and in guarding the several benefactions from embezzlement and misapplication for the
future.' To the corporation the charge was clear: 'no
power whatsoever ought to be maintained and supported at
the expense of charitable gifts.' This work also contained a detailed 150-page list of benefactions, the text
of a Chancery decree, and an appendix with rentals and
other information. (2)

Some accounts were in surprising detail. Richard
Izacke was Clerk of the Peace for Exeter, and he published
a Register 'digested from the records deposited in the
council chamber of Exeter.' (3) Izacke commented throughout on the 'misapplication' of the charities and hoped 'to
restore them to the uses for which they were given.'
The Register had 131 donors listed, and as well as the
outline of each gift, the author appended both the arms of
the donor and the ailments of the trust. For one there
were 'above thirty years arrears, now in 1732, in the hand
hands of Mr Adlerman Hickman; 'for another, 'these alm-
houses, by neglect of the chamber, fall'n down, the stones,
timber, &c by them sold, and the ground sold;' for
another, 'this charity is decay'd;' and for many others,
the forlorn notation, 'sunk.'

In a number of cases, local committees were formed to
investigate charity abuses. In 1743, the town of Ipswich
formed a committee 'to inquire what donations have from
time to time been given to the town.' When the fathers
balked at printing the eventual report, some members went
ahead on their own, deprived of official sanction and of
the use of documents. The authors sketched the history
of several major charities, with notes on their present
operation and recommendations for the future. The dis-
sidents also gave a singularly balanced statement of the
problem of charitable trusts: 'It is reasonable to expect
that the original design of the donors of publick
charities, should, in process of time, be forgotten or
mistaken; from hence the mismanagement and misapplication
of them must needs arise.' (4)

No such reserve was evident in John Watts' tract:
'A Black Scene Open'd: being the true state of Mr John
Kendrick's Gift to the Town of Reading.' Watts asserted
that the town had 'not applied one shilling' to the
charity, though directed to do so by an Exchequer decree.
He estimated a total fraud over 110 years of something
approaching £19,000. But Watts himself was seeking a
verdict at the time in an Exchequer suit, and he embel-
lished his (probably self-serving) account with a sweeping
allegation:

> If one single gentleman's charity hath been subject to
> abuses, of breach of trust, of negligence, of mis-
> employment, of not employing, of defrauding, and of
> misconverting, what may be thought of forty-three
> other pious gifts to the poor of Reading (most of which
> are misapply'd). (5)

Part of the problem which the charity inquirers
addressed was the adjunct of sensational allegations -
public ignorance and apathy. They were of course aware
of this, as their publications showed. Some made that
awareness even clearer, as did Rowland Rouse when he
wrote of the charities of Market Harborough in 1768.
He searched local archives, and he made something of a
study of local inquiries such as his own. He cited a
journalist's observation that 'in most parishes the
inhabitants in general have but a very im perfect knowledge of the charitable endowments &c belonging to them.'
In many cases the documents were unknown, some were
'irretrievably lost,' others were 'almost unintelligible.'
Rouse thought that documents ought to be recovered and
printed in the original form, being 'the most proper
method of preserving the clear and true sense' of the
documents. Rouse defended his ideas of preservation and
publication, first with reference to the precedent of
published annual statements (such as those of the SPCK and
the SPG). He went on to argue the general value of
publicity:

> Charitable trusts cannot be made too public, nor the
> proceedings of those who are interested, as by those
> means, if any, men will be fearful of perverting their
> trusts, when the eyes of a whole parish if they are not
> willingly shut, may be upon them. (6)

Of course some 'inquiries' were made without a legal
object. They were essentially descriptive, either for
promotional or for historical purposes. For example, in
1709 the churchwardens of Enfield published a broadsheet
with detailed information on sixteen parochial charities.
(7) In a different form, and for different reasons, Rev.
William Hanbury published 'Charitable Foundations at

Church Langton,' which is best described as a philanthropic autobiography. (8)   It detailed Hanbury's trials
and success as a nurseryman, and his use of the profits
of this enterprise to endow a whole range of charities.
On a corporate footing, we have the example of the Bristol
Corporation's pamphlet 'to inform the poor touching the
emoluments' of some thirty-eight foundations. (9)   An
interesting variant of this was in Castle Morton
(Worcestershire) where a table of 'lands belonging to the
church and poor' was erected in the church in 1801, and
'the property is about to be mapped (1829), and ... the
map will be hung up in the church.' (10)

Many accounts had neither legal nor promotional
features but were simply written in the interest of historical description. The Charity Commissioners found
'papers and letters' of Thomas Rudd, schoolmaster in
Durham (c. 1700), who looked into the origin of Bishop
Langley's School, and who 'had evidently taken great
pains inquiring into these matters.' (11) Local historians and antiquarians, whose ranks were swelling in the
18th century, made extensive accounts of charities, either
separately, as parts of local histories, and sometimes in
collected work. (12)

All local charity accounts were similar in that they
were records of trusts, their terms and conditions.
Their authors' purposes were varied, but the accounts were
nevertheless essentially descriptive and isolated. It was
therefore of great significance when parliamentary sanction was given to a national survey of charitable trusts.

II

The origins of charity inquiry at the national level were
random and unclear. In Ireland, two different types of
inquiry were begun, and both were institutionalized at
the turn of the century. In England, one abortive survey
of charities occurred in the 1780s, and it went almost
completely unnoticed for thirty years.

In 1763 the first major Irish experiment began with an
Act for the Better Discovery of Charitable Donations and
Bequests. (13) It was aimed at the kind of publicity
which concerned the local inquirers, 'Whereas the pious
intentions of many charitable persons are frequently
defeated by the concealment or misapplication of their
donations or bequests.' The remedy supplied was mandatory
registration of charitable donations, which registrations
would be presented to the Bishops at their annual visitations, while copies of wills and administrations would be

submitted 'to the clerk of each House.' Moreover, the
heirs, executors or trustees were to 'publish in the
Dublin Gazette three times successively every charitable
donation or bequest.' The fines provided were £5 for not
making a return and £50 for failing to publish in the
Gazette. The charity was to bear the expense of publication.

The Act seems to have flushed out several wrongdoers.
In 1764 the Irish House of Lords established a committee
of inquiry 'to take into consideration the several
charities and charitable donations in this kingdom.'
The Committee 'discovered several charitable bequests ...
which had been withheld, embezzled, and concealed, and
caused the same to be sued for, paid, and recovered.'
These statements were made in 1800 when, as the Act of
Union promised the demise of the Lords' Committee, the
Irish Parliament incorporated a body to be called the
Commissioners for Charitable Donations and Bequests. (14)
The Commissioners were to include all Irish prelates,
royal justices, the provost of Trinity College, the Vicar
General, and all the incumbents of Dublin parishes. The
Commissioners were granted full legal powers to recover
and apply donations. The terms of registration previously
enacted were renewed, excepting publication in the Gazette
and submission to the clerks of the Irish Parliament. The
Commissioners for Charitable Donations and Bequests continued to function until 1921. While their direct connection to the later English Charity Commissioners remains
difficult to establish, there can be little doubt of a
general precedent.

In another development the Irish offered an example.
In 1788 the exposure of scandalous conditions in the
Chartered Corporation Schools spurred the creation of a
commission 'for enquiring into the several funds and
revenues granted by public or private donation for the
purposes of education in this Kingdom, and into the state
and condition of all schools in this Kingdom on Public
or charitable foundations.' (15) The Lord Lieutenant was
to choose seven unpaid commissioners, who were to examine
any schools, their properties, circumstances and administration. Their work was assisted by giving them authority to summon witnesses, subpoena documents, and to fine
those who disobeyed a summons.

This inquiry commission was to expire after one year,
but it was renewed twice (1790 and 1791). Then it was
reconstituted after the Union, as 'The Commissioners of
the Board of Education (Ireland).' In spite of the
altered title, the statute made it clear that it was 'to
revive and amend an Act, made in the parliament of Ireland,

for enabling the Lord Lieutenant to appoint commissioners for enquiring into the several funds ... granted for the purposes of education ...' In its revived form, the Commission had eleven members, six appointed by the Lord Lieutenant and five designated by the Commissioners for Charitable Donations and Bequests. The new Commission published fourteen reports between 1807 and 1812. (16) In the course of its work, the Commission turned to 'extending and improving the education of the lower orders' and developed a scheme for 'a system of general education.' (17) Parts of this scheme were assigned to the new Commissioners of Education created in 1813 to manage the Irish schools. (18)

By comparison, the same time period saw little activity in the way of English moves toward national charity inquiry. In 1777, Thomas Gilbert the poor law reformer introduced a Bill to survey charitable donations in England. Ministers and Churchwardens were to be asked to make sworn returns on all donations. As the preamble put it, 'it may be proper that the Legislature, who are extending their Enquiries into the state and condition of the poor, should be informed of the several charitable donations for the use and benefit of poor persons.' (19) This Bill passed the Commons, but was defeated in the Lords. Nine years later a similar measure was enacted, with a companion Act requiring returns from overseers of the poor. (20)

The law required that a circular be sent to every parish or place, asking the officiating clergy the following questions:

(1) What charitable donations have been given, by deed or will, for the benefit of poor persons within your parish (or place); by whom, when, in what manner, and for what particular purposes were they given, to the best of your knowledge, information and belief?

(2) Were the said respective donations in land or money; in whom are they now vested, and what is the annual produce thereof respectively, to the best of your knowledge, information, and belief?

The Act set a deadline of October 15, 1786. The replies were quite complete in numbers, perhaps because the Act provided fines for non-compliance. But the answers were not complete, and over 4,000 supplementary inquiries had to be sent out. The combined result of the returns was printed in June, 1788. (21)

There was little indication of the intent behind the Gilbert survey in the debates, the Act, or later events. Whatever the intent may have been, the outcome must have been a disappointment, for nothing was done with the

returns. The Commons had to appoint a Select Committee
to 'study' the returns and supervise their preparation
for printing. (22) That work done, the returns were
simply allowed to gather dust until they were 'discovered'
about twenty-five years later - by which time they were
seriously out of date.

Why was there such a glaring failure? First, this
method of information-gathering was only becoming developed, and was quite new for the legislature. Its whole
process had not been thought through; there were no
plans for general reform of charity, there was no proposal
which the returns could have been used to support. The
main interest was clear in the Bill (1777), that is a
simple interest in an estimate of charitable resources
as an accessory to poor law data. Behind this desire was
a hope that such a survey would show the way to some
legislative action. In either case, there was no sign
that once the data were collected, anything further was
done. For twenty years after Gilbert's survey, there was
no follow-up at the national level. And when some
activity began in the 19th century, it seems to have owed
as much inspiration to the Irish experiments as to the
English tally of trusts.

One English writer who acknowledged some inspiration
from the Irish experience was William Beckwith. In 1807
he wrote a pamphlet urging the formation of a subscription
society to establish a central registry of charitable
trusts. (23) The 'Plan' was introduced with a set of
school scandals reminiscent of earlier local inquiries,
but Beckwith's object was radically new. He envisaged a
central registry office, under royal charter and statutory
sanction, superintending county assessors, whose work
would be scrutinized at the local level by JPs. The
Justice would also have summary jurisdiction in charity
cases, with appeals to the central office. Beckwith left
open the possibility of further appeal to higher courts.
He also proposed that trustees be paid, and in return
they would make annual public accounts for which they
would assume legal liability.

Beckwith's 'Plan' was too far advanced in its legal
concepts and machinery. He said in another work that it
had been inspired by the Irish Commissioners of Charitable
Donations and Bequests. (24) That may be, but there were
no bishops in Beckwith's central office, and there was no
comparable administrative power in the Irish Commissioners.
At any rate, Beckwith's ideas were not taken up very
avidly. He received favourable notice in the 'Literary
Panorama,' and in that periodical readers were asked to
form local societies, and to respond if interested in

pursuing this work. (25)   At least one community did so.

A society was established at Stamford (Lincolnshire) in December 1809 'for the reform of various abuses of charitable institutions.'   This was the organization which backed the publication of a survey of local charities in 1813, by a barrister, Thomas Blore.   The work was a careful survey of thirty charities originating or functioning in Stamford - schools, hospitals, almshouses, and general charities.   Blore gave no endorsement to the Beckwith 'Plan,' however, and his conclusion rather paralleled those of the 18th century chroniclers:

As the object of this work is to obtain a just, temperate and necessary reform in the management of those things which have been piously given by our forefathers to charitable uses, and works of local utility; it is hoped that it will receive a candid interpretation from those whose duties are pointed out, or whose errors, whether of negligence or of ignorance, are the subject of discussion, so as to lead them to the faithful discharge of their duties in future. (26)

Meanwhile, if Beckwith's 'Plan' gained little momentum, a new kind of local inquiry had appeared.   A Quaker solicitor named Zachary Clark had compiled terriers from the office of the Bishop of Norwich with the returns from the Gilbert survey for the county of Norfolk. (27)   His work was a parochial index of the charities in the county. He included the descriptions from his main sources and added numerous observations on the lapsed or abused cases which he discovered.   While no pretense was made that this was a prototype inquiry, it so appears in retrospect.   Yet Clark printed his research results apparently with the same naive expectation of automatic reform demonstrated by Blore and the 18th century inquirers.

III

The charity inquiries of the 18th century had moved some distance from the local to the national level, even if the English experience of the latter type was close to impotence.   There was perhaps more justified hesitation here because of the jurisdiction of Chancery and the power of the senior endowments or their trustees.   In any case, the circumstances were sufficiently altered in the second decade of the 19th century, and an effective inquiry was brought closer by two important developments. The first was the successful application of the Select Committee procedure to some topics closely allied to charity.   The second was a series of legislative measures

on charity which simultaneously drew attention to the
subject and, upon failing, set the stage for stronger
measures.

The Select Committee, as already noted, was a potential source of effective power in the area of social
problems. Some of that potential was clearly demonstrated
in the last years of the Napoleonic era. Committees
working in areas close to charity conducted effective
inquiries, and a review of several examples will indicate
the state of the inquiry method and show how some social
issues were gaining attention.

One of the problems which drew the attention of the
legislature was that of the parish apprentice. The
parochial authorities were empowered to bind the children
of persons on the rates to a master, principally to avoid
perpetuation of poverty, as well as the 'burden' on the
rates. (28) The exercise of this power was not always
enlightened, and among the more notorious practices was
that of sending pauper children some distance from their
parents at an early age. (29)

Around the turn of the century, a revised method of
registration was established for apprentices bound by the
parish overseer. (30) In 1811, efforts were made to
further amend the laws on parish apprentices, and these
resulted in a Select Committee of Inquiry. When the Committee reported in May 1815, it had collected the registration figures from some fifty parishes in the metropolitan area. These gave the information that between
1802 and 1811 some 5,875 apprentices were bound by the
parish authorities. Of that number, 2,026 were bound to
masters in the country. Of those, over half were under
the age of eleven. (31)

The Committee sent precepts to those persons to whom
the parish apprentices were bound, inquiring into the
current situation in each case. They summarized the
responses (nearly eighty per cent replied) in some detail.
In the opinion of the Committee, the practice of removal
of parish children was unnecessary, as their average
number of about 200 per year 'might, with the most
trifling exertion on the part of the parish officers, be
annually bound to trades and domestic employments' in
or near the metropolis. Their proof of this had no connection to the evidence, but rested on their finding that
some of the parishes 'have never followed the practice of
binding their poor children to a distance.'

The work of the inquiry was apparently effective. In
1816, a new law governing the process of binding parish
apprentices was enacted. (32) Among its novel features,
it required careful supervision of Justices of the Peace

for any case where the apprentice was to be bound outside
the home parish. In such cases, it was to be a 'reasonable distance,' which was defined as something less than
forty miles. Also, no parish apprentices were to be
bound at an age of less than nine years. The Act was
clearly influenced by the inquiry process, and the collection of data under an earlier act had as clearly
facilitated the passage. The Committee was conscious of
a novelty in the subject matter as well:

> This enquiry has been prosecuted with as much per-
> severance as was required by a subject of so much
> importance to the happiness and wellbeing of a large
> class of the community, though hitherto but little
> made an object of the attention of Parliament. (33)

If the parish apprentice was closely scrutinized,
there was even more attention paid to the lunatic.
Whether this was due to the royal malady or not, the
entire matter of lunacy - treatment, institutions, the
pauper and criminal insane - drew considerable notice
in the legislature during the reign of George III.

In 1774, the basic law on lunacy was adopted. (34)
It required the housing of lunatics in licensed madhouses,
with heavy fines provided for violators. The Act was to
be enforced by JPs in the country, and in metropolitan
London, licensing was put under the control of Commissioners who were to be chosen annually by the President and
Fellows of the Royal College of Physicians, from among
their own number. The Commissioners were to inspect and
note conditions in the madhouses, and to report defects in
any of the licensed establishments to the college.

There were numerous difficulties in administration,
but in the particular area of criminal and pauper lunatics,
action was more urgently needed than elsewhere. In 1807,
a Select Committee reported on the subject. (35) It found
inadequate or nonexistent provision for separate confinement for criminal lunatics, a class recognized by the
approval of the plea of criminal insanity. (36) The Committee found that in that class some thirty-seven persons
were in confinement, but in most cases in a common gaol.
As to lunatic paupers, there were returns under an earlier
Act showing a total of 1,765 persons in workhouses or
other public institutions plus 483 persons in private
custody. The Committee recommended construction of
asylums, the cost to be borne by the county rates. The
following year an elaborate Act set up procedures for the
Justices of the Peace to do just that. (37)

The general matter of madhouses remained an issue,
partly because the Commissioners for Licensing were
strictly a metropolitan body, partly because the manage-

ment of lunatics was poorly provided for, even after the Act of 1808. In 1815, another Select Committee was created 'to consider the provision being made for the better regulation of madhouses in England.' (38) After hearing testimony from thirty-five witnesses, including physicians, officials of asylums, and magistrates, the Committee concluded that a new law was 'indispensably necessary.' In this instance, however, no new legislation was forthcoming for England. Ironically, the same year saw an Act on Scottish madhouses, and in 1817 an Act providing for the Lunatic poor in Ireland was passed. (39) Only in 1819 did some legislation emerge on the English problem, and it was not until 1828 that significant innovations were enacted in the area of lunacy. (40)

A social problem which vexed the nation for generations, and one which was as great an affront to the evangelical conscience as to that of the earlier puritan, was the case of the sturdy beggar. Vagrancy had been dealt with in the early 18th century in draconian terms. The Vagrant Act (41) identified three classes of miscreants: 'idle and disorderly persons' (who could be committed for up to one month's hard labour in the workhouse); 'rogues and vagabonds' (who might be whipped, confined up to six months, or removed from the parish); and 'incorrigible rogues' (might be confined up to two years, and repeat offenders would be guilty of a felony, which could carry a transportation of up to seven years). For each offence bounties were provided in the Act.

In spite of this 'remedy,' vagrancy and mendicancy were still in evidence at the turn of the century, and a milder disposition toward the beggar encouraged efforts to make an objective distinction between the honest unfortunate and the sturdy beggar. A subscription was taken up in 1801 to form an inquiry into mendicity in the metropolis. The chief officer of this enterprise placed himself under the direction of the Home Secretary (as he later reported) and tickets were circulated among the mendicant population, redeemable upon surrender at the office of the chief inquirer, after submission to a set form of interrogation. Matthew Martin explained this procedure, and gave his findings, to a Select Committee in 1815. He was joined by about forty other witnesses who testified as to the amount and nature of vagrants and beggars. (42)

When the Committee was reappointed in 1816, it prepared an abstract of the previous year's testimony. It concluded that 'the laws are sufficiently strong, if they were put in execution.' (43) While it supported the motivation of the scheme which Martin had conducted, and it endorsed an extension of that operation, the Committee

was less than optimistic. Indeed, some of its observations despaired of any solution, and it cast its eye over
other sources of provision for the poor.

The Committee observed that 'money to the amount given
in charity, in different ways without injury, would
probably be sufficient to afford considerable relief to
those who may appear to be entitled, on inquiry, to
receive it.' Yet such hopes were not enough for the
Committee.

> The serious danger to society from the neglected state
> of the children in the streets of the metropolis, is
> in the opinion of your Committee so pressing, that
> they cannot close this report without again calling
> the attention of the House to the necessity of some
> immediate provision being made for care being taken of
> them.

As for concrete suggestions, the Committee offered an
unusual idea for the salvation of the children:

> A great difficulty certainly opposes itself, from the
> want of a place for receiving them. Your Committee
> therefore ventures to suggest, whether an expedient
> may not be found by fitting up some old ships of war,
> and mooring them close to the shore in the Thames, as
> floating schools. (44)

The idea of a floating school, a grim analogy to the
prison hulk, had in fact been employed in one instance
known to the Committee. Yet the legislators refrained
from seizing this novel plan, and no other specific
measure emerged directly from this Committee's labours.

Our examples indicate something of the range of possibilities which existed with legislative inquiries. In the
case of parish apprentices, there was a close correlation
between inquiring and legislating. With lunatics and
madhouses, on the other hand, extensive inquiry was only
sparsely reflected in legislation. As to mendicants and
vagrants, we see an inquiry from which there was no
apparent consequence. Of course the production of legislation was and is not the sole criterion (even if it is
the most prominent) for assessing a given inquiry and its
results. Indeed, it is too easy to pair off inquiries
and laws in close proximity and to assume a causal
relationship.

On a careful comparison, however, the significance of
the legislative variations diminishes beside the importance of the extent and nature of the investigations.
The social problems which were being studied were of long
standing; the novel method of public (and published) testimony, evaluation and recommendations was new.

By a curious inversion, when we move to the legislation

specifically aimed at charities in the early 19th century, we find that results were only erratically forthcoming. The main significance of a series of Bills and Acts from 1810 to 1815 was their contribution toward the institution of a prolonged and vigorous inquiry - by a Select Committee.

The first comprehensive legislation for English charitable trust reform was introduced in 1809. A group of evangelicals, Samuel Whitbread, William Wilberforce, George Rose and Scrope Bernard presented a Bill for 'registering and securing charitable donations for the benefit of poor people in England.' (45) The measure bore some resemblance to the Irish pattern, in that it provided for registration of all new charitable trusts with an episcopal registrar, and for joint vesting of funds in the name of the bishop and the trustees. This was shortly modified to give the joint title to the *custos rotulorum* and the registry to the clerk of the peace. But in either form, this was too stiff a dose for the House of Commons. The Bill was belaboured with delays and obstruction, while petitions were brought in against it from several London Hospitals. The Bill was finally killed in Committee on 13 June.

In 1810 a revised Bill was introduced, the sponsors having dropped the provision for joint investituture, and settled for requiring trustees to call in cash funds and invest them in government securities. (46) During the session, the Commons ordered reprinting of the 1787 Report on the Gilbert Returns. Meanwhile, several authors joined the debate: Beckwith lent support in his tract addressed to Sir Samuel Romilly, which work was primarily concerned with delays in Chancery. Beckwith praised Wilberforce in connection with the proposal of 'a Board for inquiry into the management of our Public Charities' - though there was no trace of such a board in the Bill before Parliament. (47) Whatever the accuracy or pertinence of Beckwith's tract, Romilly was lending his support to the Bill's sponsors.

The opposition was fortified by two pamphlets from the pen of Anthony Highmore, a solicitor who was just completing a London charity survey, 'Pietas Londinensis.' (48) Highmore was connected with some of the governing boards of the London hospitals, and he challenged assertions that charitable trusts were negligently run. He also argued that the proposed registry simply duplicated existing stamp office and probate registries, and hence would mean unnecessary cost and harrassment to trusts. The Bill was defeated again. In 1811 the Bill came in with a new provision for trust registration, and through

its several stages, the list of exemptions in the Bill
grew substantially, suggesting that passage was imminent.
But once again the Bill failed.

When the Bill appeared again in 1812, the registry
provision was accompanied by a daring innovation, probably
the work of Romilly, 'providing a more summary remedy' for
chancery suits on charity abuses or administrative orders.
By this provision, any two individuals could petition (via
the Attorney-General) to be heard by the Lord Chancellor,
Lord Keeper or Master of the Rolls. This hearing was to
result in a prompt, final decree, subject only to appeal
to the House of Lords. As this constituted virtually a
new subject, the Bill was divided into two parts. Both
the registry and the summary remedy measures passed
without difficulty and received the royal assent in July
1812 (52 Geo. III, cc. 101 and 102).

The campaign for charity reform legislation (1809-12)
had no doubt publicized and generated support for its
object. But the proposals, in the several forms presented
to the legislature, were limited in their design. All
versions advanced the simple solution of registration,
and the final form added summary judicial process.
Registration alone, assuming it could be carried out,
would only do what the 18th century inquiries had endeavoured to do, namely to make a trust publicly known
and less easy to violate. The addition of the summary
remedy was a much more advanced idea, aimed at reducing
the time and expense of ordinary Chancery proceedings.
However, the last-minute addition and imperfect preparation of the plan were to prove fatal to its operation.

The aftermath of 'Romilly's Acts' was a serious disappointment. Enrolments never approached a reasonable
level, and the summary procedure never became an effective
tool. Within two years the reformers had returned to the
task, and new measures were being pressed to achieve
reform, among them further schemes for inquiry.

The poor response to the registration Act was clearly
outlined in returns as early as 1814. An account of
registration in Middlesex was ordered by the Commons on
30 July. Further steps were taken to obtain complete
returns between November 1814 and March 1815. This action
resulted in a return from the Deputy Clerk of the Chancery
Inrolment Office which showed just over 400 registrations
in the first two years of the Act's operation. (49) In a
later report, the Home Office gave the full text of 562
registrations of trusts which had been received by 27 June
1815 (50) Much later, a return in 1829 showed a total of
only 696 registrations. (51) Part of the reason for
failure was the absence of adequate enforcement provisions

in the Act. But there was also a debilitating clause
which probably rendered the law meaningless. One of the
exemption sections excluded charitable trusts not secured
on land, and also excluded

> any charitable donation whatsoever which by the direc-
> tion of the donor thereof, or by the lawful rules of
> any charitable institution whatsoever, may be wholly
> or in part expended in and about the charitable pur-
> poses for which the same may have been given, at the
> discretion of the Governors, Directors, or Managers,
> or the Trustee or Trustees of such charitable institu-
> tion at any time whatsoever.

It is only surprising that nearly 700 trusts did register,
for this clause exempted any charity whose trustees
bothered to read it.

The summary remedy was equally unlucky, though not
through any flaw in the drafting of the Bill. As written,
the Act allowed any two persons to petition for relief.
The Court swiftly built a wall of case law around the new
process, and the only cases which could hope to penetrate
were those where 'a plain breach of trust' was present.
(52)   In Eldon's own words, the court 'found so many
difficulties in the application of the Act, that in their
opinion, and that of almost every gentleman at the bar who
had been in any way concerned, they could do nothing else
but desist.' (53)   Surely the 'difficulties' were placed
there frequently by the Court; moreover, the summary process was no guarantee of justice and certainly not of
economy. Romilly testified before the Select Committee
on Education (of which he was a member) in 1816 that the
Act might have little effect, for 'it is not likely that
many (informations) would come to a hearing in that period,
since the Act was passed in the present state of the
business in the Court of Chancery.' When asked by the
Committee what the effects of his Act were on court costs,
Romilly made the surprising admission that 'I ought to
say that I really know very little of the amount of
costs.' (54)   There were others who had more than enough
familiarity with this point: for example, the trustees
of Sir John Norris's Charity (Bray, Berkshire) claimed
that they presented a petition under Romilly's Act, the
expense to the charity being 'upwards of £350' - and they
lost. (55)

In view of these disappointing results, the reformers
were anxious to amend and extend the Acts of 1812. As
early as December of that year, John Lockhart and Wilberforce introduced a Bill to prevent trustees from 'granting long and improvident leases' but the session ended
before the Bill reached its second reading. (56) As the

discouraging results of the Acts became clearer, an amendment Bill was brought in by Henry Wrottesley, Richard
Preston and Romilly in June of 1815. It passed the Commons in July, but was 'not proceeded in' by the Lords.
This Bill rashly threatened disqualification of all trustees who failed to register. (57)

As the 1816 session opened, an order was made to
reprint the Select Committee Report of 1787 (15 February)
and to reprint the Gilbert Returns (26 June). (58)   On 1
May, Lockhart, Wrottesley, Charles Wetherell and John
Courteney received permission to bring in a Bill to amend
Gilbert's Act and Romilly's Act. Introduced on 28 May,
this Bill passed the Commons on 17 June but died in the
House of Lords. (59) The measure was a lengthy scheme
enlisting all ranks of local officials in a state-run
mandatory version of Gilbert's inquiry. This was the
most ambitious measure yet attempted in charity reform,
and its failure came at a time when another course of
action presented itself in the form of a new Select
Committee.

Enactment of the Charity Commission

On 21 May 1816, Henry Brougham induced the House of
Commons to appoint a Select Committee 'to inquire into
the education of the lower orders of the Metropolis.'
In one sense, this was yet another of the metropolitan
social inquiries which had appeared in the years 1810 to
1815. It was also important as a major step in the early
career of educational reform. But the prime importance
for our subject was that this Committee was to have the
distinction of recommending the commission of inquiry
into charitable trusts.

I

There is little hard evidence on the reason for the formation of this Select Committee. Brougham was eagerly
trying out issues on his return to the House of Commons
in 1816, seeking both personal and party advantage, and
also displaying a genuine desire for reform. (1) He had
been active in one cause or another during his time in
London since 1804, including educational and other benevolent societies; one of these was the West London
Lancasterian Association, many of whose officers and
members would testify before the Committee. Brougham
also was clearly interested in advancing schemes for
educational reform, as attested by his writings and
legislative proposals. (2)
    In addition to these immediate and obvious incentives,
Brougham's background suggested further reasons for his
inquiry proposals, first the Committee and then the
Commission. As a Scot and moreover a Scottish advocate,
Brougham brought a fresh and radical perspective to the
problem of English charities. The Scots had no body of
trust law comparable to the English, indeed Scottish

courts did not recognize a separate equity jurisdiction
until the 19th century, so that charity cases were dealt
with by the ordinary courts in much the same manner as
other forms of property. Given his training in this
system, Brougham was far less sensitive to the difficulties in treatment of endowments than his English colleagues.
Likewise, his view of the state's role in Irish and
Scottish education was favourable, and on more than one
occasion he spoke of those systems as good examples for
English legislators. (3) Finally, in his own experience,
Brougham was aware of Scottish legal reforms which had
been under discussion for a decade, among them an overload
of Scottish appeals which further burdened the English
Lord Chancellor. These problems had already been the
subject of Royal Commissions of Inquiry in 1808 and 1815,
examples not likely to be lost on Brougham.

In the immediate situation in 1816, the membership of
Brougham's Select Committee probably spurred the suggestion of a charity inquiry. One week after the Select
Committee was established, the Charitable Donations Bill
came up for its debate and passage in the Commons (28 May -
17 June). Several leading charity reform sponsors were
also on the Committee (Romilly, Wilberforce, and Wrottesley) and they must have urged the Committee's attention
to inefficient and wasteful handling of educational
resources in endowed schools - if any such suggestions
were in fact needed. (4) However, the evidence taken by
the Select Committee (22 May to 19 June) was chiefly
related to unendowed schools (only 22 out of 117 witnesses
were connected with endowed institutions). The story they
told was of busy volunteer work and hopelessly inadequate
provision of schooling for the poor who needed and wanted
it. The Committee was mainly engaged in probing several
destitute London districts, and the themes which emerged
in testimony were the difficulty of providing satisfactory
non-sectarian education, and the inequity of small wealthy
(endowed) schools surrounded by masses of illiterate poor.
But the witnesses gave no evidence at all of trust abuses
- at least none which was printed in the Committee
reports. (5)

When the Select Committee reported on 20 June, it had
not been appointed to examine, nor had it examined, nor
did it publish, any abuses in charitable trusts, educational or otherwise. And yet its report concluded:

Although your Committee have not been instructed to
examine the state of Education beyond the Metropolis,
they have in addition to what has appeared in evidence,
received communications, which show the necessity of
Parliament as speedily as possible instituting an

inquiry into the management of charitable donations
and other funds for the instruction of the Poor in
this country, and into the state of their Education
generally, especially in the larger towns: and your
Committee are of opinion that the most effectual as
well as least expensive mode of conducting such an
inquiry, would be by means of a Parliamentary commission. (6)

In his statement to the Commons on 20 June, Brougham
claimed that 120,000 poor children were without schooling
in London alone, 'in all sects and descriptions of persons
in the lower orders.' He boasted that the Committee 'had
not rested' at surveying the charity, parochial, subscription and Sunday schools, but had gone on to the higher
endowed schools. But Brougham cited no authority for
this critical decision - because there was none. The
only pretext for the Committee's encroachment was the
presence of 'abuses,' and this point was itself in some
doubt. Brougham said 'abuses were known, but they were
not properly denounced.' Perhaps this was so, but the
Chairman gave a faint display. First, he conceded that
'no instance of flagrant abuse occurred in London,' which
of course had been the Committee's principal zone of
activity. Brougham claimed that he had 'received many
communications on the subject from different parts of the
country.' But he gave only a single example, an allegation of corruption at an unnamed Essex grammar school
(Brentwood). Since this account was to be repeated
several times, and as it was the only instance cited here,
we may examine it at length.

He stated one flagrant case where £1,500, which was
left for the endowment of a school, was managed by
the lord of the manor, who appointed his own brother
schoolmaster with a large salary, while he again
shifted the duties to a deputy schoolmaster, in the
person of a joiner, with the small income of £40 a year
year, and left this ignorant person to educate the
children. (7)

These facts alone did not constitute any crime or even
necessarily any violation of trust law. Brougham's story,
as we shall see, would improve, and would be challenged,
later. Its purpose here was presumably to startle his
listeners. He followed it with the unsupported estimate
that 'by various accounts he had received, £70,000 might
be stated as the sum to which the (abused) charities he
alluded to might amount in all; and there was every reason
to believe that little benefit was now derived from them
in administering the blessings of education. This
deserved inquiry.' Whether this estimate was total worth,

or annual income, or for that matter, how the estimate
was made, we cannot say. But no doubt it reinforced the
story of the ignorant joiner of Brentwood.

Brougham went on to explain the rationale of a commission of inquiry, arguing for its efficiency and economy
as the strong attractions.

A Committee above stairs was inadequate for the task
as it could not examine upon oath; and as it would be
impossible, or very expensive to call up persons from
all parts of the country to give evidence, the only
remedy was, to appoint a commission with power to go
from place to place, and examine witnesses upon the
spot. More money would be saved to the country, or
dedicated to its most important interests - education,
than would be expended by such a commission. He had
no desire to create new places, or to aggravate the
public burthens, but he would propose that this commission should be paid for its labours, as the only
means of ensuring its activity, and bringing it under
the control of the House.

The case, given the existence of 'flagrant abuses,' was
a good one. Wilberforce urged that the inquiry begin at
once; Canning offered 'to contribute all his assistance
to the object of the report, satisfied that the foundation
of good order in society was good morals and that the
foundation of good morals was education;' Castlereagh
agreed 'that abuses existed' and 'he thought there would
be no great difficulty in the next session of appointing
a committee (sic) for examining into the administration
of the charities of the country.' Thus action was not
taken, but the prospects were good. In the next session,
the Education Committee was reinstated (22 May 1817).
But due to illness of the Chairman, no witnesses were
called, and a formal report was presented in July. (8)

On the occasion of the 1817 report, Brougham repeated
his Brentwood story, only changing his joiner to a carpenter, and he added the story of Pocklington school (see
below, p.111). Shortly afterward, Brougham received a
letter from Charles Tower, the Master of Brentwood,
denying that he was guilty of Brougham's allegations and
protesting the use of an anonymous 'tip' which Brougham
had not checked with the parties. (9) Brougham responded
by repeating the story in the Commons in 1818, raising
the value of the endowment, and making the carpenter a
mechanic. Referring lamely to Tower's denial, Brougham
said 'he understood, however, that before the time of the
present incumbent such a misapplication had taken
place.' (10)

Those remarks were made as Brougham moved for the

renewal of the Select Committee on 5 March 1818, this
time for inquiry into the 'education of the lower orders'
for England and Wales. In moving this extended renewal,
Brougham made several statements in favour of 'another
tribunal' on educational charities, and also warned that
'the House would find that they were but entering on their
task; for they ought to inquire generally into the misapplication of all charitable funds; this was a matter of
absolute necessity.' (11) The Select Committee took
evidence only once before their first 'Report' on 17
March, which promised a Bill for 'commissioners to inquire
into the abuses of charities connected with the education
of the poor in England and Wales.'

Hereafter events moved quickly, virtually overtaking
the Select Committee, which completed its hearings some
days after the commission Bill had passed both Houses.
But before turning to that Bill, it may be well to summarize the work of the Education Committee in 1818. Only
taking one day in March and three in April for evidence,
the Committee sat on ten days in May, and five of the
first eight in June. There were five Reports: the first
has been noted (17 March); the second (dated 25 May and
8 June!) covering about fifty pages of testimony; the
third had the 'final' report, dated 3 June, the date of
the final passage of the Commission Bill, and also 170
pages of testimony; the fourth and fifth 'reports' were
documentary appendices, dated 5 and 8 June, with documents
from Eton, St Bees, Trinity College and St John's College.
The Committee had its mandate extended to Scotland (8 May)
and this allowed it to include the northern kingdom in
its survey of schools, conducted through circular letters
to clergymen in April and May 1818. This project was also
overtaken by events. The Digest of the Returns was only
being printed in late 1818, and it was published as a
parliamentary paper in 1819. (12) This census of schools
was surely useful in the work of the Charity Commissioners,
but it could have had little impact on the actual creation
of the Commission.

The long years of discussion, the tedious legion of
bills and the endless debates were suddenly caught up in
a mood of urgency in 1818. Indeed, commissions of inquiry
had been an unusually prominent subject during the Spring.
In February, millowners unsuccessfully petitioned for a
commission 'for the purpose of examining upon the spot
into the actual condition of persons employed in factories.' (13) Later that month a motion was defeated for an
inquiry into the conduct of spies and informers. (14)
This was followed shortly by an unsuccessful motion by
Brougham for a commission of inquiry into the destruction

of income tax returns. (15)   Thus there were ample signs
of the current interest in inquiry, cropping up in the
principal areas of partisan tension.   It was not unusual
therefore for an interest in inquiry to appear in a less
partisan area.   Also, the appearance in a neutral zone
might explain the unusual show of cooperation between
Brougham and the government. (16)

II

The most significant fact in the enactment of the Charity
Commission was ministerial support for an opposition Bill.
The cabinet supported the principle of the inquiry, and
it naturally wanted to control its form and function.
Disagreement over details, and inveterate partisanship
of 'ultras' like Eldon, brought the alliance to the breaking point.   The House of Lords nearly emasculated the
Bill, and Brougham retaliated with motions for an Address
to the Regent.
     But the Bill passed in June 1818, just before the House
was dissolved for the coming election.   The Commission
itself was issued in August, after the election was ended.
Brougham was smarting from his defeat in Westmorland,
when he attacked his erstwhile ministerial allies in a
long pamphlet in the early Fall.   This sparked a minor
literary war for the next six months, but the fighting
was cut short by the government's introduction of a new,
and wider, and tougher Commission Bill in May 1819.
     The curious alliance was reflected in, and perhaps
explained by the debates on 'the Education of the Poor
Bill.' (17)   The main issues were avoided, the lesser
ones were mis-stated by both sides, and the detailed provisions were poorly discussed.   Before writing these
faults off as standard parliamentary procedure, they may
be worth examination for their evidence on the issue and
the alliance.
     The question of the education of the poor raised two
fundamental issues which were carefully muted or avoided
in parliamentary debate: religious education and endowment
reclamation.   This brilliant circumspection could hardly
have been accidental, and it hints strongly at an accommodation between reformers and ministers.   For questions
of religious instruction and the implied robbery of
resources for education were at the core of the Select
Committee's evidence.   Brougham apparently saw the commission of inquiry as a tactical manoeuvre in his march
to educational reform.   Instead of a frontal assault, he
would first attack the weak flank of corrupt educational

endowments. Brougham miscalculated here, for ministers
so completely supported his flank movement that his forces
were assimilated. (18) Only the impetuous Lord Chancellor
fought on, and his commanders nearly took revenge on him
in their legislation in 1819.

The chronological outline of the proceedings was
simple. The Bill was brought into the House of Commons
on 8 April. After several delays, it was committed on
27 April. Discussed on six occasions, it went to the
Lords on 20 May. The upper house also took up the Bill
six times in the fortnight before its passage on 2 June.
Final amendments were approved on 3 June, and the royal
assent was given one week later, on the day that Parliament was dissolved.

Some legislation is debated on principles, some on
details. Even though a major debate might have seemed
appropriate on the 'education of the poor' Bill, the real
fighting was over details. Consequently, the manner in
which both sides dealt with the principles was less than
edifying. The discussion featured on one side Brougham's
persistent flogging of abuses. On the other side, Eldon
majestically interposed on behalf of beleaguered trustees.
Both rhetorical excursions - Brougham's much the longest -
made small contributions to the real struggle over
detailed provisions.

The titillation and condemnation of scandal were
Brougham's major rhetorical resource. His rehearsal of
abuses was designed to prove that the machinery to
correct them was ineffective, and an inquiry was
'absolutely essential' because earlier reckonings were
inadequate. No serious opposition was put to Brougham's
evidence, first because the evidence to disprove scandals
is always hard to find, but also because there was really
no argument with the points which the scandals were being
used to 'prove'. Brougham's arguments were well known
they were plausible, and there was a general disposition
to accept the charges, if not all the conclusions.

Brougham's scenario had not varied from the initial
discussion in 1816, but now the ignorant mechanic of
Brentwood was joined by a large cast of villains, and at
long last, a definition of 'abuse.' In a speech later
printed for national circulation, Brougham gave an outline
of principal types of abuse (8 May): (19)

(1) Insufficient powers for the profitable management
of the funds;
(2) loss of property through defects in the original
constitution of the trusts;

(3) negligence ... including carelessness, ignorance, indolence;
(4) the large head of wilful and corrupt abuse in its various branches.

Having thus separated abuses, Brougham quickly lumped them together again and described them without any regard to category, masking the proportions between categories, and indeed regarding all as evil: 'to let and take a fine is an abuse,' or a 99-year lease 'of itself I hold to be an abuse.' Beyond careless distinctions, Brougham exploited a range of devices in citing the abuses: referring to them only by county of origin, his language was suggestive and sarcastic.

A certain corporation in Hampshire has long had the management of estates devised to charitable uses, and valued at above £2,000 a year by surveyors. They are let for 2 or 300 a year on fines. How are the fines disposed of? No one knows; at least no one will tell.

In another case, 'In Nottinghamshire there is a free school, the funds of which our reverend informant scruples not to say are grossly abused. The scholars are wholly neglected, and hush-money is given to the master.' After a series of these stories, Brougham reached an even higher (lower?) level. 'I hold in my hand forty or fifty more instances of abuse, extracted from the numerous returns made by the resident clergy.' He referred to the returns to the Select Committee's circular on schools, being sent to about 10,000 clergymen in England, Wales, and Scotland. He said he trusted that the House would treat these reports as 'beyond suspicion of exaggeration.' His trust was not misplaced. Yet even if the clergy could be trusted, perhaps their new-found spokesman could not be. Brougham himself admitted, much later in his speech, that 'many abuses exist without blame being imputable to anyone.' Surely this was true of the badly-constituted trust, or in any class of abuse where 'some remote ancestor' was to blame.

Brougham was not challenged on the small number of cases which he cited, nor was he tested on the point that his 'sample' represented a tiny fraction of trusts. This may be because Brougham had artfully pre-empted the ground by attacking the Gilbert Returns, saying they 'were known to be exceedingly defective.' In other words, a new inquiry was essential to determine the total number of trusts and the number and identity of the abuses.

There was no real challenge to Brougham in the Commons. Indeed, the real adversary, Lord Eldon, did not challenge

Brougham's case when the Bill was debated in the Lords.
Whether from deference to his ministerial colleagues, or
out of other motives, Eldon confined himself to a public
defence of trusteeship and property rights. Later he
engineered a withering amendment campaign in private.

Eldon's defence of trustees was in a way more deceptive
than Brougham's attack on abuses. The Lord Chancellor's
main point was that inquiry was an encroachment. But if
trustees were encroached upon when legislators inquired,
what could be said of a judicial inquiry? Surely the
'encroachment' which most worried Eldon was the one which
he saw on his preserve as Lord Chancellor. The trustees
were his line of defence. He argued that 'if a more
temperate measure than this were not provided, no man
would in future take upon himself such arduous and hazard-
ous duties.' (20) Eldon spoke as if the measure gave
unlimited powers: 'there was nothing in the nature of a
charity that was not within the cognizance of these commissioners' and he cleverly crossed the point of capacity
with one of jurisdiction: 'even the national schools would
be subject to them, and tomorrow the Archbishop of Canterbury himself might be summoned before them to give an
account of his demeanour.' No doubt Brougham would have
enjoyed such a prospect, but it was nonsense on any
reading of the Bill. And Eldon was after all not opposing
the committal of the Bill, with its 'suspicious and
vexatious inquiries.' He allowed that 'he despaired of
making it unobjectionable' though he would do quite a lot
to it in committee. The Lords mustered in serried ranks
to vote the second reading, approving by ten to eight.

Away from the arena and its flourishes, complicated
negotiation and manoeuvring determined the contours and
nearly terminated the career of the Bill. In this region,
there was as little concern for Brougham's abuses as there
was for Eldon's embattled trustees. Here the very hard
questions, and harder answers, were being shaped. If an
inquiry was necessary, what would be its composition, its
power, and its scope? Implied in the answers to these
practical questions would be a general answer to that
unspoken problem lurking in the 'Education of the Poor
Bill - how would charitable resources be used to meet
pressing needs of national education?'

The composition and configuration of the Commission
received far more attention than had similar bodies to
this time. (21) This was chiefly because the original
proposal was radical, and it was from the opposition.
Asking for paid, professional, non-official, and mobile

commissioners was bold, particularly when the request did not come from ministers. That these commissioners were to be named in the Act raised even more concern, although such procedure was quite common for ministerial proposals for inquiry. As it was, Brougham surrendered the naming provision (perhaps having only included it as a bargaining point), and he confessed 'this did not appear to him so indispensible as it did to some of his friends.' (22)

To compose this Commission, Brougham wanted 'active men of business, chiefly lawyers,' but Castlereagh insisted on including 'men of rank and consideration,' offering the Irish Education Commission as a model. (23) This question was compromised by having one part 'rank' and one part 'business.' There were eventually six honorary and eight stipendiary commissioners, a compromise slightly in favour of the inquiry's supporters.

Once composition was settled, the next question concerned the manner in which the stipendiaries would operate. Brougham wanted them to travel in pairs, thus giving the Commission much greater range and capacity. He took great pride in this innovation:

> I confess, that I am very sanguine in my expectation of the benefits to be derived from this part of the measure: I consider it as a contrivance of eminent utility and universal application; and I trust that no new board will ever henceforth be created without the adoption of this principle. (24)

When his pet scheme was tampered with by the Lords in committee, and the travelling board's quorum was raised from two to three, Brougham was incensed:

> The superior nature of the minds, who laughing to scorn the rashness of the original projectors, had perfected, by their grave deliberations, the present model of legislation, thought that the figure 3 was a better divisor of 8 than 2, and afforded a larger quotient of boards. Now as the crude scheme of the House of Commons was framed, there were four boards of two each calculated to proceed in their labours with expedition and emulation. As the Bill stood originally amended, as was the phrase, there were two boards of three each, with two useless members over. So much for the arithmetic of those elevated legislators who scouted the original bill in its rash imperfect state. (25)

The payment of salaries was provided in the text of the Bill. However, the provision of continuing payment for travel and expenses posed a problem. This was overcome by a special resolution on 15 May.

> Resolved, That the Lords Commissioners of His Majesty's
> Treasury be authorized to issue out of the Consolidated
> Fund ... an annual sum of money, not exceeding four
> thousand pounds, for allowance for the travelling
> expenses to the Commissioners for inquiring into the
> abuses in charities in England and Wales, and in
> defraying the salaries of clerks, messengers, and
> other officers, and all other charges incident there-
> to. (26)

In 1819 a similar resolution was passed, but this one also
covered the salaries of Commissioners (11 June 1819):

> That there be issued and paid out of the Consolidated
> Fund of the United Kingdom ... the annual sum of ten
> thousand pounds for the payment of salaries ... and
> also the annual sum of eight thousand pounds for the
> payment of the travelling expenses ... (27)

On the powers of the Commissioners there was also some
early agreement, but it melted rather quickly in the heat
of controversy. The function of inquiry required the
acquisition and recording of testimony. The initial
model was the Naval Inquiry of 1803, the powers sought
included subpoena, oaths, fines, and committal. The
latter was for uncooperative witnesses, and it was dropped
at an early stage, as were provisions for fines. The
subpoena power was nearly made inoperative by an amendment. Only the power to administer the oath to witnesses
remained unaltered, though the penalties and procedure
for perjury had to be strengthened in later legislation.

As to the record of testimony, it was accepted throughout that the Commissioners would report regularly. The
six-month interval was agreed by 8 May. In the original
Bill this was to be simultaneous reporting to the crown
and both houses of parliament. This provision was
approved, but then altered in 1819, when a clause was
introduced waiving the reporting directly to Parliament;
thereafter both houses regularly addressed the crown for
copies of the periodic reports. (28)

The Commission was not to have at first any real power
over its objects of investigation. The original Bill
proposed to empower the Commissioners to sue 'for compelling the due performance of any matter or thing touching
estates of funds destined and intended for the purposes
of Education' over which courts had jurisdiction. This
was dropped entirely from the Bill, and only restored (in
separate legislation) in 1819.

Finally, the last major question about the inquiry was
its scope. Being produced by an Education Committee, it

was accepted that it should include schools; but all
schools? or all education? or all charities? Each of
these ideas was advanced during 1818, but only the first
was adopted. The last became law in 1819.

The coverage of the Bill was seriously restricted, and
the restriction accepted by Brougham, on the schools
involved. Exemptions were important but far from crip-
pling. Many of the oldest and richest foundations were
exempt, and an effort was fought off (8 May) to drive a
host of lesser schools through this loophole. The arguments for exemption were legal and pragmatic; the statute
of Charitable Uses gave precedent to recognizing the convention of royal and special visitorial immunity; and
Brougham admitted that while exemptions were against his
better judgment

> beside the apprehension that a refusal might have
> endangered the bill in certain quarters, the reason
> which has influenced me in acceding to the proposed
> exemption is, that those great establishments are
> placed conspicuously in the eyes of the public, and
> may be examined by the ordinary proceedings in
> Chancery, and by the inquiries of this House. (29)

Brougham wanted the inquiry to be an extension of his
Select Committee, and so the Bill called for an inquiry
into 'the state of education generally.' The original
Bill said that 'it is expedient that an inquiry should
also be made into the state of education of the poorer
classes of His Majesty's subjects throughout England and
Wales.' This was dropped in the version prepared by the
House of Lords in Committee (27 May). This broad inquiry
was never restored to the mandate of the Commissioners.
While it only was to produce 'such observations and
suggestions' as might occur to the Commissioners, and
while similar 'observations' were always expected, this
loss was still significant.

On another front, a major alteration was inserted in
the 8 May version, only to be caught and removed by the
vigilant Peers. To the preamble had been added the words
'and to other charitable uses,' describing the objects of
charity under the Commission's jurisdiction. Either
Brougham had hoped to slip this enlarged definition
through unnoticed after the first two readings in the
Commons, or more probably, he had made some accommodation
with ministers: perhaps trading the power to sue for the
extended mandate of inquiry only. Whatever the source,
this offensive provision was rooted out by the Lords. It
would be restored in 1819, when the Commission was
extended to cover all charitable trusts.

The paradox of this legislation was the smooth compromise through much of its passage, and the violent clash just before its conclusion. Eldon and Brougham contrived to bring things close to a breakdown at the last stage (1-3 June 1818). What apparently happened was that Eldon, with some colleagues on the episcopal and judicial benches, tried to drown the Bill in amendments (27 May - 1 June). There were so many and such extensive alterations, that Brougham and his allies decided to oppose the Bill, and to move the House for an Address to the Regent to create a Commission. Brougham later claimed that he had the votes to succeed, though this was doubtful. In any case, the Lords were prevailed upon to drop two of their disabling clauses. (30) Brougham accepted the revised Bill, but he still gave a token display of fireworks on the third reading, arousing a good pre-election squall; constitutional thunder and lightning, but no rain. He determined, in spite of his enemies' concessions and his own support for the Bill, to move two resolutions for Addresses to the Prince Regent. The first motion was for an Address to request appointment of a Commission to inquire into the state of education of the poor. The second motion was for an Address praying the Prince Regent to instruct commissioners to inquire into charities not connected with education. These were both easily defeated - the first by a vote of fifty-four to twenty-nine, and the second without a division.

The general issue was regarded by ministerial spokesmen as a constitutional monstrosity, first by attempting to override amendments, and so the will of the other house, by an appeal to the sovereign; next, by proposing to set up prerogative and parliamentary commissions side by side, and as he threatened, to have also a revived version of Brougham's Select Committee, all sitting at the same time.

The energy generated in the debate was quite beside the point, but probably a good warmup for the election. Brougham delivered himself of scathing ridicule of the Lords, a searing indictment of Chancery, and a threatening plan of joint operation between his committee and the Commission. He was answered calmly by Castlereagh who called for 'temper and moderation' and by Canning who suggested that no urgency existed to justify Brougham's radical procedure, that Commissioners could be given a wider mandate in future, and they would have 'enough to occupy them' in the interim. To support the Addresses, said Canning, 'would go near to overturn the fixed barriers of the constitution.'

After the resolutions were defeated, there were some

angry exchanges, and the Lords' amendments were finally
moved by Castlereagh, the Bill was passed, and it received
the royal assent a week later. In the next two months,
the Commissioners were selected and the Commission itself
was issued on 20 August. By early September it was organizing and beginning to take evidence, but the matter of
its constitution and powers were still under discussion.
The next phase of that discussion moved into the public
domain.

III

After the fires of a gruelling election campaign in which
he failed in a challenge to the Lowthers' grip on Westmorland's county seats, Brougham returned to the earlier
rebuke of his charity inquiry bill. In August, he wrote
'A Letter to Sir Samuel Romilly ... upon the Abuse of
Charities. (31) In the ensuing six months, a dozen
pamphlets and a number of articles appeared in response.
They served to engender and sustain interest in, if not to
enlighten the subject. They also made the ministerial
support of the inquiry stand out more clearly than ever,
for neither Brougham's charges against the government,
nor the vigorous replies written against him, dissuaded
ministers from bringing in their new inquiry Bill in May
1819. And that Bill was one which would actually extend
and fortify the scope and power of commissioners. Finally,
these pamphlets uncovered one of the unmentionable issues
- the 'poor scholars' question - and gave it a good
airing. But by this time, it was too late for it to
become, other than indirectly, a matter for inquiry.
    Brougham published his 'Letter' as an attempt to
accelerate the charitable trust inquiry and to expose more
fully its connection to educational reform, his primary
concern. The 'Letter' was the first clear sign of his
underlying strategy: the reclamation of educational
resources. The loosely-drafted 'Letter' was three tracts
in one: a pungent commentary on the behaviour of ministers
toward the Bill, a catalogue of the sins of trustees,
and a radical proposal for the conversion or reclamation
of foundations. It aroused ire on every point, and the
anger mixed with panic on the last.
    With regard to ministers, Brougham affected the feeling
that he had been led down the primrose path and had bar-
gained away valued points only to be deserted by ministers
when the Bill reached the upper house. But he was most
aggrieved by what he saw as blatant jobbing and packing
of the Commission. He complained that his Select Com-

mittee's list of nominees, including himself and
Babington, had been passed over for a list of government
appointees, including two enemies of the inquiry.
Brougham made threatening noises about renewing the Select
Committee and giving it a mandate to investigate charities,
but his argument, while interesting, was only bluster.
It overlooked two simple but salient points: first, the
Bill and its principle had been accepted and supported
by the government; second, no ministry had ever surrendered the appointment power, and this ministry in this dry
season of patronage was not likely to be a pioneer.

In his catalogue of trust violations, Brougham was
using the 'case histories' he had formerly employed in
reports and speeches to fill a dual purpose: first, to
reveal evils and abuses in administration; but also, to
demonstrate the deficient organization of the present
Commission, barred from general educational inquiry,
limited to educational charity, and bypassing many
charitable trusts - but worst of all, omitting those with
special visitors. The trust violations he described
were of varied origin and severity. As in Parliament, so
in print, Brougham was careless of such distinctions, and
where he had sufficient ground to support his case for
inquiry, he could not refrain from loading the evidence
still further with accusations of abuse, charges which
the facts could not always support.

The most shocking section of Brougham's 'Letter' was
the unveiling of the 'poor scholars' question. The
fundamental issue was whether or not old endowments for
education were indeed for the poor, in a simple, straight-
forward sense. If so, then grammar schools and universities had been systematically expropriated over the years,
and the poor had been robbed. Brougham asserted that
founding documents were clearly in support of this view.
But Brougham, as was his wont, was not content to leave
it at that. Reclamation or restoration was a serious
enough challenge; Brougham rendered his case doubly
threatening and simultaneously hopeless by going on to
assert that founders' wills could and should be overturned
in changed circumstances. He crippled his own argument
for honest, or at least literal reading of wills and
statutes. In his words:

> It may therefore be fairly assumed that the inquiry
> will end if rightly conducted, in throwing complete
> light on the state of charities, and in correcting
> all the abuses to which they are now liable. The
> estate of the poor will be, as it were, accurately
> surveyed, and restored to its rightful owners; or
> rather rescued from the hands which have no title to

hold it, and placed at the disposal of the Legislature,
the supreme power in the state, to be managed in the
way most beneficial to those for whose use it was
destined.

Fortunately for the inquiry, Brougham had not stated his
objectives in this way earlier, although it may well have
been behind the work of his Select Committee all along.
Now, with the Commission established, Brougham elected
to open the deeper questions. Lest there by any doubt, he
elaborated his view of trust conversion in the concluding
section of his 'Letter':

The will of the donor, which ought to be closely pursued, may often be better complied with, by a deviation
from the letter of his directions.

No rights are in reality infringed by taking a fund
destined to support the poor in a way likely to
increase their numbers, and using it so as to perform
some act of charity without increasing the number of
charitable objects. (32)

Brougham was obsessed with the Malthusian notion that
generous relief produced poverty. But his idea of charity
was confused on this score as on others. It was Brougham
who argued that the endowed school which fed and clothed
its pupils should instead apply its resources to the
largest possible number of 'charitable objects.' In other
words, opening trusts to Brougham's proposed 'deviations'
was unlikely to lead to any simple resolution.

The row which followed Brougham's pamphlet was staffed
by authors of no particular eminence, but often men who
were directly affected by the charges or the challenges
which Brougham had issued. The quality of argument is
beneath notice, but the facts(so far as we can ascertain
them) are not. As the focus of all the respondents was
Brougham's tract, we can fairly analyze them around the
three major themes of the 'Letter to Romilly:' the attack
on ministers, the catalogue of sins, and the radical proposal.

The ministers found no defenders among Brougham's
critics, for in truth these authors were opposed to the
idea of inquiry, hence they were loath to support the
ministerial compromise. They opposed Brougham's charges
with assaults on him, on his committee, and on his conduct
connected to the appointment of the Commission, but all
of these were wide of the mark, and quite hopeless in
view of the government's position. The leading exponents
of these views were the two major rejoinders: 'A Letter
to the Rt. Hon. Sir William Scott' and a long essay in the
'Quarterly Review.' (33) The assaults on Brougham's

character were stock political items: sneers at his
associations (Scots and radicals) and at his motivation
(as a Westmorland candidate or a putative leader of the
Opposition) and generally at his liberalism. The Quarterly summed up his views as 'a disposition to discredit or
subvert every thing' and a 'propensity to every species
of innovation.'

The criticism of the Select Committee on Education was
that Brougham had tricked the Commons into believing that
he was studying paupers and charity schools, while he had
quickly and surreptitiously elevated the inquiry. In
levelling this charge, critics cited the committee's
instruction 'for inquiring into children begging in the
streets of the metropolis,' but failed to note that this
was only a later addition to the committee's task, and
one which occurred only in 1816. Of course, if the
elevation of the committee was dangerous, it certainly
was no secret, and it had been fully reported and discussed from 1816.

On Brougham's criticism of the ministerial appointments,
the 'Review' and the 'Letter to Scott' correctly pointed
out that ministers had the right of appointment, but
instead of justifying the selection of avowed enemies,
they assaulted Brougham's list of prospective members.
This they interpreted as a clear grab at patronage, and
they gleefully played with the image of the reformer
being soiled by jobbing: the 'Letter' combined this idea
with a calculation of the total cost of the commission
(£150,000) and ridiculed it with a borrowed phrase, as
'a large economy.'

The real meat of the controversy was in the cases of
abused charities. Of some twenty endowments which came
before his Select Committee, Brougham commented unfavour-
ably on ten in his 'Letter to Romilly,' and the victims
were all defended vigorously in the ensuing discussion.
The outcome was that Brougham's general case for inquiry
was proven, while many of his specific accusations were
overthrown. Ironically, the erroneous charges were
something of a justification for inquiry, publicity, and
the lessening of rumour. A sample of the affected
charities will illustrate the nature of the discussion.

A major target of Brougham was the trust under Lowther
control at St Bees, Cumberland. There had been some local
ferment about the use (and improvident leasing) of school
lands for coal mining, and Brougham surely considered the
issue to be of some political value. The central question
was around the taking of a 1000-year lease on school lands,
and subsequently a lease on mineral rights on the same
land by the Lowther family, who were also trustees of the

school. The original incident went back to 1742; the
leases were clearly illegal, and 'Letter to Scott'
admitted this. (34) The rejoinders turned on Brougham's
alleged motives and misconduct in the inquiry. In early
1819, Rev. John Fleming, the Vicar of Bootle and a trustee
of the school, published a pamphlet in defence of the
trustees and of Lord Lonsdale, his patron. (35) Fleming
attacked Brougham and tried to impugn his motives, but he
could not explain away the embarrassing lease. The
Charity Commissioners visited the school in September
1819, and in their report of 1820 it was agreed that the
leasing was illegal. The case was certified and eventually the lease was ordered terminated by Chancery
(1827). (36)

In Croydon, the management of charity estates had come
in for criticism by the Select Committee and its chairman.
In his 'Letter,' Brougham named long and improvident
leases, the closure of a free school, and the inaction of
the Special Visitor, as the abuses here. These charges
were answered quite effectively by John Ireland, Dean of
Westminster and late Vicar of Croydon. (37) Brougham's
information had been inaccurate, for the operation of
the school had ceased c. 1760, but one had actually been
reopened (by subscription, on the national system) in 1812.
As for the work of the Special Visitor (the Archbishop of
Canterbury), Ireland noted that none other than Samuel
Romilly had given the legal opinion to the Primate that
there was no power for interference of the Visitor in
the case in question (Whitgift's Hospital). While this
was a blow to Brougham's particular charge, it surely
supported his views about the insufficiency of visitors.
The Charity Commissioners ratified the general good report
of these charities but they also noted that the leasing
arrangements were changed - and in 1818. (38)

Finally, one of the favourite scandals was the school-
room that changed into a saw-pit. In Pocklington (E.R.)
a grammar school had suffered the chronic drift of the
18th century away from classical schools, which when not
offset by new curriculum, usually meant a shrivelling
school. The Master and Fellows of St John's, Cambridge,
were visitors. In fact, two Fellows had visited the
school in 1817, held a public meeting, solicited question-
naire type information, and made a set of recommendations
to the Master. The school was 'taken down' and rebuilt
between August 1818 and August 1819. During those same
months, Brougham was protesting that

> Pocklington School, with a large revenue, had been
> suffered to fall into decay, so that only one boy was
> taught, and the room converted into a saw-pit (Note:

An attempt was made to deny this; but it seems to be
the result of the evidence taken together. At any
rate, it is admitted, that the proper school-room was
wholly disused, except for keeping lumber and working
materials) yet it has visitors who, probably from
ignorance of the evil, had taken no step to correct
it before last winter. (39)

As the 'Letter to Scott' admitted, it was 'impossible to
deny that this abuse existed.' But it was equally
impossible to deny that it was being corrected by the
traditional machinery. The school was restored, but when
the Commissioners visited in 1828 it was found to be
educating twenty boys on an income of £1,000. There was
an unbeatable case of inefficiency, as there had been
ten years earlier. But Brougham was too intent on his
customary dramatization.

The third critical issue was the true destiny of
educational foundations for 'Paupers et indigentes
scholares.' (40) The argument here was heated and inconclusive. Whatever its historical accuracy or popular
appeal, Brougham's view of the wider interpretation would
never have carried the day in the early 19th century, in
view of the way that grammar schools were already developing under middle class demand. (41) But a vigorous
counter-attack here insured the failure of the radical
view. The argument was particularly hard-fought by two
champions of Winchester School, Rev. William Bowles and
Rev. Lisconbe Clarke. They in turn were challenged by
the author (C.H. Ker) of the main tract in Brougham's
defence. (42)

The works of Clarke and Bowles appeared at about the
same time in late October 1818. Clarke was a Fellow of
Winchester, Bowles a former student. Both took offence
at the whole course of Brougham's investigation, especially his treatment of their school, and above all, the
argument that poor scholars were meant to be poor. Their
counter-arguments were both grammatical and historical.
The grammatical argument was that 'poor' and 'indigent'
were adjectives limiting the word 'scholars,' and not
indicating the literal condition of poverty. Rather
'poor' was meant in relation to scholars (and gentlemen)
in general. Historically, it was argued that scholars
had come from the higher ranks (or rarely from the lowest)
and that scholars at Winchester with up to £3 6s. (5 marks)
of their own to spend (according to the limit in the
statutes) in the 14th century, were hardly what the
founder and his contemporaries would have classed as
'lower orders.' Bowles concluded that scholars were meant
to be 'the children of those men in general who were able

to give them some previous education,' and thus the poor
in general were not intended to benefit.

These arguments were attacked by (Ker) who observed
that the matter had not attracted great concern until the
Select Committee 'scathed the proud towers, as well as
dived into the recesses of the pitiful frauds of the
village schools.' But Clarke and Bowles, with 'subtile
and antiquarian researches' failed to explain how
Winchester could admit

the children of parents in easy or opulent circumstance.
That the boys are made solemnly to swear at the age of
15, that they have not £3 6s. a year to spend, and
yet the whole seventy (with a few occasional exceptions)
give the Masters 10 guineas each year as a gratuity.

He concluded

It cannot for a moment be contended, that there is any
preference given to poverty; it is well known that
presentations to scholarships are too much sought after
to be ever attained by the poor or the friendless.

The counter-attack on Brougham scored well on every
point, and a good coherent defence could have been made,
though the pamphlets reviewed here were not of a high
enough calibre to make it. Part of the reason for this
was of course the government's support of the inquiry,
which support became abundantly clear in the Spring of
1819.

The prose salvoes stopped when ministers stepped in
with their Bill, and the 'Edinburgh Review' had the last,
sanctimonious word against its foes, who had been deserted
'by their pitiless employers:'

It is fortunate when the virulent and interested adver-
saries of any great improvement in the condition of
mankind, are at variance with each other (or with
themselves); and even when united are not found very
formidable. There are few questions in which this
felicity has more signally attended the right side,
from the beginning of the controversy, than that
respecting the Education of the Poor; and we gladly
draw from hence the augury of a decision favourable
to the best interests of the species. (43)

This may be as close as the 'Review' could come to
describing a nonpartisan question; in any case, the
pamphlet battle was no more than a diversion. But it
served to make clearer than ever that ministers were
indeed supporting and extending the inquiry. How much so
we may now begin to assess.

IV

The ministers must have either read or heard of Brougham's
'Letter' and its attackers. They may have agreed with one
of the pamphleteers that 'much is to be forgiven in that
class of men (barristers) in a long vacation.' (44) The
long vacation of Parliament ended in January 1819, and
four months later the government introduced its amendment
Bill on the Charity Commission. The Bill would strengthen
and expand the Commission significantly. While it may
have 'passed all stages ... unanimously,' (45) it was not
unchanged, particularly in one major alteration, which
saved the Lord Chancellor from suffering an unparalleled
embarrassment at the hands of his colleagues.

On 21 May 1819, Castlereagh asked for leave to bring
in a Bill to amend 58 George III c. 91. He apologized
for leaving the matter until that late in the session and
explained that he had been holding off until receipt of
the first report of the Commissioners. But that report
was signed on 2 March and printed on the 4th. And it was
unlikely that the report had any valuable clues for the
government, nor did Castlereagh elaborate on his reasons
for waiting. At any rate, Brougham happily seconded the
motion.

When the Bill went into committee on 14 June, Castlereagh spoke with some enthusiasm of the brightened
'prospects' brought by the 'successes' of the Commission.
He did not enumerate these successes, but he went on to
propose revisions; including (1) committal power, (2) en-
largement to ten honorary and ten stipendiary Commissioners, plus operation in pairs, (3) extension to all charities, (4) extension to Wales, and (5) summary process in
Chancery before the Master of the Rolls or the Vice
Chancellor, without appeal to the Lord Chancellor.
Brougham supported the ministers' Bill, only arguing for
one major revision: the elimination of the special visitors' exemption. The Bill passed through all its stages
without serious opposition. Only at the third reading was
there any attack, and Brougham was the victim. He had
spoken for a time on the question of special visitors, and
suggested that they were often the source, or at least the
screen of serious abuses: commissions of charitable uses
could not deal with those trusts, nor in most cases could
the Lord Chancellor. Parliament was the only protection.
When Brougham finished, Peel rose and began an intemperate
attack on him, on his Select Committee, and on his alleged
radical ideas. (46) Brougham's reply made much of the
fact that he was caught off guard, yet he made a long and
powerful speech, aided by Peel's poorly prepared challenge.

The sound and fury having passed, the Bill went on un-
affected.

The measure was received in the House of Lords on 25
June. When committed on 1 July there were some minor
amendments, but the major changes were made after the
Committee report on 2 July. These changes included the
deletion of the two sections which would have allowed
appeals to the House of Lords (thus giving the Chancellor
the single contact as presiding officer of that House).
Also removed was a section providing fines for uncooperative witnesses, once again under the jurisdiction of
the Master of the Rolls and the Vice Chancellor only.
These provisions were rewritten, restoring the customary
role of the Chancellor, and also allowing the Charity
Commission access to fines and further legal process: but
these were incorporated in a separate Act, introduced and
rapidly passed in the last days of the session (5-12 July).
(47) This late flurry of activity was almost certainly
the work of Eldon, seeking to preserve what the new Bill
called 'the due course of the said (Chancery) court.'
Why this incident occurred was not clear, but that it did
suggests strongly that Eldon was under pressure from
within the cabinet, over his conduct of Chancery business
or else his misconduct on the Bill in 1818. Finally, the
incident would seem to be conclusive evidence that
ministers were seriously supporting the work of the
Charity Commission.

The creation of the charity inquiry was an important
step in the evolution of inquiry and in the investigation
of charity. It is impossible to explain the action in
terms of a reform movement with popular support and partisan discipline, and it is unwise to see in it a progressive objective.

Instead, the Act for an inquiry was generated through
a study of metropolitan school problems, a strong desire
to reform education, and an idea that trusts would be a
good (i.e. vulnerable) target for reformist examination,
and a possible ready source for financing social expenditures. The ministry's support for such an inquiry was
not altogether surprising, for inquiry was an increasingly
useful device and charity was an easy neutral territory
in which it could be used.

Organization

Our discussion of the Charity Commissioners must deal with
an inquiry whose career and activity were so extensive
that they defy a simple narrative or a conventional
analysis. In certain respects, there was great continuity
in the Charity Commission, and in others there were vital
interruptions. Therefore, an unorthodox plan will be
followed in the reconstruction of the Commission's story.
First, the organization of the Commission - its establishment, its form, and its planning - will be reviewed for
the whole span of the inquiry (1818-37). This survey will
be coupled with an overview of procedures, showing in
detail how the Commissioners actually functioned in the
several stages of their work. At this point, a narrative
of the interruptions of the inquiry will give an excellent
series of glimpses of the Charity Commission. These successive exposures will be very useful in explaining the
evolution of the commission of inquiry, and more particularly, of attitudes toward it. There will then be an
evaluation which will offer several assessments of the
reforming work of the Commissioners, and some comments on
their recorded results.

The Charity Commission inquiry was as unusual in organization as it had been in origin. It was a new body which
functioned quite satisfactorily under old rules. While a
creature of Parliament, an appendage of the Home Office,
with a separate account in the Treasury, and after 1819 a
separate line to the Attorney-General, the Commission
functioned much as it would have had its members been
Chancery court agents in one of a number of traditional
roles. There was little sense of the novelty of the Commission's position. There was barely a trace of corporate
identity. There was little central direction of Commission business until 1832. Stipendiary Commissioners

were very much on their own, going about their job of
legal research with as much or as little systematic preparation and procedure as they felt was necessary or in
conformity with their continuing practice of law.   As
later chapters will show, the job was more than research.
From the outset, the phrase 'inquire and report' failed
to do justice to the actual business which Commissioners
were forced to do.   But that was the narrow meaning of
their statutory duty, a duty which they set about fulfil-
ling promptly in September 1818.   The fascinating process
which unfolded thereafter was one in which the Charity
Commission became a reforming agency, without any explicit
design, and before there were any of the 'normal' trap-
pings of central direction, bureaucratic organization, and
policy coordination.   The Commissioners never aspired to
Brougham's lofty vision of 'correcting all the abuses to
which (charities) are now liable;' in fact they felt and
said that the law simply required inquiring and reporting;
yet they were not able to stop at that, and local needs
converted them into agents of reform.

I

The Charity Commission inquiry was actually a series of
four commissions.   The first in 1818 was only for educational charities; the renewal in the following year extended inquiry to all types of charitable trust, and with
two subsequent renewals, this Commission expired finally
in 1830; the third Commission was enacted in 1831 and
expired in 1834; the fourth and final Commission was
issued in late 1835, and with a short extension, expired
in July 1837. (1)   These instruments were in effect for
all but twenty-six months of the nearly nineteen years
covered.   Throughout this period, the basic principles
and constitution of the Commission were unchanged, but
composition and powers were altered from time to time,
both by the successive enabling Acts and by other legislation. (2)
    In 1818 the Charity Commissioners were loosely tied
to several departments of government.   The Commissioners
were nominees of the Secretary of State, they were funded
on special resolution of the Commons, and from 1819 they
were empowered to certify cases to the Attorney-General
for possible litigation.   The Commissioners' semi-annual
reports were initially directed to the crown and Parliament, but in 1819 this was altered.   Reports then went
through the Home Office, and copies thence to both Houses
by Address.

This confused situation might have been the result of design or accident, but owing to the Commission's novelty, the latter explanation has more plausibility. Apparently no firm decision was reached with regard to ministerial relations, and the particularly touchy subject of the connections with Chancery made more decisive action un-likely. While it might be tempting to impute this vacuum of direction to the altruism that observers have bestowed on Royal Commissions over the years, there is no evidence whatsoever that this was a factor. We can only say, by way of negative proof, that in the prevailing climate on patronage, such a set of appointments was going to be jealously watched for telltale signs of parasitism. Thus the work of a body like the Commission would either have to be genuinely independent, or its camouflage would have to be exceptional.

The personnel of the Commission were greeted with unpleasant comment and a small stir of controversy as we have seen. Actually the appointments turned out to be fairly effective, and the system in which they were set worked rather well, especially after its remodelling in 1819. The limits of six honorary and eight stipendiary Commissioners were raised to ten in that renovation. It was in this configuration that the Commission functioned until its last phase, 1835-7. The honorary Commissioners were designed to be an effective element, but they became mainly a check on the stipendiaries. At first, since ministers saw the Commission as a device of social control, the natural leaders of society were obvious leaders of the controlling agency. This never in fact happened, but the honoraries still had a useful function and image; the 'gentlemen of rank and consideration' could certainly see that the operation of the Commission did not get out of control (say in the way the Select Committee on the Education of the Lower Orders did). The honoraries would also serve as liaison to the royal court, the cabinet, the church, the peers, the judges: they were a symbol and a channel of reassurance and respectability to men of property and the custodians of established institutions. The honorary Commissioners' principal tasks were to attend general board meetings where they might oversee policy decisions, approve requisitions and communications, and sign the semi-annual reports. Each honorary Commissioner had the same powers as a stipendiary – without the stipend. But rarely did honoraries act in any capacity other than supervisory, and even there, their contribution was limited. There was no separate vehicle for honorary Commissioners, and when their equal numbers were offset by their high absenteeism, they gave stipendiary Commission-

ers a regular majority at all meetings. How important
this was remains uncertain, for few internal divisions
were recorded, and none on the strict lines of status.
The honorary Commissioners provided the chairman, or
equivalent; only in 1835 was this post a matter of law.
A de facto chairmanship was exercised by the Speaker of
the House of Commons, Charles Manners Sutton, from 1818-31;
this was assumed by Brougham as Lord Chancellor until 1834,
and then he was made formal Chief Commissioner for the
period 1835-7.

The honorary Commissioners were men of considerable
position: bishops, privy councillors, judges, and King's
Counsel. (3) Several of them were quite active in the
early days of the Commission, though of this number, few
were the feared foes whom Brougham had cited. Those
members tended to avoid their duties, rarely even attending regular meetings. (4) After a few years, business
settled into a routine, so Commissioner Henry Holbech
wrote Brougham in 1831 that 'the principal duty of the
honorary commissioners' was the attendance at semi-annual
meetings.(5) Holbech was writing to decline the offer
of an honorary post, which was later pressed on him. In
all, six former stipendiary Commissioners were so 'elevated,' which indicated that gradually the original role
ceased to be valued, and the upper echelon became a useful
receptacle for discarded stipendiaries. In 1831, Holbech,
Wilkinson Mathews, James McMahon, William Roberts, and
John Warren were promoted, whereas Daniel Finch managed
to resist the offer. Later (1835) Nicholas Carlisle,
once Secretary, then stipendiary, also was promoted. The
last phase of the Commission saw a doubling of stipendiaries but only an increase to thirteen honoraries.
Allowing for party differences, the men of the last group
were from the same small political elite: churchmen,
lawyers, and politicians of high standing.

The workhorses of the Commission were the stipendiary
Commissioners. (6) With few exceptions, these men were
practising barristers with experience at the Chancery
bar. (7) Some, indeed most, gave up their practice over
the years. The Commission business took about two-thirds
of their time, so that none of the stipendiaries could
keep up a really active London practice. A few combined
charity with other Commission assignments. But in the
last phase, with pressure mounting to complete their
survey, all salaried Commissioners were expected to devote
full time to the work (1835-7). The salary of the
stipendiary was originally £1,000 per annum. This was
reduced to £800 in 1831, but it was restored to the original amount in 1835, on the understanding that they worked

full time. In addition, a per diem allowance was paid
while they travelled.

Of the original eight, two remained as paid members of
the Commission throughout its full term (Daniel Finch and
William Grant). Eight new Commissioners joined in 1831,
and of the latter number, two remained when sixteen
recruits were added in 1835. Of that sixteen, four had
to be replaced owing to resignations within five months
of appointment. Thus a long period of settled membership
was followed by a more hectic spell with high turnover.
The barristers were generally mature and experienced. On
average, they were thirty-nine years of age and had
eleven years at the bar when they were appointed. There
were some large variations, as when the 55-year-old George
Long joined in 1835 with his twenty four years of service,
and 28-year-old Charles Humfrey came on at the same time,
with less than a year since he was admitted to the bar.
But distribution confirms the average, for a third had
less than five years service, a half less than ten, and a
third over fifteen. Likewise in age: five were under
thirty, six were over fifty, fourteen were in their
thirties, six in their forties. (8) For the thirty-one
for whom some family information was available, one was
the son of a Peer, one of a colonial governor, seven had
professional parents, and twenty-two were gentlemen's sons.
At least eighteen were (English) university graduates. It
is difficult to generalize about their legal training,
though most members had practised in common law or equity,
and many had experience on assize circuits. In all, the
Commissioners were a well-trained group of lawyers, but
as their job was one for which no precise professional
preparation existed, it is almost impossible to evaluate
them as potential Commissioners.

The Commissioners were allowed to employ a secretary,
four clerks, four messengers, and two 'other officers.'
(9) The staff and travel expenses were allotted £4,000
for the first year. In 1819, with one more clerk, this
allowance was doubled. But in 1835, when the clerks were
increased to twenty - one for each new stipendiary - the
expense allowance was actually cut to an annual rate of
£7,500. (10)

The staff of the Commission were men of some legal or
professional qualifications. The Secretaries in particular held a responsible and demanding position. The
salary was £500 and was raised to £650 in 1835. The first
Secretary was Nicholas Carlisle, a librarian and antiquarian. (11) Carlisle remained at his post of under
librarian in the King's Library (British Museum) during
his term (1818-31). His researches made him something

of an authority on antiquities, and his archival connections no doubt helped to offset his lack of legal training. In 1831 Carlisle was made a stipendiary Commissioner,
and in 1835 he was raised to an honorary post, the only
man to have gone through all the ranks.

James L. Hine was Carlisle's successor as Secretary.
With a different background, Hine was more suited to the
work of the Commission. Trained as a lawyer, Hine was
made the first solicitor to the Charity Commissioners
under the Attorney-General; he was the official who
handled cases referred from the Commission to the Attorney
General, and so he was well-versed in the business of
the Commission, or at least one aspect of it, when he
became Secretary. The two men were very different in
temperament as well as training. As Secretary, Hine on
his own initiative sent proposals for Charity Commission
reform to Lord Chancellor Brougham in 1834. Later he
published these in amended and extended form, and the
contrast could not be clearer between these forward-
looking proposals, and the backward-looking antiquarian
studies of Carlisle; what is fascinating is that the two
apparently did equally effective jobs in the position of
Secretary, and that their proclivities had relatively
little bearing on the actual product of the Commission.

The work of the Commission clerks was arduous. Theirs
was the duty of organizing trips, handling correspondence,
taking notes in hearings, and copying documentary extracts
and drafting reports. For this they received £250-300
per annum plus a per diem allowance when travelling. It
was difficult to retain well-qualified men at these posts.
The turnover was high and at least thirty seven men served
as clerks at one time or another. The clerks were 'regularly bred to the profession of the law' according to
Hine. (12) Commissioner John Warren told a House of
Commons Finance Committee in 1828 'they are most of them
gentlemen, intended, I believe, for solicitors, or actually such, and one who means to come to the bar.' (13) Of
course their formal qualifications were not everything,
as Commissioner W.A. Miles made clear, when he confident-
ially requested a replacement: 'a combination of the man
of business, the lawyer, and a gentleman - quiet and
unassuming, which is not the case with my present man.'
(14)

The Commissioners held their first two meetings at the
home of Charles Manners Sutton (4 and 7 September 1818),
and after inspecting other offices, they took up quarters
in a building occupied by the Church Building Commissioners at 13 Great George Street, Westminster. In these
offices, the Commissioners accumulated their papers, pre-

pared their reports, and held hearings on London charities over the next two decades.

II

Beyond enacting the inquiry and specifying its personnel, how far did Parliament go in its design? Statutes laid down the major questions to be answered, stated the duties of the Commissioners in general terms, and provided them with specific powers. But by not going further into the outlining of procedures, Parliament left the Commissioners to follow natural precedents, which is what they did.

The prime targets of the inquiry were delineated as follows:

(1) the amount, nature, and application of the produce of any estates or funds;

(2) whether any breaches of trust, irregularities or abuses have been practised or happened, and;

(3) whether by change of circumstances or by other causes, the same (trusts) cannot be beneficially applied for the purposes originally intended.

The Commissioners were to 'examine and investigate' the said matters, to 'report and certify' their findings and 'observations' on the modes of recovery, and 'suggestions' for avoiding 'any future misapplication.'

How were these tasks to be executed? The Commissioners were given general powers to travel, to call witnesses, to demand documents (or extracts) and to administer oaths. In short, they were given some elements of judicial authority. But they were also denied powers of judgment and were directed to examine all trusts (unless exempt), whether abused or not. What the statute did was assign a judicial research function in a totally new context. To discover donations, abuses thereto and anomalies therein was a perfectly normal task for a trained solicitor or barrister. (15) But putting this research on such a scale, and placing its results into the modern setting of published reports (and recommendations) was a drastic innovation. A very new job was undertaken under an old set of rules and assumptions, producing a result which resembles - and significantly differs from - modern kinds of governmental studies.

In this setting, Chancery experience dictated the evolution of Commission procedure. After all, the specialized commission was a standard tool for taking evidence, and sometimes for making preliminary judgments in Chancery jurisdictions. Parts of several pieces of

court machinery were reflected in the Charity Commission:
the Commission of Charitable Uses was an especially apt
precedent, while Commissioners of Bankruptcy, lunacy, and
the ordinary 'country commission' for taking evidence were
related structures whose experience may have influenced
the Charity Commission.

The basic purpose of these commissions under the Lord
Chancellor was to take evidnece, and in some instances,
to render a judgment. The commissions enjoyed varying
degrees of independence and power. In the country commission, the court was using solicitors chosen by parties
to suits. The court simply sent directions to these
solicitors to obtain sworn answers to specific questions
on a single case. These written replies were sent in
through the Examiner's Office and used as evidence. (16)
Further along the scale, the Commissioners of Charitable
Uses had, until their demise in the late 18th century,
been appointed by the Chancellor to conduct hearings and
give decrees on charity cases. Finally, commissioners of
bankruptcy and lunacy represented distinct, but function-
ally related cases of Chancery jurisdiction, and commission usage. Commissioners of Bankrupts came under the
Chancellor's power of appointment in the 16th century
(13 Eliz. I c. 7) but only in the 18th century did the
Chancellor take a major role in bankruptcy matters. By
then, the Commissioners were quite independent as judges
and had to be extensively overhauled in the 19th century.
(17) Commissions of lunacy were being incorporated in
Chancery jurisdiction from the 17th century, but the
Metropolitan Lunacy Commissioners were a significant
departure. For the question at hand, the Lunacy Commissioners were yet another example of autonomous, yet
centrally-managed jurisdiction, concerned with routine
legal business of the Court of Chancery. (18)

The similarity between these tasks of evidence-taking
and judgment and those of the Charity Commission was plain.
The key difference was that instead of a formal legal
judgment, the Charity Commission's work was embodied in
published reports to the crown, via the Home Secretary.
For the purposes of basic operations, surely the barristers and their clerks were well-conditioned by these
examples. They did not need elaborate rules or plans, if
their work was to follow traditional patterns. (19)

III

In 1818 it was perfectly clear that the inquiry would
move along well-established lines of investigation. There

was no master plan because none was seen to be necessary.
But because of the periodic reporting requirement, the
published reports of the commission created an impression
of disorganized mayhem, where there was in fact an orderly, if decentralized, process of work. The Commissioners
worked in pairs, (20) and as their inquiries for parishes
or towns were completed, the accounts would go into the
next semi-annual report. Therefore, if three to five
groups had worked steadily in one county each, variable
rates of work would still have created an erratic publication pattern. But of course it was an illusion to
imagine that it was possible to 'go through' a parish,
town, or county. In fact, the work involved numerous
obstructions, diversions, recapitulations, and other un-
controllable delays. No symmetrical pattern was likely
to emerge, and certainly not when the call of the printer
came at regular six-month intervals. (21) What did emerge
was a scattering of segments, some counties being split
into twenty different reports. Critics confused this
reference-nightmare (later solved by indexing, and reprints in County volumes) for an unsystematic method.
Indeed, the Select Committee examining the Commission in
1835 found that the system had tended to 'delay redress
and render access to the reports difficult and expensive.'
(22) This critical view was actually about as fanciful
as the opposite notion of planned disorder, put forward
by Brougham: 'It was never known where the Commissioners
would next alight. Very judiciously they did not take
the counties in any regular order.' (23)

Actually, the Commissioners were guided by mundane
concerns. Daniel Finch said that he and William Grant
worked on a northern county in the Summer and a southern
one in Spring. (24) Sometimes town or circuit business,
or other commitments intervened. A further air of carelessness or even chaotic dispersal came from completely
legitimate causes of delay, such as printing problems,
negotiations with trustees, or with the office of the
Attorney-General. But there was neither a planned lack
of system nor were the Commissioners truly unsystematic,
certainly not to the extent which their reports made it
appear.

Behind the unstructured reporting, there was a deliberately independent strategy in the working arrangements
of the Commission. Because the Commissioners were not
full-time (or did not think they were) and because it
would be impossible to dictate local movements of Commissioners from London, some operational expediency was
obviously necessary. The Commissioners early on elected
a general pattern of expediency from which they rarely

strayed, and then only under pressure for meeting dead-
lines of expiration. At one of its early meetings, the
General Board considered a resolution 'respecting the
execution of the Act in the Country.' In the draft
resolution, the Commission directed one board to visit
Reading and the other to investigate Canterbury. But in
the final version, the resolution said simply 'That two
divisions of the Board, each consisting of three Commissioners do proceed to the execution of the powers of
the Act in such places in the country, as may be expedient.' (25) Thus the Commission renounced formal control
and detailed supervision of the movements of its members,
leaving them to govern their own acts individually or in
informal consultation. This general decision was ratified
in 1819 after the new statute and the reissue of the Commission. On 23 July, the members resolved 'That five
divisions of the Board, each consisting of two commissioners do proceed to the execution of the Act in such places
in the Country, as may be expedient.' (26) When asked
about the Commission's procedure in 1828, John Warren
explained: 'We received no instructions at all; we met as
soon as the commission was issued, and considered what
mode we should proceed in, and our proceeding has been on
our own suggestion.' (27) The only signs of interference
or central planning occurred when pressure rose for completion of some phase of the work. Thus the Board, in
signing its twenty-third report on 30 June 1830, said
   having taken into consideration that there are some
   counties in which the Inquiry into charities was commenced long ago, and is not yet completed, particularly the counties of Nottingham, Northampton, and
   Warwick, It is resolved, that *it is desirable* that such
   counties should be completed as far as possible, previously to the next general meeting. (28)
This 'interference' with the Commissioners' autonomy was
only occasioned by the imminent expiration of the current
Commission, and was not a sign of reform in procedure.
However, it might have been a portent, for as the inquiry
drew to a close, the same kind of pressure and planning
appeared in more developed form.
   There were serious attempts to introduce more planned
and directed activity in the later stages of the inquiry
(1830-7). The results of planned or coordinated activity
were not strikingly different or better, although to some
extent the belated application of planning may have diminished its effectiveness. There were several different
features in the increase in planned activity:
   (1) more direction or assignment of Commissioners,
   (2) more management and standardizing of work, and

(3) more checks on the progress of work, and

(4) attempts to apply the results of the inquiry.

These attempts at organization were understandable. The
Commission was embarrassingly slow, and after 1830 the
embarrassment became the property of the Whig ministers.
They could hardly disown it, for where Brougham had once
been only a shadow influence, he now was Lord Chancellor
and titular head of the Commission. There were no easy
answers to the problem, but on review of the efforts to
direct the Commission, we may find that the laissez-faire
decision of 1818 was more sound.

On the actual movement of Commissioners, more central
control was asserted after 1830, but still the basic
question remained whether part-time investigators could be
directed, without regard to local circumstances. When the
new Commission was getting organized in 1832, it was
recorded that 'The following Commissioners *communicated
their intentions* of proceeding into the country shortly
on the examination of the charities in the counties undermentioned.' (29) There followed a list of Commissioners
in pairs, and names of counties opposite each pair. But
there was no indication of how the selection or assignment
had been made.

In 1835 some early resolutions showed more determination. On 11 November 'Resolved that the stipendiary
commissioners shall forthwith proceed to the examination
of the charities in the several counties of Berks,
Cambridge, Chester, Dorset, Essex, Kent and Lincoln.' (30)
As soon as these 'arrangements' were made, there were
changes being recorded. Within a few months, another
entry suggested that old informal methods were being
adapted to the new centralized framework:

> The Commissioners present proceeded to make arrange-
> ments of districts in the counties of which the char-
> ities have not yet been examined and for the examin-
> ation of charities remaining uninvestigated ... such
> arrangements to be subject to modification as circum-
> stances require it and after communication with the
> Chief Commissioner and such Commissioners as are at
> present in the country. (31)

Finally, as the end of the final phase, or rather its
four-month extension, approached, the strongest directive
on Commissioners' movements was issued, because the funds
for travel had almost run out:

> no journey should be undertaken, during the remaining
> period of the Commission, by any Commissioner, for the
> purpose of making or reviewing an inquiry in the coun-
> try, without his first making a representation to the
> Chief Commissioner, or to three, at least, of the other
> Commissioners. (32)

Thus we can see more 'planning' of movements, but it was
hardly systematic or complete. Furthermore, the value of
what was done is impossible to assess without much more
evidence than we have. Finally it appears that what was
done was much more the product of external pressures than
internal design,

The later stages of the Commission also saw attempts
at greater management and standardization of the work of
Commissioners. Steps were taken for training of Commissioners, attribution of reports, standardized corrective
action, and a centralized advisory board. In general it
must be said that the character and personnel of the Commission changed so quickly between 1830 and 1837 that such
measures might have been necessary under any regime. But
this was after all, not any regime, but the reform Whig
ministry.

To train a new Commissioner, nothing could have been
simpler than to have him observe some of the regular
sessions on London charities held at the office in Great
George Street. When eight Commissioners were drafted in
1831, such a provision was made. Following organization
meetings on 18 and 21 February, the members assembled on
the 27th for an examination of the parish officers of St
Martins in the Fields (Middlesex) and Walthamstow (Essex)
Instead of the normal two attending Commissioners, there
were two groups of five each. The interviews were
recorded in detailed notes in the Minute Book (unlike
other interviews), (33) and it was noted that a copy of
the minutes was to be sent to the Lord Chancellor. Likewise, when the Commission was renewed in 1835, there were
sixteen novices, and once again, a few days after the
initial meeting, there were regular 'inquiry' sessions,
this time with seven and eleven members in attendance. (34)

Another step toward standardizing or control was the
signed report. At the initial meeting of the 1835 Commission it was resolved 'that each Commissioner shall sign
his own report.' No discussion was recorded, but presumably the interest was in accountability, reliability and
perhaps even competition between investigators. Also, it
was relevant that for the first time, Commissioners were
now authorized to make solo investigations and reports.

Finally, the central board was going to be converted
into some sort of clearing house, according to resolutions
of 1835. At a general meeting on 16 November, the board
decided that it was 'very desirable that there should be
as soon as convenient a Board in London, to whom at all
times the Commissioners in the country may apply for
advice as emergencies arise and for preserving thereby an
uniformity of practice.' (35) Out of context, this sounds

like a significant innovation, but a 'board' simply meant
a formal sitting of one or more Commissioners, and ordinary boards were always being held at Great George Street.
This directive was an attempt to add an element of stability to the process. Whether the boards sitting in
London actually behaved in this fashion was not recorded.
What was clear was that the Secretary acted, as he always
had, as a coordinator and channel of information in intervals between the general meetings of the Commission. There
was in fact slight opportunity for a board in the central
office to perform as anything other than an ordinary
inquiring unit, and this seemed to remain the practice
throughout. (36)

In all, the suggestions and steps toward more managed
or standardized activity were of limited value. They may
have increased the appearance of control and uniformity,
but there was nothing in the reports or other acts of the
Commission to indicate a substantial alteration in the
performance results. (37)

Another element of central control which was introduced
late in the Commission's career was a system of monitoring
movements, work, and expenses. In 1835, Brougham
instituted a reporting system under which each Commissioner in the country was to submit a 'Weekly Return of
Progress' and an accompanying 'Memorandum of Expenses.'
(38) These were printed forms which were to be sent in
to the office each week, where an abstract was made up
and sent on to the Chief Commissioner. The 'Return of
Progress' had columns for: place/charity/when begun/when
ended/no. witnesses examined/no. of documents produced/
days and hours at the board/and remarks. The memorandum
of expenses had blanks for per diem (Commissioner and
clerk), travelling expense, and contingencies.

The institution of these returns was greeted with a
mixture of ridicule and hostility. Commissioner George
Long wrote to Secretary Hine on 5 December 1835

I have just finished the troublesome business of making
the weekly return of progress. That there is some
occult utility in this mysterious process, I cannot
presume to doubt, and can only regret being unable to
conjecture in what it may consist. (39)

On the same date, Charles Tucker, one of the clerks, wrote
more caustically:

Inclosed I send you this most juvenile and ridiculously
useless return, if the form does not suit, we can make
no other. Anyone acquainted with the nature and the
work of the inquiry must see how absurd this kind of
return is. That is, if they have any sense at all -
in what column is the time wasted in making it to be
noted? (40)

These views were echoed in the coming months by others.
Charles Humfrey mildly complained that '"entre nous"
making said returns is an unmitigated bore,' while Arthur
Buller offered the stronger opinion that 'a more hum-
bugging document never passed thro' the Post Office.'
These and numerous other remarks survive in the Commissioners' correspondence. (41) But the returns were
established and continued, not without some pressure.
What did the returns achieve? They provided a standardized record of activity, but there is no evidence that
this record was ever used as such. No doubt one of the
functions of the return was automatic nagging, and in
that it was surely a success.

We can detect some late-developing interest in general
planning in the area of application of the results of
inquiry. Whereas in the early stages of the Commission,
no steps were taken beyond the printed reports, after
1830 a new, action-oriented policy emerged. One facet of
that policy was evident in the creation of powers by
which the Commissioners could vest trusteeship of small
rent-charges in the Minister, Churchwardens, and Overseers
of the Poor. (42) Another project was a plan to appropriate undesignated trust funds to the service of education. In November 1833, the Lord Chancellor asked the
Commission to prepare a tabulation of two complete but
dissimilar counties, showing the place, donor or title,
object, date, revenue, property, number of benefactors,
trustees, total revenue of those under £5 per annum, and
observations. (43) The object was to locate the small,
undesignated, potentially convertible trusts. Then a
circular letter to trustees was made up 'with questions
for their consideration as to the expediency of a more
extended application of the funds to the purposes of
education.' The Commissioners recommended and prepared
surveys of Gloucester and Hampshire. On a further request
they also recommended Staffordshire. But the Commissioners asked that the circular letters not be sent out
under their names, as they felt it would be an abuse of
their authority. Instead, questionnaires were sent out
from the Home Office beginning in December 1833. (44)
The questions asked were (a) were those charities without
specific directions being applied in a manner 'most beneficial to the poor?' (b) could such proceeds be applied
'more beneficially for the poor in the education of their
children?' and (c) if there was a charity for education
which also provided clothing or maintenance, would it 'be
more beneficial for the poor to extend education to a
greater number of children, instead of giving clothing
or maintenance?' The questions had a familiar ring, for

they were the ones to which Brougham had long ago given
'answers' in debates on education, but they were now
being tested in the field.

Apparently nothing beyond simple collation was ever
done with the replies to the Home Office questionnaires.
The matter of conversion of trust funds, a potentially
explosive issue, was not taken further until a series of
bills which Brougham began in 1835 (see below, p. 172).
Nevertheless, this attempt did show a serious (and unparalleled) effort to determine 'whether by change of
circumstance' the trusts could 'not be beneficially
applied for the purposes originally intended.'

Whatever else they did, the struggles of the last years
of the Commission showed how little control had been
exercised, and how hard it was to superimpose controls
at any stage after inception. The Commission operated
like a judicial fact-finding body, a cross between a
country commission and a Commission of Charitable uses
with the novel twist of national publication. It could
not be centrally controlled nor could its activities
be carefully planned. As we shall see, the value of such
control no doubt seemed greater to the self-conscious
reformer than it actually was. The vital fact in reforming was not the central regulation of inquirers, but the
way in which the inquirers acted in the local situation,
individually and collectively.

6

Procedure

The Charity Commission carried out its function as a legal
research unit with consistent procedure for nearly twenty
years. Its auxiliary function as an agency of reform,
on the other hand, developed extensively in the same
period, and within the framework of ordinary inquiry.
Our task here must be to sketch the working of the Commission: the local inquiry, the follow-up and reports,
and the general boards. While doing this, we must bear in
mind the dual nature of the Commission's work, and show
how the job of legal research developed into and encouraged widespread reform.

I

The basic operating unit of the Commission was the travelling board, usually two Commissioners and a clerk. At
most times, one of these units sat in London, while the
others toured the country. In thousands of sittings, the
Commissioners took evidence and testimony on the past and
present state of the charitable trusts. (1) The session
of a board was ordinarily set up at least a few days in
advance, witnesses and documents having to be assembled,
and in the country, a site having to be set. Preliminary
work was extremely important in determining how thorough
a particular survey would be. The actual hearing consisted of a sworn statement by witnesses, part usually in
the form of documentary extracts, and part in answer to
questioning by the Commissioners. At the end of the testimony, if there had been any suggestion of improper
management, the Commissioners might make recommendations
for ad hoc correction, or indicate the need for an equity
proceeding.
   While they worked to no set pattern - or as Warren

said, 'our proceeding has been on our own suggestion' -
there were clear lines of legal and logistic preparation
developed and followed by the Commissioners. These lines
were not so much the product of calculated design or
systematic development, but a rather obvious blend of
common sense and tradition, dictated or sanctioned by
the task itself.

The first requirement was the identification of
charitable trusts and potential witnesses. The Commissioners adopted from the outset a two-pronged initial
procedure. Circulars were sent to officiating clergy to
acquire knowledge or information bearing on charitable
trusts, and the response was compared with what was
available in existing records: the Gilbert Returns, and
the Digest of the Select Committee returns of 1818 in
particular. (2)

The circular used by the Commission was a printed form,
sent under the clerk's signature sometime well before the
visit.

> Sir, I am desired by the Commissioners for enquiring
> into Charities in England and Wales to request that
> you will favour them with a list of all the Charities
> in your parish, stating by whom and when they were
> founded, and for what purpose; and likewise, that you
> will state what persons, as trustees, or otherwise,
> will be best able to give information with respect to
> each charity. (3)

The replies to circulars were checked against the available records, the most useful being the 1816 reprint of
the Gilbert Returns. These were supposed to show all
charitable donations, based upon a circular letter similar
to the one used by the Commissioners. But the more recent
letters also sought the identity of qualified witnesses;
and one of their principal tasks would be to clear up
discrepancies between both sets of returns. The Commissioners tried to use the Gilbert Returns as a basis for
planning, but there was some disagreement as to their
value. William Grant found them 'extremely accurate' in
connection with his inquiries, (4) whereas others reported
cases overlooked, misstated, or otherwise misleading.
George Long wrote from Derbyshire, 'I fear there was much
roguery in the returns under Gilbert's Act in this county.'
Henry Gunning in Chester complained that the survey 'is
worse than no guide.' And Francis Eagle while touring
Cornwall said 'I find the returns so little to be depended
upon that it is impossible to fix my movements prospect-
ively with any degree of certainty for a lengthened
period.' (5)

The Gilbert Returns, being thirty years old at the out-

set of the inquiry, were bound to be incomplete. The most
recent survey, that of Brougham's Select Committee in 1818,
was newer but also incomplete - it only dealt with schools.
(6) But its utility was appreciated, and the Commissioners were anxious from the very first to put it to use.
The board was corresponding with the clerk to the Select
Committee in November 1818, requesting and obtaining
early copies of the returns as soon as they were printed.
(7) It was also evident from later internal correspondence that Commissioners were still using these returns
in the closing phase of the Commission. (8)

The Brougham returns having only recently been sent in,
some resistance was encountered in early months from
respondents who thought the Commission's circular was
redundant. The Board wrote to several London clergymen,
asking them to 'take the further trouble to send a circumstantial account ... as the Commissioners are not (yet)
in possession of the returns made to Mr Brougham's circular letters.' (9) And of course, after 1818 the Commissioners would require new replies, as their mandate
swelled beyond that of the Select Committee.

Once equipped with a (provisional) sketch of the
charitable trusts in a town or an area of a county, Commissioners would authorize the preparation of a visit.
The clerk then had to take the next preparatory steps of
advertisement and summons, the two basic means for re-
quisition of witnesses. Advertising was used from the
earliest days, both for London and county investigations.
Grant explained in his 1835 testimony: 'An advertisement
is always inserted in the county paper, that the Commissioners will be at certain places on or about the days
therein named, and all persons are invited to give information.' (10) The Commission papers contain numerous
drafts, printed copies of and receipts for newspaper
advertisements. They may have been less than perfect in
following this procedure, and that was suggested by one
critic in 1828.(11) Nevertheless, there was ample evidence of the use of advertising. The earliest surviving
record was this rather awkward announcement that the Commission was open for business, given out three months
after the initial meeting, and recorded in the minutes:
(12)

Sent copy of the following advertisement to be inserted
tomorrow in the undermentioned newspapers

Morning Chronicle	New Times
Morning Post	British Press
Times	Morning Herald

Commissioners of Inquiry Concerning
Charities
No. 12 Great George St.
Westminster
11 December 1818

The London Board of Commissioners, appointed by the Act
of Parliament of the last session, to inquire concerning charities for the education of the poor, meet
regularly at their office, No. 12 Great George Street,
Westminster, where any communications to them may be
addressed.

Nich^s Carlisle
Secretary

Aside from giving the wrong address (no. 13 was correct),
this advertisement, like most of them, probably produced
very little response. Grant testified that the number
who came forward with information was 'but few.'

Advertising was as uncertain as it was novel, yet the
method of summons was as reliable as it was traditional.
The Commissioner or the clerk sent letters to clergy and
precepts to all other potential witnesses, identified by
the circulars or by other means. The precept's form was
as follows:

Sir,

I am directed by the Commissioners appointed to inquire
concerning Charities in England and Wales, to request
the favour of your attendance at
on   at   o'clock in the   noon,
in order to give any information in your power
respecting   and to
desire that you will bring with you any papers from
among the parish documents, or from any other source
in your power, which you think may assist the Commissioners in their investigation. And also a copy of the
Table of Benefactions if any. (13)

The precept might be sent out, or delivered by messenger,
after the Commissioners arrived in town, or it might be
mailed either from Westminster or an earlier stage on the
Commissioner's circuit. Some Commissioners had a supply
of precepts signed and ready for mailing from Great George
Street, and Finch once instructed Hine: 'If you should be
deficient in precepts to send out to my flock - please to
forge my name to others, but do not send a genuine and a
forgery to the same Parish.' (14)

Having issued precepts, the Commissioners then awaited
compliance, which seems to have been generally good,
although no true measurement of compliance is possible.
In any event, Commissioners were limited in their capacity
to force the attendance of witnesses or the production of

documents. There was some power in the former case, but virtually none in the latter. A test case in 1819, and the passage of the Equity Facilities Act (59 Geo. III c. 91) apparently settled the Commissioners' power to compel attendance. Early in 1819, two witnesses refused to appear; the General Board in a special meeting, the first with full attendance, directed a letter to Home Secretary Sidmouth on 27 February. The reluctant duo were subsequently indicted, at which point they agreed to be examined. (15) Thereafter, no further legal proceedings of this kind appeared in the minutes. But that alone would not justify our assumption of a complete power to compel appearance. The Commission could defeat outright resistance, but it was relatively powerless against evasion. Many witnesses were conveniently unavailable or unable to attend, and Commissioners were not always capable of repeated visits, or of exercising great authority away from London.

In the matter of compelling documents, the position of the Commissioners was even weaker. This had been an area of great contention in 1818, and was to remain so throughout all discussions of a charity regulating agency. Could government agents pry into private papers? On what grounds and to what extent? The original Act empowered Commissioners to call for 'any deed, paper, writing, instrument, or other document' in custody of trustees or managers of funds or those concerned in trust estates. But the Act specifically protected trustees or owners from revealing deeds or other documents (a) if the charitable trust was unknown to the purchaser of property; (b) if there was a lien on the property, and the mortgagor was exempt under the Act; (c) in all cases of exemptions; and (d) in cases of self-incrimination. (16) Moreover, when deeds were called for, Commissioners were only entitled to examine the relevant parts, or extracts. Warren said in 1835, 'I have never felt myself authorized to call for title-deeds unless they were voluntarily produced.' (17) Thus the trustees or owners or tenants of trust property were at liberty to reveal what they felt was relevant to the trust. If an owner had anything to gain from concealment, and if he controlled the only incriminating documents, the Commissioners were poorly equipped to expose him.

The legal preparations, locating trusts and summoning trustees, were accompanied in the country investigations by logistical preparation. The clerk's job was to ssemble necessary references and supplies, to arrange for transport and accommodation. In the way of reference materials, they carried copies of the Gilbert and Select

Committee Returns for the counties they were visiting.
They also made use of other government sources (Returns
under Romilly's Act, census records) and local histories
and inquiries. (18) Of course in their travels, inns,
coaches, and postal arrangements occupied the clerks'
busy days, when they were not present at hearings, or
working into the night transcribing documents. Once
witnesses and documents were assembled, the hearing would
be opened. The Commissioners called witnesses before
them, administered their oath, received their testimony,
interrogated them, and made recommendations. To this
basic outline, we are able to add slightly, thanks to
Commissioners' testimony. The kind of information sought
by Commissioners fell into a set pattern: the origin
and descent of the trust, the management of the property,
and the application of the revenues. As John Wrottesley
told the 1835 Committee:

> I will mention the precise order. Having taken the
> abstract of the original deed or will, the first point
> is to trace the legal estate into the then existing
> trustees, and that completes one part of the report.
> Then we examine into the property, the tenants, the
> rents at which the property is let ... and also examine
> the leases of the property. The next point is the
> application of the revenue. In this order we have
> usually reported. (19)

The Commissioners would read over, and extract as necessary, the documentary information, which was transcribed
by the clerk, and often this exercise in transcription
had to continue outside the actual sittings of the board.
For the oral testimony, there were early efforts at a
verbatim record, but these were soon given up. As John
Warren explained, when asked why the Commissioners did
not use shorthand writers:

> We endeavour to take the evidence as that it shall in
> some measure form a preparation for the report; the
> examinations are not in general taken down in question
> and answer, they are gone through with the witness,
> and when we learn what the witness has to state, the
> answers are dictated by us to the clerk who takes the
> notes, and are taken down in the form of a narrative;
> the witness, of course, hearing and confirming it. (20)

In addition to this modification of ordinary procedure,
the Commissioners experimented a little, especially later,
with different configurations. Trials of single Commissioner hearings and more than one clerk per Commissioner
were discussed and carried out. (21) But the vast majority of work (excepting only 1836-7) was carried out by
the troika of two commissioners and a clerk.

The meetings were semi-private. William Grant said, 'I do not consider it an open court; but I am not aware that anybody was ever refused attending it.' (22)   In fact, since the meetings were advertised, they were theoretically open to anyone with information on charitable trusts. Only rarely did this produce a crowd, and when it did, it may be guessed that the amount of information was not in proportion to the size of the crowd. James Hume reported on a most unusual turnout from Holbeach, Lincolnshire:

> I think I mentioned to you the interest taken here in the investigations of the charities. I have not had less than an hundred any day that the Long Sutton charities have been under consideration, and with not more than 10 or 12 summons out. (23)

The attendance of those giving evidence was sometimes augmented by their solicitors and others. On several occasions there were attempts by these observers to record proceedings. William Grant recalled one where he had objected to note-taking. (24) Another case was noted by Francis Martin, who intimated that the General Board had ruled against such notes in 1835, and he thereupon denied permission to an attorney. (25)

If there was any secrecy in charity affairs, it was not inside the hearings. As the Vicar said in the Peacock novel: 'The state of the public charities, sir, is exceedingly simple. There are none. The charities here are all private, and so private, that I for one know nothing of them.' (26) What was done in the hearing before the board was not secret, or certainly not destined to remain so. Commissioners could have suppressed nonessential matter, but not any relevant information. The mass of material, edited and refined to be sure, was going to be printed and in the public domain.

When the actual hearing was complete, there were some few cases where further local information was acquired, in meetings with authorities, through correspondence, or on a few occasions by retaining aid of surveyors. There were only a few traces of such activity, but they remind us that the hearings had definite limitations as to discovery of information. (27)

John Warren testified in 1828 that the Commissioners 'have in fact no remedial powers.' But he hastened to add that 'where it appeared that the abuse could be remedied in that way, (Commissioners) endeavoured to do so by representation to the parties.' (28) Actually Warren was being too modest (or cautious). The Commission had in fact a wide range of responses and remedies, even though it had no remedial 'powers'. Simple admonition or

suggestion was the most common remedy. Where there were
local arguments, the Commissioners might act as mediators.
And where there was evidence of circumstances or acts
requiring a court ruling, the process of certification
to Chancery would be initiated.

In the most common instance, that of admonition, Commissioners made observations, suggestions, and criticisms,
mainly for the benefit of the trustees who had in some
way faltered in their duty. In Daniel Finch's opinion,
this kind of activity was common:

> I think there is hardly a parish in which we do not
> make some recommendation or other on the spot, in which
> there is not something or other to be corrected, that
> would be quite idle to bring before the (General)
> Board, being matters with which we are perfectly
> acquainted, and more advantageously made objects of
> recommendations to the parties on the spot. There is
> rarely a parish which comes in which there are not
> some observations to be made in the mode of administer-
> ing the charities. (29)

As trust advisers, the Commissioners were versatile
and usually helpful. Their advice appears in various
survivals, especially their printed reports. As those
reports may have been written to throw the best light on
the Commissioners' actions, and as sometimes the reports
were themselves part of the Commissioners' leverage with
the locals, we may want to limit the faith we put in their
clauses about current conditions. Moreover, those clauses
mainly appeared in reports which dealt with difficulties
or 'abuses,' and they were easily the shortest sections.
Nevertheless, we can safely reconstruct a number of
admonitory approaches used by the Commissioners, grouping
them roughly into observation, suggestion, and criticism.

The observation was a simple report of a problem,
where the clear impression was that a solution was
imminent (in the opinion of the Commissioners). In their
report on the poor allotment in Elstree (Herts), the
Commissioners plainly found an anomaly, but one where
they equally plainly thought everything was under control.
Citing an enclosure Act and a consequent augmented rent-
charge of £2 10s., they observed:

> The management of the funds of these charities had,
> previous to the year 1822, been left to the farmers ...
> who do not appear to have kept any accounts. The
> several deeds and documents belonging to the parish,
> and deposited in the church chest, have suffered much
> from damp, and are in many parts illegible.
>   Although regular account books have not been kept
> of the receipts and disbursements of the several

charities, nor audited annually by the proper authorities, yet the charities are known to have been
publicly distributed, and their general amount to
have been fully applied.

Account books will, however, in future be provided,
and audits regularly observed. (30)

So with Astley School in Lancashire, where a schoolmaster,
appointed in 1772 had become truly superannuated. The
report of 1828 said 'for a great length of time he has
been wholly unfit for the situation' and they 'found the
school reduced to a very low state.' But although the
inhabitants had the power of removal under the founder's
will, the Commissioners' silence was tantamount to
endorsing the decision to let the old master die in har-
ness.(31) In the case of the grammar School of East
Retford (Nottinghamshire) the Commissioners spent long
hours unravelling the undesignated properties of the
corporation, which had been indiscriminately lumped into
a 'united fund.' They finally laid out the figures and
simply said 'since the year 1762, when their accounts
commence, the bailiffs and burgesses received more than
they have paid.' The specific income of the school was
estimated at £300, and the school salaries were only
£100. (32) The Commissioners went no further than observing the discrepancy.

But numerous other cases brought forth a wide array of
suggestions, repeated no doubt for emphasis in the printed
reports. The simplest and most direct (if not the most
easy) advice was on restarting a defunct trust. When the
Commissioners visited Launton (Oxford), they found that
a town cottage had lost its charitable character:

The rent, till about 10 years ago, was one guinea,
which used to be distributed amongst the poor, together
with the sacrament money.

For the last ten years no rent has been paid, the
cottage having been chiefly occupied by poor widows
put in by the parish, and two or three years ago it
was let to William Long, who was to put it into repair,
and he was to hold it free until he was repaid the
expenses, taking the value at £1 1s. a year, which is
as much as it is worth. He is lately dead, and it is
now occupied by his widow, who is very poor and unable
to pay rent.

Under the circumstances above stated, we apprehend
that as soon as the expenses of the repairs are repaid,
a rent ought to be taken from the occupier, or paid by
the parish, and distributed as it used formerly to be,
with the sacrament money, to the poor. (33)

The basic object here, as in most cases, was to restart

the charity as it had been originally established. But
due care was taken where other obligations had been
reasonably incurred. When the Commissioners proceeded to
examine Tackley in the same county, they studied Hill's
Charity. This was a gift of £20, the interest on which
was given to the poor in bread. There was some question
as to the best manner of handling the funds, to which the
Commissioners gave one of their favourite suggestions.
'The rector being very desirous of placing out this money
in the best manner for the poor, we suggested to him the
expediency of placing the sum of £20 in a savings bank.'
(34) The early Savings Banks owed a good deal of their
patronage to the Commissioners.

On several occasions Commissioners were able to intervene in circumstances where the 'self-help' of old might
have led to problems. At Tiverton (Devon) the trustees
were hoping to divert the funds of the Market Trust into
the widening and repair of the Exe bridge. The Commissioners vetoed that idea, and gave alternative suggestions. (35) In Farnworth (Lancashire) they discovered a
trustee who had placed the £40 stock in his son's care,
and had made up a deed for a new trust, composed of his
two sons and two grandsons. But he had neglected to
inform the other surviving trustee. The Commissioners
called this 'highly improper,' and they notified the
other trustee themselves. (36)

Unfortunately we have very few insights into the
methods by which the Commissioners wheedled, cajoled, or
browbeat local authorities or individuals. It must be
recognized, however, that recoveries of arrears, corrections of errors, and other constructive results, may have
been the consequence of unattractive methods. What looks
like an unsavoury example appeared in a letter from
Commissioner P.F. Johnston, regarding an allegedly unpaid
charity in Brecon: 'The widow is a very sick, old, almost
blind and very parsimonious woman, and I should therefore
think we had better demand 40 years arrears, and if she
demurs, compromise the matter.' (37) Something better
than compromise occurred, for the report on this charity
stated that the trust had been properly managed for many
years. (38)

When Commissioner James Sedgwick visited Fishtoft
(Lincolnshire) he too found an elderly person, in this
case an old man who claimed he had purchased land without
knowing that it belonged to a charity. Sedgwick offered
several possible solutions, but he confessed to Hine:

I am unable to bring him to any compromise, but I am
nevertheless of opinion that if a letter came from

London *clothed with official authority,* it might have
the desired effect, at least I should be willing to
try it, and with a view to the experiment I have
written the enclosed letter which if addressed to him
with *your* signature, may induce him to accede to terms.

In a postscript, Sedgwick added, 'have the goodness to put
the large official Seal, which in this part of the Country
produces all the alarm of a Messenger at *Arms.*' Sedgwick's
ruse apparently did not work, for the printed report
conceded that legal action had to be taken. (39)

There were quite a few cases where the Commissioners'
criticism became blunt, especially in their comments on
the practices which were perennial and which underlined
their powerlessness. In the early days of the Commission,
this kind of criticism took a lot of mustering, as for
example in the following scolding on the application of
Reeve's Charity (London) for general parochial purposes.

It appears to us to be wholly unauthorised, either by
the will of Mr Reeve, or by the order of court which
was made for carrying that will into effect; and we
feel ourselves called upon the more seriously to
animadvert upon such conduct, which we cannot but consider a manifest misapplication of the funds, since it
has been the source of heavy loss to the charity,
which we do not perceive any prospect or means of
repairing. (40)

Perhaps even more disturbing to the Commissioners were
those cases of misapplication which seemed to have the
sanction of tradition. Henry Gunning wrote from Wrexham
(Denbigh) in regard to such a case:

The Parish of Gresford is now in the state that Wrexham
was - a rent charge of £13-6-8 a year - one farm left
to the Poor, and another purchased by the Parish with
monies left to the Poor - and producing between £70
and £80 a year, are and always have been paid to the
Overseers and added to the Poor's rate. The purchase-
deed cannot be found - nor any draught or abstract
thereof.... But they have a copy of the deed of 37th
Elizabeth, granting the rent-charge, expressly given
to 10 of the poorest people of Gresford. And this had
never been done I presume. Certainly not in the time
of the Curate who knows the Parish 40 years - but who
as long as he gets his roast mutton and his sherry
doubtless cares but little for the souls and bodies of
his lisped-at flock. (41)

The diversion to parochial funds was a frequent source of
irritation. Less frequent but more dangerous was the
mixture of the roles of tenant and trustee. In reporting

on the Chapel Lands in Great Barr (Aldridge, Staffordshire) Commissioners found charity land which had been
enclosed in 1795, but the rent had not improved:

> We have noticed as we have gone along, the incorrect-
> ness which appears to us to have prevailed, in many
> instances, in the management of this charity, partic-
> ularly in the mixed character which, in so many of the
> transactions, Sir Joseph Scott has borne as a trustee
> of the charity, and at the same time, as an unthrifty
> occupier of the trust property, and in one instance, as
> an adverse claimant. This has, perhaps, naturally
> arisen from the circumstance of his being a very
> extensive proprietor of land in the township, the
> greater part of which belongs to him. It appears how-
> ever to us, that the value of the timber growing upon
> the Clerk's Hills should be accounted for by Sir Joseph
> to the charity, and that in the case of Grove's cot-
> tage and garden, unless the title under which Sir
> Joseph purchased them should be more clearly made out
> than we conceive possible, they should be restored to
> the trustees, as part of the property originally
> belonging to the charity. (42)

The Commissioners sometimes had rather pointed suggestions
for trustee action. In one of the all-too common cases
of inept schoolmasters, they found at the 'High Style
School' in Kearsley (Lancashire) a master 'habitually
addicted to drunkenness' and 'unfit for his situation.'
He 'was reprimanded' by the Commissioners, who called on
the trustees for their 'immediate and active interference.'
And their scolding was broadened by an admonition on
'large sums of money retained in the hands of trustees.'
(43)

When the Commissioners completed their review of
Walthamstow parish (Essex), their painstaking account
showed a large diversion of over £640 from the charity to
the church account, during the period 1820-6. In words
quite literally true they said, 'we cannot but animadvert
upon the blameable inattention to the due application of
these charitable funds.' (44) In truth, the Commissioners
were powerless, but their advice was often powerful.

The second principal form which the Commissioners'
recommendations took was that of mediation. Many charitable trust problems originated or culminated in local
feuds. The Commissioners were inadvertently put in the
middle of some of them, and the resulting reconciliation
was often effective. Commissioner Samuel Smith felt this
part of their work was very significant.

> I consider the good we have done indirectly to have
> been very great, by acting as a court of reconciliation,

giving to the parties complaining and the parties complained of an opportunity of coming together, without
compromising their feelings, where a little might be
necessary to be conceded by each to the other. We
afforded an easy channel for such arrangements. (45)
In Plymouth the inquiry ran across one of the local poor
relief Acts, which had given some authority over trusts
to the Guardians. In the case of Rowe's Charity, the
estate had been given for specific charitable uses with
a residual grant to general charitable uses. The Guardians had sued the trustees for the entire estate, but the
Commissioners were sure that the Guardians only had a
right to supervise general use funds. To resolve matters
'it was agreed, that for preventing further expenses of
the charity money ... (the trustees) should convey to the
Guardians and their successors, the said field, in trust,
for the charitable uses mentioned in the will of the said
William Rowe.' (46)

In another Devon case, the Commissioners took the very
unusual step of treating at length with a case then before
a court. The Ottery Trust was the focus of a very complex
dispute, and in their report the Commissioners unravelled
the story at great length. Their review of all the
charges in detail was clearly aimed at bringing a reconciliation between parties. (47)

In the Bristol parish of St Peter, a charity property
had been 'Improvidently' leased for ninety-nine years in
1785. The tenant admitted to the Commissioners that the
lease was unfair, 'attended us with his solicitor, and
engaged to make a surrender of the above lease.' The
Commissioners reported that at a subsequent vestry meeting
the matter was considered, and the new terms were
accepted. (48)

The Commissioners were not always so fortunate, because
not all tenants or other troublemakers were so easy to
handle. An extreme case came from Cheshire in the Spring
of 1836. Edmund Clark visited Northwich and found himself
the arbiter of a bitter feud between a schoolmaster and
a board of trustees. Clark's letters to Hine gave in
vivid detail the nature and progress of this extraordinary
case.

It is impossible to describe the spirit of fury and
recrimination that actuates the parties. The Master
declares that one of the trustees has committed three
murders - that he heard another propound a scheme for
assassinating him which was only defeated by his pro-
curing a body guard, that another has been convicted
of perjury - In fact such a nest you never heard of.
Don't say anything about this - for my impression is,

that the poor schoolmaster is, at least on this subject,
slightly touched in his intellectuals. (49)

Clark's opinion grew stronger as he went through two weeks
in the town and several days of hearings with the schoolmaster, Mr Hand. The Commissioner had warily approached
the case, asking Hine whether intervention was proper,
but in the end, he despaired of success and confided, 'I
am sick and tired and should die but for the prospect
of quitting these infernal shades.' The schoolmaster had
filed suit against the trustees (1834), so Clark reported
with relief that 'we are released from the painful task
of reporting the transactions.' (50)

   Where the Commissioners could not succeed with re-
presentations or with reconciliation, they still had
resort to legal action. The ultimate weapon was certification to Chancery. But even here, the usage was more
diverse than it appeared. In the first place, suits could
be friendly or hostile. If Chancery was the only authority which could resolve a property or trust settlement,
an uncontested petition might be entered. On the other
hand, if an abuse was stubbornly maintained, the Commission could bring suit by an information through the
Attorney-General. Certification of either kind was approved by the General Board on the recommendation of
reporting Commissioners, and it meant a copy of their
report was sent to the solicitor for the Attorney-General,
who took opinion from counsel, and if that proved favourable for trial, the Attorney-General's endorsement put
the case into Chancery.

   But preceding certification itself, there was an area
of influence in which Commissioners exploited the threat
of legal process. We can observe the operation of this
activity from two angles: actual threats made by or in
the name of the Commission, and suspension of proceedings
prior to certification. The threats to go to court were
both in printed reports and unpublished correspondence,
though naturally the former were less common. One instance occurred in the report on Sir George Monox's Alms-
house and School in Walthamstow. Commissioners found that
the parish had wrongly conveyed some charity land in 1782,
and was operating on the assumption that the school was
classical only, allowing the Master to take fees for non-
classical instruction:

   We should therefore suggest to the trustees ... the
   propriety of calling on Mr Roberts to afford gratuitous
   instruction ... Should Mr Roberts decline to do so, it
   may be questionable whether this point also should not
   be referred to the consideration of a court of equity.
   (51)

In their correspondence, the Commissioners and the staff were less circumspect in their threats. The Secretary once wrote to a trustee in Yorkshire:

> I am desired by the Commissioners to inform you that much complaint is made on the subject of the letting of the lands belonging to Jefferson's Charity (School and Almshouse) at Hook, of which you are the sole trustee, the same being let at £24 a year, although as represented a rent of upwards of £40 a year might be obtained. The Commissioners request to be informed by you what is the real annual value of the land, what means you have taken to obtain the fair value, and whether it is your intention to take steps for getting a better rent if the present rent is too low. The Commissioners think this information material for enabling them to judge whether it is expedient they should recommend the adoption of measures to remedy the complaint that is made. (52)

Nor were the communications from the Commission always veiled as this was. Indeed they could be unmistakably clear, as when they wrote to a solicitor in Wellingborough:

> Commissioners consider it their duty to certify the particulars of this charity (Marriott) to the Attorney General with a view to an information being filed for recovering payment of the arrears and securing the future payment of the annuity, unless they shall learn from you on or before the 6th Nov. next that Mr. J. Robinson has paid. (53)

The threat of certification was therefore used as a tool, and we can also see how in some cases the responses led to interruption of proceedings. For Commissioners were able to and did withdraw cases up to the actual time of transmission to the Attorney-General. There is good evidence that this was considered in at least thirty-six cases, which is about nine per cent of the number eventually certified. In the general minute books, against the lists of cases to be certified which were made at nearly every semi-annual meeting, there were notations indicating that certain cases were held up. The earliest was in 1823, when on 23 January four cases were marked 'if necessary.' At the next meeting, three had the notation 'withdrawn conditionally,' and similar notes appeared regularly thereafter until 1833. Sometimes specific Commissioners were identified, as in the note of 30 January 1830, where one was 'postponed by Mr Roberts;' or the case of the July 1833 meeting where one was noted; '1 Feb 1834 Mr Finch directed the sending of this case to be postponed.' (54) The last suggests a fairly sluggish pace of proceedings, as well as showing the ability of Commissioners to interpose in cases under certification process.

When cases did proceed to the Attorney General, they were
arriving at the same destination from several different
routes. For the case might be a 'friendly one, or indeed
if 'hostile' it might be a matter of resolving doubt
rather than proving guilt. The Commissioners often faced
situations where they could not interfere lawfully, yet
some interference was essential to correct non-criminal
error or alteration of circumstance. For example, a
frequent case was a stymied foundation like that of
Captain Stone of Sandhurst. When he died in 1823, Stone
left £100 in Navy four per cents in trust with three
officers of the military college. The interest was to
pay for cleaning his tomb, with the residue (of the interest) to go to the poor in bread. If the college failed,
the trust was to pass to the minister, churchwardens
and overseers of Sandhurst. The college authorities
'declined to receive' the gift, the case went to Chancery,
the money went to the Accountant-General, and the parish
offered to take over the trust. Commissioners noted 'we
have submitted these facts for the consideration of His
Majesty's Attorney General.' (55)

At the other end of the scale, some trusts had outlived
the machinery set up for them. In Howden (Yorkshire,
E.R.) Richard Garlthorpe left an estate in the 16th
century to support a minister, a chapel, a waterworks,
and the poor of Howden. In 1619 the charity was regulated
by a Commission of Charitable Uses, and an elaborate
system of management was instituted. But in 1827, the
Commissioners found the system inflexible and incapable
of producing sufficient and reasonable rents. They recommended examination by a court of equity to obtain 'other
and better regulation in future.' (56)

Even when certification was not 'friendly' it was sometimes less than an outright accusation of abuse or irregularity. There were some cases where the passage of time,
the decay of documents, and the loss of memory had thoroughly confused a trust, and the Commissioners sought
equity assistance as the final arbiter.

In the parish of Penn (Buckinghamshire) the Commissioners found a reference in Gilbert's Returns to a gift of
£1000 by Nathaniel Curzon; in the parish a record of the
charity was discovered which expired in 1797. The owner
of the land in question was Lord Howe, who claimed 'he
had searched his papers, and could find nothing relating
to the charity.' But the Commissioners felt there was
too much circumstantial evidence.

> It seems probable that some deed of declaration of
> trust was in fact executed by Sir Nathaniel, which has
> either been lost by the parish officers of Penn, or
> has been somewhere mislaid.

The case is however involved in much doubt and
mystery, and it appears to us most conducive to the
interests of all parties that it should be finally
set at rest by the decision of a Court of Equity. (57)
Another example of confusion requiring court action was
uncovered by Daniel Finch when working through the Drapers'
Company charities. The specific case was Sir John
Milborne's Almshouses. The donor had given thirteen
houses to one William Dolphin, who in turn gave them in
trust to the Company. The property however had been
mingled with all the company's holdings. Finch found
that some property which was conceivably under this trust
was very much appreciated and the charity deprived thereof. But if the will of Dolphin only required fixed payments, the Company might be overpaying by 'upwards of
£400.' Finch felt that only a court decision could
clarify the situation. (58)

Of course most certification cases were quite unfriend-
ly. They varied greatly in the amounts at stake. For
instance, two annuities were thought owing from the lands
of the Marquis of Downshire to charities in Easthampstead
(Berkshire). These were the princely sums of 12s. and
14s., and the case was certified. (59) Where the Commissioners found serious 'improvidence' in letting, the
cases might be carried forward as was that of the Christs'
Hospital Almshouses of Abingdon:

By the existing mode of leasing both houses and land
it is obvious that the charity does not derive the
income it ought from the property; and, as considerable portions of the property are held by individual
gentlemen under such leases (21-years with fines), it
is deemed fit to submit the case to His Majesty's
Attorney-General. (60)
Elsewhere in Berkshire, the Causeway Charity at Steventon
represented a more serious abuse. A large balance of
funds was neither accounted for nor secured. The trustees
had made a profit of £450 from tree-cutting, were holding
a balance of over £300, had lent some on personal security,
had spent £4 or £5 on their annual dinner, but only £8 or
£9 on schooling for the poor. The treasurer promised
(in 1836) a full account 'next Summer.' As the Commission
was due to expire in March 1837, this was small satisfaction, and Commissioners 'resolved to submit the case to
the Attorney General.' (61)

Finally, some cases left the Commissioners with no real
choice. One such was Richard Gaitskill's Charity of
Dalton in Furness (Lancashire). Their report needs no
amplification:

Considering all the circumstances of this case, that

the house for the pensioners has been suffered to fall into ruin, and the site of it sold; that the whole of the income, except what may be considered as laid out in the improvement of the property, has been misapplied; and finding that in the conveyance of the Billincoat land to trustees, and in the declaration of trust, all reference either to the trusts of the charity, or even to the name of the founders, has been omitted - we think that the management of this trust is a proper subject for the consideration of a court of equity. (62)

The flaw in the matter of recommendations was that there was only one case where there was certain (if slow) follow-up; and in order to obtain that, the problems of the trust had to be serious enough to outweigh the known risks of Chancery proceedings. However, there was a 'follow-up' of sorts in the publication of the Commission's Reports, the making of which we must examine next.

II

John Warren said that after country tours 'the Commissioners then return to town, and there they digest their Reports, and a great deal of additional matter is frequently collected in London.' (63) The 'digesting' was an arduous and very important part of the Commissioners' work, probably consuming as much time and energy and possibly affecting the final report as much as the original hearings. The course of the Commissioners' 'digestion' encompassed collection and correction of evidence, drafting of reports, and correction and adoption of reports by the General Board.

The time spent in preparation of the reports was estimated at about forty to fifty per cent of the total work of the Commissioners. This was a central item of the questioning in 1828 and again in 1835. The Commissioners were quite agreed as to the need for this amount of time, whereas their questioners seemed perplexed by it. (64) But after the local inquiry in which the bulk of the raw data was received, a great deal of hard labour remained before a finished report would be ready; moreover, the labour was beset with a series of delays and difficulties.

Returning to London with a portmanteau stuffed with documents, transcripts and notes, the Commissioners and their clerks had first to determine which charities were in need of further evidence. The most frequent situations were those where (1) no deed of trust had been found locally, though there was a trust in operation; (2) there was some dispute or confusion over original or subsequent documents (leases, exchanges, sales, etc.); or (3) there were relevant documents in London not available in the country (decrees of Commissions of Charitable Uses, Chancery decrees, charters, etc.). Of course, all of these situations, with a geographic difference, applied to London charities as well.

There were several possible clues and traces for pursuing unknown foundations. If the name of the founder and the date of foundation were known, a search of the relevant probate registries might be requested. If the foundation had been made since 1736, a check of the Chancery Inrolment Office was made (for a deed under 9 Geo. II c. 36). In the case of disputed terms or other questions, several government offices might have relevant information: the State Paper Office, the Stamp Office, the Tax Office, the Poor Return Office among them. Finally, there were many records which were sometimes copied locally, but were generally available at the main repository in London. These included the various records of Chancery proceedings and other court papers. They also included the acts of parliament and a host of more recent classes of departmental information: census and poor law returns, etc.

In searching and extracting all this material, the Commissioners and their clerks were on their own, with only a small amount of financial assistance from the central office, which after all only had a staff of a Secretary, a messenger, and a housekeeper. As Hine explained to Commissioner John Fellows:

It is wholly out of my power to make the numerous searches which become necessary for wills and other documents of which the Commissioners have not sufficient evidence produced to them in the course of their inquiries and I have no one I can depute to make the searches. As to such wills as there is reason to believe are proved in the Episcopal, Archidiaconal, or other Provincial courts, it is usual for the Commissioners' clerks to write to the Registrars of those courts requesting searches and extracts; and wills in the (Doctors') Commons are searched for by the clerks after their return to town. (65)

When all the documents were collected, drafting of the report could be completed. While the Commissioners may have used John Warren's system of paraphrasing so as to have drafting already underway, even that could not save long hours of preparation. The drafting might proceed in any cases where documents and other evidence were complete or nearly so, even as negotiations continued between

parties, Commissioners, and/or other authorities. Often
the only reference to current status was a sentence or
short paragraph; the great bulk of each report was devoted
to foundation and history of the trust. Those trusts
which were in any difficulty naturally had more detailed
sections on current management.

Drafting itself involved the clerks writing out, on
folded quarto sheets, the dictated extracts and comment-
aries of the Commissioners. Some of this was done in the
country, but much of it had to be done in town. These
draft reports were first edited and corrected by the
Commissioners and then filed in the office in Great George
Street. The surviving drafts, or most of them, have been
preserved as they returned from the printer. (66) It
appears that in the early stages the reports were taken
directly from the individual Commissioners to the General
Board, and thence to the printer. While editing was done,
it was not systematic. Only in the last stage of the Commission did the reports become subject to the screening
of a formal drafting committee. This body was first
mentioned in a letter from James Hine to Commissioner E.B.
Sugden. The Commissioners had been concerned that a
number of the entries in the 31st Report failed to give
'the information required by the Act.' (67) The members
of the drafting committee were William Grant, Daniel Finch,
John Wrottesley, George Long, Samuel Smith, and Frances
Martin.

Ironically, and not perhaps by accident, this committee
was instituted at the time that Commissioners began signing their own individual reports. James Hume was one
Commissioner who complained bitterly to Secretary Hine:

I do not know whether I shall be singular in expressing
surprise at finding the finishing process they (reports)
all have to undergo but I was surprised, because I had
believed each Commissioner was to sign his own report
which he could hardly do with propriety, supposing it
to be subject to being 'settled' by another person. (68)

The avowed purpose was uniformity of reporting, which Hume
sarcastically called 'uniformity of omission.' He was
troubled by passages which his reviser, George Long, found
objectionable, including statements as to 'whether money
in arrears be recoverable or not.'

If I understand, which I do not, whether the Revising
Committee have the power to strike out what may appear
to destroy the uniformity of the Reports, I need not
say that I should not attempt to justify or plead for
a word marked as objectionable.... I hope that a Commissioner, who, having to sign his own Report, and
therefore, for so much solely responsible and com-

promising no one, may be permitted to express an
opinion he strongly feels.

The critiques were not always taken so seriously, at
least by the members of the Committee.   Long wrote a
humorous note about one clerk's predilection for capital
letters

which he substitutes on many occasions for small
letters which have no title whatever to be raised from
the ranks.   As all those letters must be re-altered
before the draft goes to the press, which will be a sad
loss of time to my clerk, I should be very glad if a
hint from you should prevent in future the commission
of these capital offenses. (69)

And Finch jokingly appealed to Hine that revision was
driving him to extreme lengths:

I am in the middle of Mr Johnston's reports - and want
some little assistance to get through them - will you
have the goodness to send to the Stationery Office for
a bit of rope a razor or a pistol - it is too cold to
walk down to the Thames. (70)

Naturally enough, the only recorded case of serious
internal criticism in the Commission coincided with the
appearance of the Revising Committee.   It may have been
the Committee's cause - or an early consequence - for the
chronology was not completely clear.   Particularly harsh
comment came from several quarters in the Commission
regarding the work of Commissioners William Peter and
John Fellows (in Berkshire and Lincoln).

Grant wrote to Hine on 12 July 1836 and said that Peter
'does not seem to have read the Act of Parliament to see
what we are required to note.' (71)   Peter had however
left the Commission in May to go on a diplomatic mission
to Germany.   Fellows had been with him in Berkshire in the
preceding December and in a letter to Hine on 18 July he
acknowledged defects in their work.   But a week later he
protested strongly against Grant's criticism.   After prolonged discussion, and a showdown between Grant and
Fellows in December 1836, it was agreed that the work
would have to be redone. (72)   Comments from those who
did the new work confirmed Grant's original opinion.   In
January 1837, Arthur Buller wrote from Sleaford (Lincolnshire) 'We are at this moment in the middle of a great
grammar school which Fellows had made a most extraordinary
hash of.' (73)   In February, James Whishaw from Lambourne
(Berkshire) wrote of Peter's work: 'All reference to some
of the most important instruments has been wholly omitted
or supplied in such a manner as to render the information
given in the reports almost worse than useless.' (74)
These were the only cases of serious revision, or for that

matter, of anything like internal hostility. It is not
possible to say that they were the only major errors or
oversights, for before 1836 there was no comparable internal machinery, only a more perfunctory review by the
General Board, the semi-annual meetings of the Commission's
full membership.

III

The ruling body of the Commission was the full board
meeting, which made procedural resolutions, authorised
official interdepartmental communications, and ratified
(and signed) the Commission's Reports. In all of these
functions, there were no signs of overbearing leadership
by either the Chief Commissioners or the Honorary Commissioners, nor of dissension in the ranks. The partici-
pating members shared legal training, and no doubt they
carried from this some unspoken marks of seniority. These
at no time appear to have ruffled the working of the
Commission, and indeed may have had the opposite effect.
It must be noted that there was no record of votes in
the minutes, thus it is not possible to detect or document
divisions or unanimity.

The procedural actions were constitutional or routine.
The former consisted of refining and implementing the
terms of the statutes. In the first months of the Commission a series of resolutions dealt with the Special
Visitor exemption, the limits of inquiry, the ordering of
travelling boards, and the enforcing of summonses. Thereafter there were few traces of Commission action of this
kind, which either meant that a routine was quickly
settled, or that later decisions (of which there was no
external evidence) were made outside the general board or
not recorded.

One of the earliest 'constitutional' acts was the
definition of the exemption of special visitors. In this,
as in so much else, the Commissioners followed their Chancery experience.

Our attention was first directed to the consideration
of so much of the twelfth section of the said Act of
Parliament as relates to Special Visitors, Governors
and Overseers, in order to ascertain how far our powers
of inquiry were limited thereby. Adopting the rule of
construction which has been applied to a similar provision, in the Statute of Charitable Uses of the 43
Eliz. c. 4, we were of opinion, that this clause does
not extend to such Special Visitors, Governors and
Overseers, as have themselves the administration of

any funds belonging to Charitable Institutions for the
purposes of Education. Upon this construction we have
acted in the course of our proceedings; and where we
have met with charitable foundations provided with
special visitors or governors thus circumstanced, we
have thought it proper to pursue our inquiries concerning them. (75)

This decision was taken on 7 September 1818, and it was
carried on into the second and wider Commission of 1819.
Thus there was some narrowing of the troublesome restriction on special visitors, one which the Court had recognized, mainly because the control of funds reduced the
visitor to the role of a superior trustee.

There were also some early questions put to the General
Board about the limits of inquiry. On 28 September 1818

The Commissioners in Kent having submitted to the Board
this day the two following questions, viz,

Have the Commissioners authority to inquire into the
application of money left to bind apprentices to be
taken from a school over which they have no jurisdiction?

Can the Commissioners inquire into the amount or
management of scholarships or exhibitions of which the
Head and Fellows of a College are trustees to be given
to scholars taken from a school over which the Act of
Parliament extends?

The Board having considered those questions decided
each in the negative. (76)

The Commissioners here were encountering the first of
innumerable borderline questions, impossible to anticipate
in the law. Actually, this early notation was unusual,
and the general minute books ceased to be bothered with
such things before very long. We are left with the puzzle
of whether the communications from Commissioners stopped,
or whether they were simply no longer entered in the
minutes. The answer surely was a combination of both.

The minute books suggest that a fairly stable routine
had developed by 1820, and by 1821 the Board was meeting
only twice a year. In the regular gatherings of the
General Board a quorum was five, but all Stipendiaries and
a few honoraries were usually in attendance. The focal
point of the meeting was the approval of the general and
parochial reports. After the first four reports, the
introductory or general section was simply a formality,
and the bulk of the board meeting must have been devoted
to discussion of the cases to be certified, or to any
discrepancies which might have been apprehended in any of
the individual reports.

The other important statutory power came to the General

Board later in its career. In 1832 the Commission was
enabled to vest rent charges in local authorities as
trustees. On 21 July, the Board adopted 'a form of power
to be given to the resident minister' in pursuance of the
Act. (77) The first usage of the new authority was approved within days by a Board resolution of 1 August.
But there was no recurrence of such entries and on 5 February 1833 it was resolved that Commissioners should
recommend vesting rent charges

> in such cases only in which the Commissioners who shall
> have so inquired shall think the granting of such power
> expedient for enforcing the payment or due application
> of the Rent Charge or Rent Charges or for any other
> particular reason. (78)

Thereafter the rent charge powers appear to have been
slightly used until the last phase of the Commission. The
surviving duplicates of rent charge powers indicate that
at least 627 charitable endowments were vested in parochial authorities, mainly in 1836 and 1837, under this
authority. (79)

Outside of its regular routine, the General Board was
the natural agency of formal communication between the
Charity Commission and other departments of state. There
may have been any amount of informal contact, from Cabinet
level on down, but the recorded contacts were in the
domain of the Board, and those are of course our principal
evidence. The major areas were the Attorney-General, the
Home Office, the Treasury, and other Parliamentary agents.

The Home Office was the department responsible for the
inquiry. As such it was the channel for the reports of
the Commission, it was in charge of the composition and
the renewals of the Commission, and in the later stages,
it managed the special survey of education. Considering
the importance of these relationships, there was very
little formal communication. This meant either that the
Commission was independent, the Home Office was uncon-
cerned, or that there were private channels through which
business was transacted. There was some truth in each of
these possibilities. The formal requests made for information before renewals of the Commission showed a certain
aloofness and lack of current understanding of the Commission's work; the Home Secretary and his aides occasionally dropped clues that they were unfamiliar with the
Commission, and as our discussion (Chapter 5) has shown,
the Commission was quite independent in its operations.

The treasury relationship was even more remote. As a
temporary agency, and a recipient of funds on special
resolutions, there was little occasion for any major contact. But it is still somewhat surprising to find the

Secretary of the Commission writing to the Treasury in 1828, and explaining to them his procedure for receiving funds. Carlisle explained that he had periodically written (under the authority of the General Board) to obtain a warrant for a draft on the exchequer.

> When any sum is received at the Exchequer, it is instantly deposited with Messrs Drummonds, the bankers, from whence it cannot be drawn but by the signature of the Speaker and two other Commissioners in whose name it is lodged. (80)

The occasion of this letter was a move to tighten up the system of internal accounting, and the fact that Carlisle had not had any earlier occasion to inform the Treasury (or as far as we can tell, anyone else) of how the funds were handled, only proved that the Commission had enjoyed a loose supervision in its finances.

The General Board was also responsible for other official communications, most of which concerned the inquiries of members of Parliament, and returns thereto, but at a later stage came to include correspondence with other (parliamentary) commissions of inquiry. This category grew considerably after 1830, and especially in 1835-7. In the latter period, there was a very sizeable correspondence with the Poor Law Commissioners, (81) and scattered contact with others such as the Municipal Corporation commission.

The formal responsibility for the reports lay with the General Board, though as we have seen, there was no administrative machinery connected with them until 1836. Every semi-annual report was signed by those in attendance at the general meeting, which usually included all of the stipendiaries and perhaps half of the honoraries. Until 1837, when a Final Report summarized the findings, there was little added to the basic parochial accounts (and appendices). Two important procedural points arose in regard to the reports. In 1821 it was resolved to send copies of reports to parishes. (82) This was probably not carried out systematically. Carlisle was asked about it in 1836, and he said he could not find a list of 'those gentlemen to whom we promised to send copies of our reports' but 'I think Mr Nicholas (a clerk) kept a list.' (83) The other important procedural decision was that in which the last commission directed individually-signed reports, which has been discussed above.

The General Board had a vital role in formal terms, but it was not a body, by design, temperament, or circumstance, which would be likely to act with special inspiration or vigour. In fact, its formally superior position disguised a certain impotence; the real powers were in the individual members, and particularly those who were the most active.

The proceedings of the Charity Commissioners were remarkably consistent and flexible. The basic discovery of charitable trusts and abuses thereof was a matter of legal drudgery which the Commissioners did uniformly and well. At least their methods were perfectly adequate to the type of inquisition which they conceived proper (i.e. a title-search and not a complete screening). While its individual members probed the trust-community, the Commission ought to have been developing as a unit. Yet as a parliamentary creature, with functional ties to the Home Office, the Attorney-General, and the Treasury (plus an anomolous relation to Chancery) the Commission had weak institutional bearings. There was no strong outside or superior imprint on Commission activity or procedure. This could have led to indolence and/or jobbing. In fact, we find innovation and intervention. As Commissioners inquired, they tried to correct, to compromise, to chastise. In other words, the Commission was an instrument of reform by experience and not by design.

At this point, we need to examine the Commission's activity in the wider perspective, particularly observing the interruptions and inspections during its long two-decade career. These highlights will fortify our understanding of what the Commission did.

Interruptions

The Charity Commission was a novelty but it drew more attention and criticism as it ceased to be one. The length of its career virtually insured its interruption and periodic reassessment. These intervals were more significant as stages in the developing perception of the Commission, than as stages in its own growth or development. What emerged in the series of breaks (1824, 1828, 1830, and 1835) was a heightened consciousness of Commissions: on one side, more scepticism as to their cost-effectiveness; on the other, more concern for their effective design and operation. Meanwhile, at every stage there was a good exposure of the Charity Commission's working, its activity as a reforming agency, and its reception by the political community.

I

The 1819 Commission was due to expire at the end of the session of 1824. In April, Henry Hobhouse wrote to the Commissioners and reminded them that Peel would be responsible for moving the renewal. On 14 May, Hobhouse forwarded Secretary Peel's request for the following details: (1)

(1) What was the income of the trusts so far investigated? from land, from other property?
(2) How many charities had been investigated in each county, and how many counties were complete?
(3) How many cases were there where complaints were found?
(4) How many charities were of an annual value of less than £40, less than £10, less than £5?
(5) How many cases had been begun, how far advanced were they?

Within two weeks, Carlisle had assembled answers to most
of these questions. He sent a detailed chart of data and
a list of cases to the Home Office on 26 May. The investigation had so far dealt with 10,736 charities. Their
aggregate value was £239,205 7s. 9d. in land and
£83,504 0s. 1d. in other property. Carlisle estimated
that approximately 7,000 charities were under £10 value,
but he said he could not determine the other categories
without more time. The Commissioners considered seven
counties complete at this point. Carlisle also forwarded
a list of seventy cases which were being considered for
certification: including those awaiting decision, already
certified, and already on trial. But the Commissioners
were not able to answer Peel's question about complaints.
No running score was being kept, either owing to the professional approach of the Commissioners or their disinterest in dramatizing abuses. Perhaps if the question had
asked how many corrections had been made, it would have
received an enthusiastic reply. Finally, Commissioners
were at a loss to define 'complaints,' for these existed
everywhere, where serious 'abuses' were in fact quite
rare. (2)

Armed with this information, Peel was able to obtain
the renewal of the Commission with little difficulty.
The same day his request went to Carlisle the Bill was
introduced in the Commons. Within a week of the Commission's return, the Bill cleared the lower house, and
it passed the Lords on 4 June. (3) There was no debate
worthy of mention in Hansard, and from all appearances,
renewal was taken for granted. The new Act extended the
life of the Commission for four years. In view of later
developments, this unopposed and liberal extension was
notable, but in the immediate circumstances it was probably unnoticed. There were several reasons. First,
although the Commissioners had studied more than a third
of the charities which they would eventually cover, they
had only put one tenth of the eventual total of cases into
court. By their eleventh Report (17 June 1824) the Commissioners had only completed seven counties, although
they had entered twenty-one, including the metropolis. (4)
Their impact had thus been fairly widely dispersed. Also,
in the earlier stages Commissioners were less sure of
themselves and less aggressive than later. But the general
reason for easy acceptance of the renewal was that the
conditions of the origin of the Commission still prevailed,
and there had as yet been no serious questioning of the
Commission process.

From 1821, however, there was a growing campaign for
economy led by Radicals. In 1826 one of the targets of

this campaign became the proliferating new parasite of
patronage, the Royal Commission of Inquiry. Joseph Hume
was the leader of this enterprise, and part of his
economic scrutiny produced Returns to the Commons on the
burgeoning new Commissions. The first occasion was a
return presented on 2 May 1827 giving the 'Expense of
Commissions of Inquiry in the last Twenty Years.' (5)
The contents were something of a revelation. A total of
thirty-eight commissions were listed, and the total cost
was nearly £957,000. The size of the annual bill had
risen from £38,000 in 1807 to £92,000 in 1826. (6) The
range of individual cost was great. The cheapest was a
prison inquiry listed at £44; the most expensive was the
Record Commission at £126,000. But since that sum was
expended over a twenty-year reporting period, the Charity
Commission, listed at £121,248 for its first nine years'
expenditure, was well in the lead on average annual cost.
From this point on, casual acceptance of commissions was
replaced by cold analysis and caustic criticism. The
returns on commissions became a regular practice, and
because of the new awareness, the next renewal of the
Charity Commission could not be like the first.

II

When the Charity Commission was once again approaching
renewal in 1828, it had to run a rough gauntlet. Legal
returns were angrily demanded by one MP, one commissioner
was summoned to testify before the Finance Committee, and
a mere one-year renewal bill in 1829 encountered resistance.
    On 5 March 1828, the House of Commons was moved to
order a return of informations filed on behalf of the
Charity Commission. The mover was Daniel Whittle Harvey,
Member for Colchester. (7) Harvey was to be an important
if erratic critic. His positions encompassed outspoken
hostility to the Commission and assiduous place-hunting
inside it. On this occasion, Harvey launched the first
of several critiques. Professing 'the most friendly
feeling,' he nonetheless found that 'of all the Commissions which had ever been issued at the desire of Parliament, no one had ever been attended with such costly
results, and with such slight beneficial consequences.'
(8) He called it 'lavish and extravagant,' he doubted the
need for voluminous reports, and he darkly hinted that
they were being used to cover up abuses. Further, when
cases were certified, it was 'for the benefit of cunning
lawyers.' This was ironic in veiw of charges which later

would be made against Harvey himself, but there was little
evidence to support his charge. (9)   Harvey's attack was
taken lightly, and it was confidently handled two days
later by those rare allies, Peel and Brougham, who corrected some of Harvey's erroneous remarks and refuted his
allegations. (10)

But the time of testing was not over. Within the next
ten days, while Peel was beginning to assemble renewal
data., (11) the Select Committee on Finance was inquiring
into the work of the Charity Commission. Commissioner
John Warren appeared and testified on 18 March 1828. (12)
He brought with him a return of the Commission's expenditure (£138,000). The Committee, chaired by Sir Henry
Parnell, examined Warren in some detail on the organization and proceedings of the Commission. The hearing was
in a way an audit of the Commission, its methods and its
finances. It produced a picture of part-time, practising
barristers, under no system of rules, no regular accounting, and with little idea of what their subsequent recommendations might be. That was a fairly accurate if somewhat incomplete picture.

There were several repercussions from the hearing.
Warren was asked to obtain answers to a set of questions
which arose at the Committee hearing; some internal steps
were taken to tally the sittings of the Commissioners; and
the Treasury began to put pressure on the Commission to
improve its system of accounting. In the first instance,
Warren had been rather unimpressive in answering some
questions about 'preventing abuses in future.' The Commissioner had also been asked about the possibility of a
cheaper and more summary process. For this and the other
questions, draft answers were prepared (by Daniel Finch)
and circulated within the Commission, and remarks by the
Commissioners were sent to Carlisle. Probably none of
these views were heard outside the Commission, but they
provided a valuable insight into the thinking of the Commissioners. (13)

To the question of whether or not Commissioners could
take 'a more summary view' and save money, the answer was
that it could only be done at the expense of authoritative
reports. Finch went so far as to outline a plan in which
only the more wealthy trusts were actually visited. Rely-
ing on circulars for the rest would not, however, reduce
the time of inquiry by, say, the same sixty per cent which
trusts of less than £10 represented.

The Committee had also asked about establishment of
county charity boards, a proposal which the Commissioners'
remarks did not favour. The boards would be too expensive,
and they would not be capable of handling the 'nice and

difficult' questions of trust law.   A third question dealt
with documents.   The Committee wanted to know how they
could be preserved, but the draft answers of the Commissioners evaded the question, and turned to trust continuity and the need for a summary method of instituting
trustees.

The answers of the Commissioners were revealing in
showing the problems they experienced when forced to
ponder the larger implications of their work.   Unhappily,
the Commissioners' answers do not enhance our impression
of their vision, though the replies make it quite clear
that the Commission was not inhibited by any preconceived
solutions.

While these answers were being written, other operations were in progress as a consequence of the Finance
Committee hearing.   On 26 March Warren wrote to Carlisle:

I think it would be well if you would be good enough
to set about at once making out a list of the numbers
of Boards held at the office in London each year.   I
should not think it necessary to return the number of
attendances of each Commissioner - indeed better not,
because frequently only one has attended, which wo'd
make a seeming inconsistency with the number of boards.
Nevertheless if such an account can without much
trouble be made out of the respective attendances on
a separate paper in going through the Minute Book for
the purpose of numbering the boards, it might save
the future trouble of going through it again. (14)

Carlisle did make up the return of the 'Number of Sittings
held by the Commissioners at their office in London, and
of the days on which they have been absent from London
pursuing their inquiries in the several counties specified.' (15)   This covered the period 1818-27, and it was
not printed in Parliamentary Papers.   This analysis,
though not made on specific instruction of the Finance
Committee, was clearly in response to its interrogation;
though without further evidence of its internal use, it
would be unsafe to assume that the return was more than a
clerical exercise.

Another development related to the Committee hearing
was growing pressure from the Treasury for reform of
accounts.   From October through December 1828, there were
several exchanges of queries and answers between the Audit
Office and Secretary Carlisle, who gave an explanation
and justification of the Commission's financial procedure.
(16)   Then in December J.K. Stewart, Assistant Secretary
to the Lords of the Treasury, wrote to Carlisle and asked
for tighter accounting, especially on travel expenses.
This was taken up in a special board meeting of 24 January

1829, where it was noted that the board

> took into consideration a letter dated the 23d of
> December 1828, rec'd from the Honble J. Stewart, Sec-
> retary to the Lords Commissioners of His Majesty's
> Treasury - and to prepare a mode of rendering accounts
> in conformity therewith. (17)

The precise change made as a result of these exchanges was
not clear, for the detailed incoming complaints do not
appear to have remained in the files of the Commission.
But it was abundantly clear that the Committee's work had
triggered the first serious examination of the Commission
by the Treasury.

When the Commission's renewal bill came up in 1829,
there was thus a considerable background of discussion
and activity. The opposition spokesman once again was
D.W. Harvey, the 'government' spokesman was Brougham.
The bill went through Parliament in a fortnight, with the
only recorded debate being a brief exchange on the third
reading in the Commons. Harvey had made several charges
which were careless and inaccurate. As the bill was for
a one-year extension, he represented it as an attempt to
conclude the inquiry in that time, when it had taken
eleven years to do only half the job. He also claimed
that the Gilbert Inquiry was unknown to the founders of
the Commission, and he implied that the Charity Commission
was merely duplicating the survey of 1786 at great public
expense. Finally, Harvey accused Lord Eldon (now retired)
of having 'nearly stifled' the inquiry by his construction
of the 1812 Act for summary process - apparently confusing
that process with the certification of cases to the
Attorney-General. Brougham easily disposed of these
flimsy arguments and wandered into an explanation of his
own continuing interest in an education bill, a revealing
preoccupation which was to reappear throughout the life
of the Commission. (18) But most interesting for the
immediate situation was Brougham's explanation of the one-
year extension.

> At the present period of the session it was not pract-
> icable to make certain alterations in the constitution
> of the commission, which alterations were, nevertheless,
> necessary; but as the period of the existence of the
> Commission was about to expire, it was imperative to
> provide for its continuance for another year, with a
> view, in the next session, to make the required
> changes. (19)

Brougham's other remarks showed a detailed current knowledge of the state of the Commission's working, but he
gave no further clue to the cryptic 'required changes.'
The one-year extension passed (10 Geo. IV c. 57), and

nothing was heard for another year.   Then on 16 June 1830,
a bill was ordered to be brought in by the Attorney-
General, the Solicitor-General, and Brougham. (20)   But
this bill was yet another simple extension, as Brougham's
comment made clear:

> As I believe there is at present no wish to discuss
> this subject, I will at once move for leave to bring
> in a bill to continue the Act 10 George IV c. 57 for
> one year.   It is under that Act, Sir, that the Com-
> missioners of Inquiry into Charities are empowered to
> act, but it has been found absolutely impossible to
> give due deliberation to the interests of all parties
> without more time than has been allotted them for that
> purpose, and it is to prolong that time that the pre-
> sent bill is intended. (21)

Whereas extension had succeeded in 1829, in 1830 the bill
never appeared before the dissolution of that turbulent
Summer, and the redesign and required changes were
obscured as the Commission collapsed on the threshold of
the new era.

III

The Charity Commission expired on 1 July 1830 and was not
reinstated until 22 December 1831.   This hiatus coincided
with distractions presented by climaxes in financial,
religious, legal, and parliamentary reforms.   But if the
Commission had not been at a stage where its own structure
was under review, it might have gone on without this
deviation.   The conjunction of uncertainty within and
general turmoil without caused the long interruption.

A series of converging and accelerating reform developments in the period 1829-31 overtook and threatened to
disrupt the deliberate and painstaking legal research of
the Charity Commissioners.   The new wave of financial
reform was the first sign of these developments.   Through
the Public Accounts Commission there was pressure on the
continuing examination of Commissions of Inquiry, and the
institution of required annual estimates and the reporting
of other data.   (22)

Meanwhile, in the same period since 1828, the several
religious reform measures - relief for Dissenters, emancipation for Catholics and overhaul for Anglicans - had very
substantial impact on charitable trusts in a variety of
ways.   Directly, there were several bills to bring Roman
Catholic charities into the ambit of existing law after
emancipation. (23)   Indirectly, the rates campaign of
Dissenters which took renewed strength from the formal

penal law grant of relief, encouraged measures to make
charitable trusts liable for local rates. (24) Also, the
concurrent impact on the established church, especially
the creation of Commissions on Ecclesiastical Courts and
Revenues, was an important collateral development. It
put church trusts under further scrutiny, which produced
further reform interest and establishment resistance. (25)

The considerable activity of twenty years and more of
legal reform efforts culminated in the late 1820s, after
Eldon's retirement, in a surge of legal reform actions:
featured elements were the Common Law Commission (1828)
and the Real Property Law Commission (1829). More per-
tinent was the Chancery reform effort which began in 1826
with the first of a series of bills advanced by Attorney-
General John Copley (later Lord Chancellor Lyndhurst,
1827-30; 1834-5; 1841-6). (26) When he became Chancellor,
Lyndhurst was able to effect a few modified procedures.

When Brougham became Lord Chancellor in 1830, he undertook his legendary sweeping of the Eldonian stables of
Chancery arrears. Actually the job had been well begun
by Lyndhurst, and was carried through by Brougham. In
any case, the workload was real enough, and taken together
with the distraction of the Great Reform Bill, kept
Brougham well occupied. (27) And it was in the midst of
this activity that the Charity Commission was renewed in
1831. Two attempts were necessary, because of the
election of 1831. The bill experienced no serious opposition, and indeed, it was ironically unimpressive. With
all of the reform currents swirling about, with the hero
of charity reform on the woolsack, having months earlier
promised a reconstructed Commission, the Commission
enacted in 1831 should have been a major new departure.
Instead, it was a reissue of the old Commission, minus the
exemption for charities with special visitors.

The first attempt at renewal was made in March, but the
bill died at the dissolution in April, 1831. Another bill
was brought in on 6 September, which passed within a month
(1 and 2 Will. IV c. 34). The extension was for a minimum
of two years. The only recorded debate in this instance
was a brief exchange on the salary provision and the
number of paid Commissioners. Hume suggested a return to
Brougham's old idea of a 'salvage fee' and Harvey supported this plan for making charity pay its own way. (28)
However the bill went through without any alteration in
its financial provisions. The new Commission was issued
on 22 December, 1831.

As reconstituted in 1831, the Charity Commission was
not fundamentally different from its predecessors. But
the world in which it operated certainly was different.

During the period 1830-5, the usage of commissions of inquiry was changing, along with the rest of the political landscape. Professional inquiry along the lines of the Charity Commission was applied to many other problems, with some constitutional alteration, but much more doctrinal dedication. The result was the 'reform commission' norm to which we have become accustomed. The Charity Commission tended to follow rather than lead this alteration. During the years 1832-4 there were some serious reconsiderations of the Charity Commission's structure and role, and two plans were forwarded to Lord Brougham as possible designs for renovation. At the same time, 1833-4 saw continued 'harrassment' in calls for Parliamentary returns. The Commission expired without renewal in 1834. It was in this atmosphere of redesigning commissions that a Select Committee of the Commons was established in 1835 to assess the Charity Commissioners' reports, to give a prognosis for completion, and to make suggestions for the future of charitable trust administration.

The growing frequency of commissions, and the corollary of expanding coverage, had made them by 1830 a familiar form of governmental change. But whereas the commissions of 1800-29 had been zealously establishment-oriented (though able and apt to reform, the two properties not being mutually exclusive), those of 1830-5 were oriented toward change. Both sets of commissions were 'programmed' to some extent by their constitution, composition, and objectives, but the programmes changed in 1830.

The new 'programming' led to important changes in function, in that the Factory Commission, the Poor Law Commission, and other latter-day bodies were meant to remodel and regulate, where their older cousins had been set up to renovate and restore. To perform remodelling required a rethinking of fundamentals; to regulate required a redesigning of duties. For those reasons, inspectors, assistant commissioners et al. were needed, as was the central office or board to which they reported.

The impact of the reorientation of commissions was not clear within the Charity Commission. While five of the ten honorary Commissioners came from promotions in 1831, thirteen Commissioners were new, eight of them being recruits at the stipendiary job. The Act of 1831 had not drastically altered its predecessors, nor had it given complete ratification to the old system. In fact, within the Commission it was clearly understood, probably from 1831 and certainly by 1833, that change was anticipated. As renewal time again approached, Brougham had requested some of the Commissioners to suggest revisions. In 1833, Samuel Smith forwarded a draft proposal to Lord Brougham's

Secretary, Denis Le Marchant 'on the recasting of the
Charity Commission.' (29)   The authorship was attributed
primarily to John Wrottesley, and the concurrence of
another Commissioner, Charles Cameron, was noted.   As the
proposal was prefaced with a defence of the established
method and its (often unseen) results, it need not be
added that the suggestions were less than radical.

The plan itself was headed Hints for the Formation of
a Board of Commissioners for the Superintendance of
Charities.   It recommended a Board of three, plus two
secretaries or clerks, an accountant, and a registrar.
Their office would be the general registry, the board
would supervise and take annual accounts from trustees,
and they would have the same power as the Attorney-General
to file suit.   The board would investigate 'by detaching
one of their number to pursue the inquiry on the spot, if
necessary.'   The board also was 'to have the powers of
Masters in Chancery in matters of charity,' hence to
report into court various statements, schemes, etc. for
the approval of the Lord Chancellor.   On its own authority, the board would be able:

1. to exercise a summary jurisdiction over charities
under £10 per annum;
2. to charge trustees retaining balances of charitable
estates for their own benefit with interest at £20 per
charity;
3. to authorize any sale, exchange, lease or other
dealing with charity property which may appear for the
benefit of the charity;
4. to authorize the appropriation of any portion of the
funds of a school not exceeding 1/4 or 1/3 of the whole
by way of retiring pension to a master incapacitated
by age or infirmity.
5. to authorize a deviation *cy pres* (30) from the
founder's intention where it cannot by possibility be
strictly performed, and the annual income does not
exceed £20.
6. to direct the revenues of charities given for the
benefit of the poor generally, or where the positive
trusts are unknown & the application has varied, to
be applied as shall appear most beneficial to the
objects, provided the annual income does not exceed
£20.

The Hints went on to propose wider powers for the Lord
Chancellor in redirecting funds, and it made him the
appellate authority for the new board.   Each parish was
to have a 'Charity Board,' including the incumbent, the
resident clergyman, the senior churchwarden, the vestry
clerk, the six highest ratepayers, and two elected parish-

ioners.   These parish boards would have trustee powers
where others failed, and the Bank of England would be
required to admit them on the books under their corporate
names.   Finally the Hints called for 'the Mortmain Act to
be repealed as to charities having for their sole object
the diffusion of useful knowledge, including scientific
societies.'

This plan was ambitious and sweeping, especially in
its local provisions.   The authors acknowledged an
inadvertent breadth: 'In our ignorance of what is contemplated, it was difficult to make them (the Hints) more
precise than we have done.'   There was no trace of a
reply or of further internal action in response to the
Hints.

Within months, another plan was forwarded, this time
from the Secretary, James Hine.   He wrote to Le Marchant
on 17 February 1834 'to offer for your perusal some
suggestions respecting provisions to be engrafted on a
bill for renewing the inquiry into charities.' (31)   Hine
justified his plan by referring to the numerous applications for help received by the Commissioners, which they
had to refer to Chancery.   And the latter course was as
bad as ever: 'during the past week an instance has
occurred in which £359, out of a fund for £380, are gone
for costs.'

Hine's plan was cast in the form of 'provisions' to be
added to a renewal bill, i.e. it was aimed at amending,
not fundamentally changing, the existing structure.   The
essence of Hine's plan was to give the existing Commission
administrative powers.   They would hear complaints, or
dispatch one or more Commissioners to investigate.   After
such inquiries and investigations, Commissioners would
file a written report 'in the same manner as Reports of
Masters of the said court.'   These reports would be the
basis for orders: for appointing or removing trustees;
'the settlement and establishment of schemes for the
regulation and management of charities, and the Estates
and Funds belonging thereto and the application of the
income arising therefrom;' removal or restoration of
schoolmasters; regulation of schools 'and other similar
objects.'   The parties would be able to file exceptions,
to be heard by the Master of the Rolls or the Vice Chancellor.   Ordinary informations would be screened by the
Commissioners.   A provision was included authorizing
payments to be taken by the Commissioners from the charitable trusts 'towards reimbursement,' which payments were
'to be accounted for to the Treasury on oath.'   Finally,
Hine also called for a reform in Bank of England procedure,
whereby trustees would be perpetual account-holders, 'or,

possibly, an officer (of the Commission) might be appointed, in whose name investments of stock might be made in
trust for any charity' - a treasurer of charities.

The essence of these two plans was to attack the problem of Chancery by introducing the Charity Commission as
a permanent adjunct to the court, and in so doing, to give
administrative latitude and to permit quicker and less
costly resolution of problems discovered by the Commissioners. Whether these court-oriented schemes were apt
to succeed before full-scale court reform was effected
may be open to doubt. But their actual failure was easily
explained. They were never adopted and put before parliament; meanwhile other proposals were being made from
various sources.

IV

During the early 1830s the increasing tempo of Commission
activity was accompanied by continued surveillance of
commissions. (32) A special inquiry was created for the
Charity Commission, chaired by none other than D.W. Harvey.
Harvey's connection to the Charity Commission was strange
in the extreme. While he publicly opposed its allegedly
wasteful proceedings, he was quietly seeking a position
on it. Harvey claimed that he had had an interview with
Lord Brougham in 1830 in which the new Lord Chancellor
had promised him the post of Commission Secretary, and
when this was not available, Harvey was offered the post
of solicitor to the Attorney-General for the Charity Commission, which also fell through. (33) In July 1831,
Harvey wrote to Brougham and suggested a new office of
assistant to the Attorney-General on charity questions,
a post which Harvey offered to fill. (34) And after the
Select Committee of 1835, Harvey was still on the trail,
asking Brougham to appoint him as the Chief Commissioner's
personal secretary. (35) Unfortunately for Harvey,
Brougham had already renounced the patronage of the Commission when he became its head, but in the same letter
he had written to Russell: 'by all means ... get D.W.
Harvey to belong.' (36)

Harvey's persistence was not altruistic. Some Commissioners were convinced that he was an outright fraud.
Samuel Smith wrote in his Hints that Harvey had picked
out likely unapplied funds from the reports of the Commission and sent them 'to an equity draftsman in shoals.
I think I am correct in saying Mr Skirrow received between
50 and 60 in one term.' Smith thought 'there are numerous
cases in which the whole funds of a charity have been

absorbed for long periods in the payment of law expenses.'
He hinted that Harvey chose insolvent persons to be
relators, and that 'in other cases the threat of proceeding has been dropped upon payment of what Mr D W Harvey
called his "expenses".' Finally, Harvey had a business
address in Great George Street which Smith asserted was
easily (and not accidentally) confused with the office
of the Commission. (37) Another Commissioner, F.O. Martin,
encountered a Harvey case in 1836 which he thought serious
enough to bring before a General Board. (38)

The allegations were serious, but they can never be
proven. Harvey was indeed quite proud of his record of
winning recoveries for trusts (and fees for himself).
From the Commissioners' viewpoint, this appeared scandalous; from the point of view of charity beneficiaries, the
scandal may have been in the Commissioners' inaction, not
Harvey's vigorous if venal action. After all, if Smith
was right, Harvey was only following the path staked out
for him in the reports of the Commission!

In any event, in 1835 Harvey was sitting for his new
constituency of Southwark. He was still looking for some
connection with the Charity Commission, and he was still
taking a tough line on the Commission's performance. It
was in that context that he proposed and was named the
chairman of a Select Committee 'to examine and consider
the evidence in the reports of the Commissioners for
inquiring concerning charities.' (39) In moving for the
Committee after alluding to Brougham's oratory, Harvey
said:

His object was to pass from learning to labour, from
speculative fancies to facts - from reveries to things
which had been revealed. It was, indeed, time that
something should be known of a Commission the labours
of which were spread over 17 years, and that a practical
character should be given them.

The inquiries commenced in 1818, and continued down
to the year 1834, thus extending over a period of time
unexampled in parliamentary history for an inquiry to
last, and presenting a body of information, at least
so far as they could be determined by the number of
volumes, he might say altogether without precedent. He
believed the result was, that these efforts, vast as
they appeared, were yielding at present little or no
return. (40)

The 'return' which Harvey's Committee promised was in
three parts: to assess the reports, to plan for and estimate the remaining work, and to consider the future
administration of charitable trusts. The first it evaded,
the second it made a feeble attempt to do, and the third

brought forth a well-conceived but premature plan for a
permanent Board of Charity Commissioners.

The Select Committee examined fourteen witnesses in
eight days of hearings. Included were five Commissioners,
Secretary Hine, his successor as Solicitor to the Attorney
General, and another London solicitor. The remaining six
witnesses were all connected with the Berkhampstead School
case, which the Committee held up as an example of mismanagement. (41)

The testimony was not organized, but it may be roughly
divided into parts, related to the Committee's principal
objectives: the reports, the proceedings, and the future.
The Committee eschewed any attempt at a full study of the
reports. Instead, they made a thorough and exhaustive
study of one case, as if to prove how laborious the job
would be. The Berkhampstead School had been referred to
the Committee, being the subject of a petition to the
Commons. It was not typical, though the Committee thought
'that case embodies most remarkably the prominent features
of a class of cases which have been investigated by the
Commissioners.' The class referred to was ambiguous,
presumably that small fraction of hopelessly inoperable
trusts. For Berkhampstead was unusually beset with
problems: a grammar school for '144 boys' which had no
pupils for twenty-five or thirty years; a charity which
had been under some Chancery supervision since 1735; and
an endowment with a special visitor, in this case the
Warden of All Souls' College, Oxford. The schoolmaster -
who was 'trustee' as well - was deeply involved in the
school properties, and his brother-in-law was the court-
appointed receiver of the rents. It was fairly clear
from the rather complex testimony, that this particular
trust had not been completely unravelled, nor truly
reformed by the visit of the Charity Commissioner. (42)

But the Committee had to confess its frustration and
impotence also:

Your Committee find that a valuable institution, with
large funds and appropriate premises adequate for the
free education of a great number of children, and the
liberal maintenance of the necessary instructors, with
a surplus fund which, rightly administered according to
the design of the benevolent founder, would afford
comfortable provision to many deserving objects, in all
material circumstances the reverse of what it ought to
be. Your Committee find a Master and Usher (the latter
the son of the Master, and appointed by him when a
minor), the incorporated trustees of the charity property, receiving to their own use considerable stipends,
the schoolhouse dilapidated, no boys on the foundation,

and the surplus revenue so exhausted by law and other
expenses as to leave an uncertain trifle for the relief
of the poor.
Against this situation, the Committee had no suggestion
for a remedy.
   The Select Committee did explore at length the way in
which the Commission operated. They had testimony from
half of the active members of the last Commission, plus
that of the senior staff man and other legal professionals.
While their questions covered most aspects of the inquiry,
the general impression was of a time-motion study. The
Committee was looking for optimum efficiency for the
remainder of the investigation: would one Commissioner be
able to work alone, would each single Commissioner need a
clerk, could Commissioners take evidence either more
quickly or less fully? The drift of the testimony favour-
ed the old system, and the witnesses agreed that completion of the inquiry might take up to four more years on
the past pattern. The conclusions of the Committee were
that 'at least' twenty stipendiary Commissioners should
be appointed in the next Commission, each with a clerk;
that the individuals concerned should sign their reports,
that there should be a Chief Commissioner, and that the
term of the Commission should expire on 1 March 1837. The
Committee in effect endorsed the effort of the Commission,
but urged that it should be fortified in order to bring
the inquiry to completion as soon as possible.
   The prognosis of the Commission explained the Committee's interest in early completion. They concluded,
with the widespread concurrence of their witnesses, that
a permanent board of Charity Commissioners was necessary.
The Committee heard the plan of Smith and Wrottesley and
that of Hine. The report recommended 'a permanent board
of three Commissioners.' It would supervise property,
call for returns, have power to summon trust administrators, power to preserve documents to make audits, to remove
schoolmasters, make schemes for revision, correct abuses
and resolve conflicting claims - in tandem with the
special visitor where necessary - and the board would
screen all cases before equity proceedings.
   The Committee did not explicitly evaluate the Charity
Commission's inquiry, but it is hard to avoid the conclusion that (by ignoring the mass of reports and looking
at one mess) the general feeling was that, as Harvey had
said 'these efforts, vast as they appeared, were yielding
at present little or no return.' On the other hand, the
Committee fully approved of the object, urged the speedy
conclusion of the inquiry, and with great emphasis (and
one-sided testimony) supported a conversion of inquiry
into bureaucracy.

Both extension of the old Commission and erection of
the new were put before parliament in 1835. The extension
succeeded, and the new board failed. The latter was
actually made the subject of a bill before the Select
Committee was done. Brougham brought in a bill on 3 July
in the Lords, which proposed a Commission of Public
Instruction that would double as a Charity Commission. (43)
This hasty and loaded measure was easily stopped, and it
probably forestalled effective action on a permanent board
after the Select Committee's report (30 July).

However, extension was duly and deliberately introduced
in August 1835. The form of the bill followed the recommendations of the Select Committee, and within a month
(9 September) it had been made law and the Commission,
with Lord Brougham as Chief, was issued 22 October and met
on 11 November. As befits a story which has no shortage
of odd twists, Brougham voted against the renewal of the
Commission in the Committee stage of the bill in the Lords,
because he objected to the fact that fourty-four posts
(twenty stipendiaries, twenty clerks, and a secretary and
three others) were being created without a maximum salary
being set. The implication was that ministers were taking
excessive patronage. (44) As these salaries were not
usually set in the statutes, but by convention, it is
hard to tell how serious Brougham was. He still supported
the bill, but since his own Commission of Public Instruction had just been killed, he may have been very sensitive.
In any event, his opposition was brief and benign - he
soon accepted the post of Chief Commissioner for the last
stage of the inquiry, though in view of his voting record,
he felt obliged to renounce the patronage. (45)

V

The appointment of Brougham was apparently over the
objections of the King. As Russell wrote to Melbourne in
September, 'You will know before that the King strongly
objects to Brougham, but I hope you will be able to overcome his objections. He considers it as a Commission to
direct education instead of an inquiry.' (46) The King
was in this case more alert than his advisers, for what
Brougham clearly had in mind was 'a commission to direct
education' - that was the subject of his bill in 1835,
and it would be the same bill in 1837 which nearly dis-
rupted the final stages of the Charity Commission. Whether
indeed Brougham expected to operate as freely with the
Commission as he had done with the original Select Committee may be doubted, though the chance of an attempt was

a fair ground for William's suspicion. But there was no
question about Brougham's plan when the Education and
Charities bill came on in 1837.

The essentials of this final disruption were that
(1) the bill excited interest in the permanent Commission,
and it caused distraction, as (2) the Commissioners struggled, needing a four-month extension, to complete the
collection of their material, neglecting an overview of
their work until (3) the defeat of Brougham's bill on the
eve of expiration (late June) led to a hurried and unsatisfactory Final Report.

Brougham's bill for a Commission of Public Instruction,
introduced on 2 February 1837, was almost identical to the
measure he offered two years earlier: (47) a body of ex
officio and working commissioners (the latter in life
posts) under ministerial guidance, and under the legal
authority of the Judicial Committee of the Privy Council.
The Commission was charged with 'promoting education and
regulating charities.' To achieve its purpose it was to
be given 'school inspectors' and certain powers in regard
to local rates. This was certainly a 'commission to
direct education,' and charity was not to benefit from the
association. Brougham's bill never even reached the
House of Commons, nor did this bill or its successors (48)
pass a second reading in the Lords.

Brougham's bills showed the kind of Charity
Commissioners he had in mind, and the picture which
emerged was not apt to gain wide support. He proposed
the membership of the Lord President of the Council, the
Lord Privy Seal, the Home Secretary, and the Speaker of
the House, plus three life Commissioners (serjeants or
barristers). The latter would exercise all the powers of
the existing Commissioners, plus power to fill trust
vacancies, approve sales, advise on funds, take applications for educational funds, assist in removal of schoolmasters, call for charity accounts, summon trustees, and
make decrees. The powers and actions of the Commission
were subject to appeal to the Judicial Committee of the
Privy Council (thereby bypassing Chancery). The 1837 bill
added ten school inspectors, with powers analogous to the
existing Charity Commissioners; a treasurer of charities
was also added to receive the charity funds held by the
Accountant General, as well as all which might be voluntarily transferred.

In the Spring of 1837, the Chief Commissioner and some
of his minions were absorbed in the new proposal, and the
extension of the old, to the detriment of an orderly conclusion to the inquiry. Two days after Brougham's bill
was introduced, Daniel Finch wrote and requested nomin-

ation as a Commissioner under the new plan. He told
Brougham that he rested his hopes on 'your lordship's
kindness to me,' and he pleaded, 'having given up my profession for the Charity Commission, this is to me of the
utmost importance.' (49) Others also expressed an interest to the Chief Commissioner, including Samuel Smith,
who wrote to ask to be considered for 'the permanent Board
contemplated by your Lordship's bill now in Parliament.'
(50) Some were less ambitious in their objective: William
Miles wrote to Hine and asked for a copy of the bill, 'and
can you (in confidence) inform me what will be the presumed salary of Inspectors of Schools under the permanent
Commission?' (51) The clerks were doubly interested in
the division of the spoils, as Charles Tucker noted in a
letter to Hine:

> I presume in Lord Brougham's Bill, when he decided on
> having a Secretary and two clerks he must have had in
> view the long & meritorious services of yourself,
> Troward & myself. The three paid Commissioners does
> not so exactly fit the number of expectants. (52)

There was some interest other than patronage. The Commissioners were considering the terms of the bill, and
making recommendations to its sponsor, as the following
from William Grant to Hine makes clear:

> The formation of the board, if properly constituted,
> will be a great blessing to the country ... you may
> show these (revisions) to Mr Finch & Mr Smith who no
> doubt have been exercising their judgment on the bill
> & giving it the benefit of their experience ... you
> will either submit our suggestions to Lord Brougham or
> not as you think meet. (53)

Grant continued to show an interest in the composition of
the bill, and wrote again to Hine a few days later:

> I have been thinking about an addition to Lord
> Brougham's Bill by giving facilities for recovering in
> ejectment against tenants & occupiers who have got into
> possession & hold in spite of trustees.... We once had
> a plan for vesting all Charity estates in some individ-
> ual.... I think in the proceedings of D.W. Harvey's
> committee it was considered desirable that the new
> Board contemplated should be a corporation, but there
> is no provision of that sort in the Bill. (54)

Of course the Commissioners had some current business on
their minds, and as 1 March drew near, they had to obtain
a renewal, or face extinction. The Commission's powers
were extended for four months (7 William IV c. 4), but
they were not granted any further funds. (55) This meant
that official travel virtually ceased from March, and the
Commissioners were turned to the final preparation of
their reports.

But with what many obviously regarded as the probability of a permanent 'extension' in Brougham's new Commission, there was no attention given to preparation of a Final Report. In June the bill ran into trouble in the Lords, and on the 26th its second reading was held up, and on the 29th the order of the day was 'discharged.' (56) Suddenly there was a need for a concluding document. On 26 June, Hine wrote to at least two Commissioners (Fellows and Martin) and asked them to prepare suggestions for a final report. (57) On 30 June the Board met, confirmed the solicitation of ideas, appointed a committee to draft the report, and set a date to meet and approve the draft. (58) The drafting committee consisted of the four senior stipendiaries: Grant, Finch, Wrottesley, and Smith, plus the only other man who had been on the Commission from the beginning, John Warren, now an honorary Commissioner.

The committee met at Grant's house on 7 July and composed a draft which was submitted and approved by the Board on 10 July. The Final Report was signed by all the stipendiary Commissioners, but only by one honorary, John Warren. Lord Brougham, Robert Eden, and Henry Milman added an endorsement

> imparting their entire concurrence in it, his Lordship
> having been of opinion that, with reference to the
> suggestions contained in the report, they should appear
> to proceed, as in fact they did, from Commissioners
> who had been personally engaged in the inquiries. (59)

But seven others also did not sign, and only one, Sir E.B. Sugden, left an account of his reason. In the Commons on 28 November 1837 he stated (when the report was presented) that he did not wish to see 'another tribunal' created. Strangely enough, the report made no direct recommendation even mention of such a board. One can only conclude that such a body had been a focus of discussion in the report's preparation, and for that and possibly other reasons, the report received only the partial support of the members. (60)

The Final Report listed eleven faults in charitable trust administration, and for most of them it mentioned a vague course of corrective action. (61) However, in no case did the Board go beyond recommendations to concrete proposals. There were some fairly clear hints in the direction of a permanent board, but nothing like the Hints of 1833.

The first flaw noted was the expense and difficulty of replacing trustees, and it was observed that 'an easy and inexpensive mode of appointing trustees ... is much wanted.' No proposal was offered. The lack of a safe deposit for deeds and the risky practice of loaning funds

on personal security were both criticised, but without
constructive remedies. The fourth and fifth points
related to the problem of trustee-turnover: that funds
with low interest ate up most of their profits in transfer-
deed costs and that claiming dividends from the Bank of
England was complex and costly, especially when trustees
had been changed. The last six observations dealt with
powers of trust management which were deemed insufficient
or badly used. For instance, Commissioners complained of
the difficulty of varying trusts. There must be 'a competent jurisdiction attended with less expense and delay'
than Chancery or Parliament 'to vary the directions of
the founder.' Likewise, to remove unfit schoolmasters,
to authorize property alterations, to correct 'indiscriminate distribution,' to keep charitable trust and
parochial funds separate, there had to be a new jurisdiction. Finally, the report complained that the Attorney
General was not supervising cases 'effectually' and thus
some frivolous cases were being brought against charities.

The implication could not have been clearer. There
must be a new power, a new agency. Why did the Commissioners not come right out and say what it should be? Why
did they not make recommendations which were more to the
point? The possible reasons were, first, that the internal debate (confined it seems to honorary Commissioners)
necessitated a moderated statement; second, that there was
genuine disagreement on what constituted 'some competent
authority;' third, the Commission was both unprepared
and disarmed by Brougham's bill: its failure meant a last-
minute rush to prepare a report; and the bill had also
prepared a bed of nails, since it was a very strong 'commission' bill. Brougham himself showed expectation of
reaction, when he divorced himself personally, but with
tact, from the Final Report.

The report was discussed only briefly in the Commons
in November. At that time, Hume asked what the government's plans were, and Russell said it was being left up
to Brougham. Then Sugden stated his objection and reason
for not signing. The report had clearly settled nothing
and probably satisfied no one.

The intervals in the career of the Charity Commission
were useful points for measurement of the Commission's
work. They were also important stages of observation, by
contemporaries, of what the Commission was doing. A very
costly job was drawing more and more attention, especially
as the Commission process became more widely used and more
closely scrutinized.

Unfortunately for the Charity Commission, the job of
legal research and ad hoc reform which it did so well was

poorly understood at the time. The Commission tended to b
be seen either as an adjunct of Chancery or as a Commission of Public Instruction. Both images showed that
the 'advanced' inquiry body of 1818 was overtaken by the
sweep of events in the next two decades. The backwash
prevented it from proceeding to an orderly conclusion.

8

◇◇◇

Evaluation

◇◇◇

When the inquiry officially expired, its work was far from complete. Reports kept appearing and the campaign for establishment went on. The latter was a long story - so long that we must reserve it for separate treatment in the next chapter. But since inquiry ended in July 1837, we ought to make an evaluation of the process at this point in our story.

What had the Commissioners done, and how well had they done it? There are two possible levels of evaluation: that of the inquiry itself, or that of its subject, the charitable trusts. The former is of primary interest to us, though the latter cannot be ignored. In the case of the inquiry, we have a generous supply of information and a reasonable prospect of digesting it. Regrettably, the same cannot be said for the 'before' and 'after' of the charitable trusts.

A contemporary analysis would no doubt have begun with a tally of the expenditure of the Commission. An evaluation by Hume or Harvey would most certainly have done so. The next focus of the time would be - indeed was - on the cases certified to Chancery in the name of the Commissioners. Beyond these, the more mundane achievements of local reform and central reporting and registration complete the picture of the work of the Commission.

When we have examined the inquiry in these respects, the work and its value will be very clear. These studies also will create an impression of the charitable trust as it was affected by the inquiry. But converting that impression into a concrete reality will be impossible, for the inquiry was quite literally incomparable -save with later inquiries. There are moreover, serious problems in quantifying the data on charitable trusts, largely stemming from the obvious fact that Commissioners were taking legal depositions, not statistical enumerations. (See p.198.)

The general evaluation of the inquiry which ended in 1837 must be that it was a worthwhile and economical enterprise, which was crucial as a beginning in renovating and maintaining charitable trusts in England and Wales.

I

The costs of the Commission, as they were measured by contemporaries, are our principal guide, though we may add some elaboration and qualification to render the sums more intelligible. The true costs will be better appreciated with the aid of relevant contemporary data on commissions, and a sampling of related costs in a special 'value-index.' Finally, costs will only be fully understood when they are juxtaposed with the benefits which they helped to produce.

TABLE 3   Charity Commission cost analysis

A   Expenditure allowed (a)

Salaries:	Commissioners	163,000
	Clerks	24,275
	Secretaries	7,773
Expenses:	Other salaries	
	Travel	
	Rent, etc.	
	@ £8,000/year	122,000
TOTAL		317,498

B   Treasury payments

Date/payment (£)		Date/payment (£)	
19/7/19	2,985	30/6/29	13,049
30/6/20	20,152	30/6/30	12,852
30/6/21	15,882	5/3/32	3,369
30/6/22	15,425	31/3/33	20,334
30/6/23	15,867	31/3/34	16,353
30/6/24	15,443	31/3/35	1,717
30/6/25	14,842	31/3/36	5,924
30/6/26	14,909	3/8/37	27,012
7/7/27	15,432	26/6/41	14,206
12/7/28	15,803		
TOTAL			261,826

Source: A Statutes and HC Resolutions; B Treasury Return
(1846.XXV.279).
(a) Figures based upon months in actual service X allowed
rates of expenditure. The 'expense allowance' for the
first twelve months was only £4000.

On the basis of the allowances and the actual disbursements, it is clear that the Commission, while very costly,
remained within its limit, in fact nearly fifteen per cent
below it. We must recognize that the allowances were
themselves only a rough estimate, but the fact remains
that the Commission did not overspend.
One item not reflected in the data in Table 3 was the
cost of printing. We have several estimates, but no hard
figures, even though there was considerable inquiry into
printing costs in the 1830s. (1) The best guides to the
particular costs of printing specific documents came too
late to yield exact data on the Charity Commission. (2)
However, the various returns generally confirm the figures
given in a speech by Daniel Harvey, who put the cost of
printing the Charity Commission reports at somewhere between £600 and £700 per volume. On this basis, the total
cost of printing, including all indexes and digests (forty
four volumes) would have been in excess of £28,000. (3)
Finally, one or two minor items were not included in
the Treasury payments in Table 3. For example, the
Charity Commissioners were recorded as receiving two payments under 'civil contingencies' in 1835(£344) and in
1836 (£131). (4) Moreover, it was reported that the
Charity Commission received the following out of the
bounty of the Stationery Office: (5)

    1836-7   £201
    1838   £93
    1839   £26
    1840   £11
    1841   5s. 11d.

With all the 'extras,' the total cost came to about
£291,000.
Whatever the precise monetary cost, we may begin to
focus the figures by a comparison with other Commissions
of Inquiry. Recognizing that all commissions were engaged
in vastly different enterprises and under widely varied
terms and conditions, we can nevertheless summarise the
gross and yearly expenditures of a broad group. The
figures in Table 4 are by no means complete, and no
general ranking of commissions of inquiry is intended.
Rather, the information provided indicates that while the
Charity Commission was one of the costliest of inquiries
in gross terms, its annual average expenditure was much
less abnormal.

TABLE 4   Cost of Commissions of Inquiry, 1807-53

Title	Total	Average
A		
Public Records	126,080	6,304
Fees (Ire)	71,500	11,916
Military	68,300	13,660
Schools (Ire)	17,337	866
Navy	10,572	3,524
Cold Bath Fields	44	44
New Forest	4,500	4,500
Bogs (Ire)	21,556	5,389
Saleable offices	177	177
Records (Ire)	85,421	5,389
Laws (Jersey)	4,543	4,543
Malta	8,050	8,050
Office of Works	9,168	3,056
Lincoln gaol	996	996
Lancaster gaol	996	996
Windsor Forest	14,838	4,946
Royal Canal (Ire)	5,727	1,432
Courts (Eng)	54,117	6,766
Guernsey	3,680	3,680
Fleet and Marshalsea	1,111	1,111
Courts (Scot)	28,206	4,029
Customs and Excise	5,539	692
CHARITIES (a)	121,248	13,472
Courts (Ire)	86,282	7,190
Forgery	676	676
Weights and Measures	256	256
Ilchester gaol	716	358
Negroes	2,647	662
Leeward Islands	17,267	5,755
Courts (Scot)	2,648	2,648
Revenue (UK)	59,125	9,854
New South Wales	10,462	2,615
Land Revenue (Ire)	9,199	1,533
Cape, Ceylon, etc.	35,244	8,811
Chancery	5,909	1,969
Education (Ire)	39,271	13,090
Law (W.I.)	20,903	6,968
Sierra Leone	2,575	1,288
B		
Justice (Ire)	3,784	3,784
Common Law	24,397	6,099
Real Property	27,500	13,750
CHARITIES (a)	79,350	15,870

Title	Total	Average
Municipal Corp. (Eng)	75,150	18,770
Law Digest	55,461	5,042
County Rates	3,453	1,727
Excise Revenue	6,000	6,000
Religious Instr (Ire)	36,800	36,800
Religious Instr (Scot)	20,425	6,808
Railways (Ire)	24,842	8,281
Handloom Weavers	5,457	2,737
Child Employment	8,761	2,920
Health of Towns	6,500	3,250
Poor Law (Scot)	7,000	7,000
River Shannon	40,643	5,809
Law (Channel Is.)	1,500	1,500
Metro Sanitary	600	600
Estates (Ire)	81,279	13,547
Corrupt Practices	16,000	16,000
Laws (Ire)	2,700	900
Slave Compensation	49,999	21,428
Turnpike Trust (Wales)	2,891	1,445

Source: A Return of Commissions 1826-7.XX.503; B Return of Commissions 1856.XXXIX.716
(a) These figures do not cover the years 1827-30.

There remains one further basis for cost evaluation. We may look at the Commission's expenditure within the context of an index of contemporary values or quantities. Representing current relevant levels of expenditure, these quantities will help to further clarify the dimensions of the cost of the Charity Commission.

TABLE 5   Contemporary value index

Equity expenditures (£)		Relevant Incomes (£)	
1. Establishment	200,000	1. Charitable trusts	
2. Legal costs (est)	30,000	(reported)	1,199,227
3. Suitors' Fund	2,146,008	2. Charitable trusts	
1832 dividends	59,243	(exempt (est)	500,000
1832 payments	45,077	3. Other charity	
4. Six clerks' com-		(est)	2,500,000
pensation (1842)	1,388,424	4. Church revenue	177,479
		5. Poor relief	6,118,000
		6. Savings Banks	734,250

Explanatory Notes

1. John Miller, 'An Inquiry into the Present State of the Civil Law of England' (1825), p.79 puts this as the lowest estimate for all fees, emoluments, etc.

2. An estimate based upon 5 per cent of all trusts obtaining some legal assistance (deed, conveyance, litigation) at an arbitrary £20 for each case.

3. These are the highest values of a series (1800-32) 1833.XXXI.253.

4. 1843.XLIV.159 (5, 6 Vict. 103)

1. A corrected total, in 1877.LXVI.15.

2. Estimate based upon an (adjusted) total of:

Universities (1873.XXXVII)	444,000
Public schools	30,000
Church, other	26,000

3. Sampson Low, 'Charities of London' (1850), p.452 (adjusted).

4. Diocesan revenue, 1830 (1851.XLII).

5. Average annual expenditure, 1818-37 (1845.XLI. 393).

6. Figure based on 3 per cent of assets reported for 1841 (Statistical Abstract 1854.XXXIX.131).

The value index shows that in the narrow field of the courts of equity, the annual expenditure of £14,000 on charitable trusts was a none too extravagant figure. In all probability the regular legal costs of trusts far exceeded the cost of the Commission. Moreover, regular legal fees brought far slower and smaller returns than the work of the Commissioners. On the wider view of equity, the cost of the entire Commission was barely up to that of the whole equity establishment for a single year! Indeed, the Suitor's Fund could have paid the annual Charity Commission bill in 1832, merely using the surplus of dividends. Finally, the great 'reform' of removing the Six Clerks cost enough to pay for the Charity Commission four times over!

The incomes involved in charitable trust investigation were as significant as the sums expended, but they were less well recorded and require more ambitious estimating. The trust income reported by the original inquiry (£1,209,394) was slightly revised by the permanent Commission, but not markedly. The true income of all charitable trusts must be estimated by the addition of those funds exempted from the inquiry. Unfortunately there were no satisfactory public records for most of these funds, but it seems likely that they amounted to another £500,000 at least. The probable total of non-endowment charity funds exceeded the endowed, and the combined charity income came to £4.2 million.

The significance of these income figures also lies in their relation to the annual Commission cost. Adopting the 'salvage fee' concept, we can see that a mere 1.25 per cent of the income (of trusts investigated) would have covered the cost of the Charity Commission.

Even allowing for wide margins of error, the expense of the Charity Commission was reasonable. Although a monetary justification was never offered at the time of the Commission inquiry, undoubtedly the responsible legal and political leaders were aware of the quantities involved (however generally), and in that awareness, approved of the costly investigation. Of course the most meaningful way of looking at the cost of the inquiry is by ranging expense against results. The latter may be taken in several classes, for convenience of analysis: the cases litigated, the trusts renovated, and charities reported (or registered). In each category there were important and sometimes measurable gains, with which we may complete our assessment.

II

Certification was the most serious, the most visible, and the most troublesome course of action which the Commissioners could take to correct an irregularity in charitable trust operation. Until 1831 it was the only legal power bestowed on the Commission. Yet its severity, or rather the severity of Chancery, was all too well known to the Commissioners. Thus, as we have already seen, the certification process was often used as a threat, and it was quite an intimidating one.

Contemporaries like Joseph Hume and Daniel Harvey saw the small number of certifications as a sign of Charity Commission softness or failure, and their attitude was echoed in the 1849 Commission 'inquiring into those cases which were investigated and reported upon by the Charity Commissioners but not certified to the Attorney-General.' (6) Of course, this judgment was the corollary of those strong impressions of corruption, whether or not they had been satisfied by the findings of the inquiry. Before we can judge the meaning of the numbers, we ought to review the reasons for certification, the process itself, and its effectiveness as a method of reform.

As noted above, there were two basic types of certification, hostile and friendly. The former were those instances where an abuse was found which trustees refused to recognize or to correct, and which Commissioners then had to put to the Attorney-General. The friendly certification was that in which the trustees did not oppose action, but rather required the formal approval of the court for some alteration or amendment of the trust.

In the actual working of the Commission we have found that certification lent itself to a form of benign extortion or blackmail, being held over trustees and others as a threat to make them reform. We can see that not only were cases held up inside the Commission, but also, there were a number of cases settled after certification but before the proceedings were well under way. These must be the slower or more stubborn cousins of those which surrendered earlier (see Table 6, column g).

TABLE 6   Returns of cases certified to Chancery, 1828-52

Re-turn	(a) Bills	(b) Set-tled	(c) Costs £ s. d.			(d) Peti-tion	(e) Set-tled	(f) Costs £ s. d.			(g) No. Pro-ceed
1828	53	7	680	17	5	18	8	779	12	6	11
1829	5	6	840	6	4	3	0	-			1
1830	16	6	904	6	5	4	4	183	3	4	8
1831	8	1	47	3	1	2	5	518	9	7	0
1833	2	6	742	9	6	2	3	410	19	10	0
1835	8	3	187	0	0	0	0	-			6
1837 -8	79	7	363	6	10	10	2	53	11	0	0
1841	56	11	699	12	0	16	3	118	3	8	0
1852	54	162	66,304	4	9	12	23	2,666	2	7	0
	281	209	70,769	16	4	67	48	4,730	2	6	26

Source: Returns of Informations, etc. 1828.XXI.7; 1829. XXI; 1830.XXIX.409; 1831.XV.45; 1833.XXXI.283; 1835.XL. 457; 1837-8.XXXVIII.1; 1841.XIII.249; 1852.XXXVIII.361.

As for the outcome, the vast majority of the cases (about ninety-five per cent) were won. (7) This reflects the reserve used in certification and the careful screening by the Commissioners (individually and at the board), as well as by the solicitor, counsel and Attorney-General. As the figures indicate, the certification process was tedious and expensive. The charity funds paid for approximately two thirds of the costs involved. As a method of 'reform' this could effect any change proven (within the Chancery rules) to be vital and legal. Moreover, this process was something more than a stepped-up version of

the old routine. By allowing another agency to interfere
in a judicial procedure, there was a considerable (if not
conspicuous) addition to ministerial authority.

On the whole, if the estimates we have were accurate,
the process of certification was a great financial success.
The Attorney-General in 1852 estimated that these cases
recovered £600,000 in charity property. (8) A few years
later, J.P. Fearon, the solicitor to the Attorney-General,
totalled the gains from 105 cases and found that they came
to over £600,000 in property after costs were deducted.
(9) And Fearon added that these were only the cases where
gain could be put in monetary terms. The other cases
where foundations were retrieved, schools reopened, trusts
reestablished, etc. were of considerable, if not measurable value. And these renovations were extensive.

. III

The second major method of reforming trusts was by amendment on the recommendation of the Commissioners. A wide
variety of legal and extralegal reforms were thus made.
The Commissioners were proud of this side of their work,
and they regretted that it was not better known to the
public at large. As John Warren told the Finance Committee in 1828:

> The Commissioners have in fact no remedial powers;
> they are only to inquire and report; but they have,
> where it appeared that the abuse could be remedied in
> that way, endeavoured to do so by representation to
> the parties, and pointing out to them in what manner
> their duty ought to be performed, and in very numerous
> cases their representations have been attended to, the
> misconduct has been corrected; that is a good result-
> ing from the labours of the Commissioners which does
> not always appear from their Reports; it has been
> silently performed, and so will have escaped public
> notice. (10)

Likewise, Samuel Smith wrote, in his letter forwarding
the draft of 'Hints' in 1833,

> We are I suppose, sufficiently unpopular, but I really
> think the world rather hard upon us, first in expecting
> immediate and direct results from the labours of those
> who are only empowered to 'inquire and report' and next
> in undervaluing what we have really done. I am quite
> sure that the indirect results of the inquiry have been
> very extensively beneficial. The numberless instances
> in which we have found the accounts of charity trustees
> commencing only with the year in which the Commission

was appointed, or in which intimation of the approaching visit was sent them has quite satisfied me on this
head.
   Their direct benefit has been very great in forming
a channel of communication and conciliation between
obstinate trustees and unreasonable parishioners, whose
small causes of offence had been aggravated into
quarrels - but more than all, in actually working out
the accomplishment of acts of justice, which tho' all
agreed that they ought to be done, yet were indefin-
itely postponed, till a convenient season. (11)
The Commissioners probably made recommendations in most of
the parishes they visited. The ones which did appear in
the reports have been collected and tabulated in Table 7;
though they do not represent the total of recommendations,
they should nevertheless constitute a fair sampling of the
whole. Some general observations must be made at first.
None of the tabulated recommendations was authorized or
required by the law under which the Commission operated.
The Commissioners were only directed to make 'suggestions'

TABLE 7 Charity Commissioners' renovations

Operations	917
Arrears	511
Investment	309
Leasing	173
Trusteeship	149
Legal Advice	53
Total	2,112

Source: Analytical Digest of Reports, 1843.XVI.XVII

or 'observations' in their reports to the crown, but
nothing was said about acting on these in local situations.
A second point was that some of these recommendations were
technically illegal or without sufficient authority to
stand up in court. It is possible that the more questionable acts were not cited in reports, and hence would not
appear here. There is no particular significance in the
numerical distribution in Table 7. It is only a rough
guide to types of recommendation. The leading category
('operations') is the most diverse, including all facets
of trust operation aside from property management and
trusteeship itself. It includes everything the trustees
did (or did wrong) in dispensing the income; in hiring,
firing and pensioning; in distribution of income; or in
accounting or record-keeping.

In the first of these areas, one of the serious problems which Commissioners encountered, and one which earned
a place in their Final Report, was the superannuated
schoolmaster. Smith included a point on pensions in his
'Hints,' to which he added this note:

There are many grades of misconduct, quite sufficient
to destroy the whole utility of a school, in which a
decree of dismissal by the Court of Chancery would be
by no means a matter of certainty. The remedy is at
all counts so slow, that to obtain any benefit from a
school, my colleague and myself (not to speak for
others) have been absolutely compelled to suggest some
such (pensioning) arrangement in 2 or 3 instances,
always however explaining its illegality.

At Mansfield we avoided (a pension) by inducing the
inhabitants to come forward with a voluntary subscription to buy out Mr Bowerbank (the schoolmaster).... At
Stourbridge we were obliged to recommend a pension from
the school funds, to a very objectionable usher - but
whose unpopularity arose from nothing criminal.

At Coventry, with the Bishop's sanction, we attempted the same thing - unfortunately we failed, the
illegality of the contract being the obstacle.

Smith admitted that the Commissioners had

total inability to deal with the worst abomination of
all - the grammar schools.... here we are quite useless
... unless by exceeding our powers and negociating (not
very legally) the removal of incapable or improperly
conducted masters. (12)

In the area of income distribution, the most common
complaint was that of improper application of funds to
public expenditure of one kind or another, frequently the
poor rate. Commissioners were quick to spot these violations, and often were able to correct them. When this
situation was discovered at Kirkby Ireleth (Lancashire)

We suggested to the parish officers at the time of our
inquiry, the impropriety of this mode of application;
and from the readiness which appeared on their part to
adopt such measures as should appear necessary for a
more proper mode of application in future, he hoped
that the different objects of these charities would
have been obtained ...

In consequence of our recommendation, there has been
a meeting of some of the principal inhabitants and
parish officers, but nothing has been settled at
present ...

From a letter sent to us by the minister of the
parish, stating the above facts, we have reason to hope
that the inhabitants will soon make a proper arrangement. (13)

Often these cases were mixed with some amount of arrears,
as for example in the case of Mary Barnes' Charity, St
Margaret, Lothbury (London). Under this bequest, two
apprentice funds were endowed, but since 1776 the account
'has been united with the Churchwardens' general account'
and the receipts of charity property 'greatly exceeded
the expenditure,' leaving a balance owing to the fund of
over £550. The Commissioners suggested a meeting, one
was held, and the vestry made an order to increase the
premiums, to resume the separate account and to reinstate
the trust. (14) Another case of fund-straying occurred in
Henley on Thames (Oxford). Robert Shard's charity was a
dole paid out of rents. The corporation held the land,
and one of its members was the tenant (and owner of the
surrounding land). The £8 rent was paid, but

> In consequence, as it appears of some mistake, there
> has been no specific application of the rent of this
> land for some years. It has been carried to the
> account of the bridge book, and disposed of with the
> other rents ... (of corporation property) This mistake,
> however, having been discovered, it was agreed at a
> meeting of the corporation, held on the 14th of Feb-
> ruary 1820, that the rent of this land shall in future
> be distributed amongst the poor, as it was formerly,
> in bread on Good Friday, and on the 5th of May. (15)

Distribution was also faulted on other grounds: that it
was 'indiscriminate' (i.e., distributed in small and useless amounts). A third way in which the Commission tried
to correct operations of trustees was to demand proper
accounts: either that they be begun, or resumed, or rect-
ified.

In the very large class of amendments as to arrears,
the Commission was dealing with the fundamental problem of
trust failure, in those circumstances where intervention
still happened to be in time to prevent complete loss; in
other words, those cases where stoppage or diversion or
other problems were of relatively recent origin.

When the Commissioners examined the charities of
Maghull (Lancashire) they found that the 'ancient poor
stock' of £120 had been laid out in the purchase of land
in 1815, but no deeds were to be found. As the current
rent was only £4, the Commissioners urged a search for
deeds, and an overhaul of the foundation. A vestry meeting was held, and the project was begun. (16)

When they investigated Lamplugh (Cumberland), the
Commissioners found 'from an entry in the parish books'
that a Mrs King left the interest of £5 to a schoolmaster
in 1722. The sum was either lost or misplaced, but it was
definitely not being paid in 1819. But the Commissioners

wrote that 'we have been informed by the Rev. Joseph
Gillbanks, the rector of Lamplugh, that a vestry has been
held ... £16 shall be raised by an equal assessment from
the several tenements in the parish' and the required
interest would be paid. (17)

Often the disruption of revenue came from complex
causes. Thus the charity of Sir Abraham Elton for teaching reading to children in Bristol, was impeded when the
two parishes involved (St Philip and St Jacob) were re-
organized in 1798 and separated in 1802. 'The tenants
were often defaulters,' the parishes hired a collection
agent, and some charity money went incorrectly into the
parish account. But the Commissioners were able to report
that

> Since our inquiry we have been given to understand,
> that the vestry has passed a resolution to pay back so
> much of this charity as has been unduly applied to
> general parish objects, and to employ such arrears in
> building or procuring a proper school room, and strict-
> ly effectuating the purposes of the donor by providing
> for the sound education of the poor children of the
> parish. (18)

Occasionally the complexity of a situation was exploited by trustees, as a means of avoiding payment. One such
case was that of Symonds's Almshouses in Hereford. When
Edmund Clark visited the city in 1836 he found that the
almshouse, given for 'four poor men,' had passed into the
patronage of one Mr Lewis:

> Shortly after Mr L. acquired the estate the only per-
> sons left in the houses were four women, the widows of
> persons legally placed in possession - whereupon arose
> a doubt in the mind of Mr Lewis whether money destined
> for poor men could lawfully be given to poor women. He
> consulted his attorney & it was settled between them
> that the widows must be ejected & four men were forth-
> with appointed to fill their places. But a decree and
> its execution are very different matters. The widows
> stood upon the defensive, and when an attempt was made
> to storm the premises, the doors were locked and the
> inmates appeared at the upper windows armed at all
> points with very offensive weapons. In short the
> widows gained the day & left Mr Lewis in a dilemma.
> He could not pay them because they were not men & he
> could not pay his nominees because they were not in
> the almshouses & he was therefore under the painful
> necessity of keeping the money in his pocket - a thing
> which has by lapse of time become habitual & he almost
> fainted when I told him he would be responsible for
> the arrears. (19)

The Commissioner advised Lewis to put the money in a
savings bank 'to await the result of future consideration.'
This done, the following was reported as the last note on
the affair:

> After some deliberation it was resolved that Mr Lewis
> should be required to pay the arrears to the poor men,
> and to continue their allowance as it became due. To
> this he has assented, and it is to be hoped that the
> intrusive occupation of the houses will soon cease, so
> as to allow the proper tenants to obtain possession.(20)

Whose 'deliberation' produced this result was not clear,
but the result was apparently a successful recovery of the
charity.

Trustees often strayed into difficulty in matters of
investment, and in a good number of cases the Commissioners took the liberty of directing some improvement. Most
cases of this kind involved money loaned on personal
security, a practice of which Commissioners invariably
disapproved. Their habitual advice was to recommend calling in such sums, and investing them in savings banks.

The leasing of charity lands posed a variety of problems. Though Brougham unhesitatingly labelled all of
these problems 'abuses,' some were understandable, and
most were correctable. The two basic grievances were the
practice of letting for lives and undervaluation. A
genuine abuse occurred in those instances where patrons
or trustees allowed favourable terms to tenants at a consequent loss to the trusts, without any extenuating circumstances. The mere existence of inadequate terms was
not an abuse. In any case, it was possible for the Charity Commission to correct many cases, either on their own
authority, or with the sanction (or threat) of Chancery.
So when the Commissioners examined John Day's Charity in
Cirencester (Gloucestershire), they found the estate
valued at £192 10s. 6d.

> This has been deemed an inadequate consideration for
> the land and tithes, and the lands have been lately
> valued by an experienced surveyor, and estimated at
> £263 10s. 10d. Upon the strength of that evaluation,
> the trustees have agreed to re-let the lands. (21)

Much less significant amounts also received the attention
of the Commissioners. When they visited Wrockwardine
Parish (Shropshire), they found a united fund which had
been used to purchase land, with the rental going to the
poor. In 1801 that rent had been set at £4.10s., but
according to the report

> The annual value of the land ... is stated to be £8;
> and in consequence of our suggestion, that the rent
> ought to be raised to that amount, it was resolved, at

a vestry meeting of the parish, held 5th May 1830, that
the sum of £8 should in future be paid by the parish
annually for the lands abovementioned, and that the
churchwardens and overseers should be thereby empowered
to distribute money to that amount among the deserving
poor on Good Friday in the next and every succeeding
year. (22)

The most serious fault which the Commissioners encountered was a failed trust. Here the case admitted of no
delay, and Commissioners acted to restore trustees either
where co-opting was sufficient, or by extraordinary means
if necessary. Often the renewal was undertaken on the
impulse of the Commissioners' initial visit. On the other
hand, some cases required further urging, as that of
Castlethorpe (Buckinghamshire). As Hine wrote to the
Vicar, William Singleton,

> With regard to the Poor's Allotment in the Parish of
> Castlethorpe a representation has been made at this
> office that ... Mr Joseph Kitelee is now the sole sur-
> viving Trustee; and that he is of very advanced age
> and is, besides, likely to remove from the parish.
> Under these circumstances it is suggested that it would
> be expedient that new Trustees should be appointed ...
> (23)

The Vicar replied several weeks later that 'a new trust
deed has been lately made and executed, and therefore
there are now four Trustees.' (24)

The Commission even moved on occasion to oust incumbent
trustees who were manifestly ineffective. When the
inquiry reached Skelmersdale (Lancashire), it found that

> ... the administration of the charities in this town-
> ship has been very much neglected. There are now very
> few resident trustees, and the persons who have lately
> had the management seem not to have been well qualified
> for the duties they have had to perform. (25)

The Commissioners recommended the resignation of the incumbents, and steps taken to relieve them of the funds in
their control were reported.

In their visit to the city of Durham, the Commissioners
found that in the parish of St Giles some charity land
had been wrongly sold, apparently because the trust had
failed. To resolve the matter, Commissioners 'recommended
that steps be taken for appointing new trustees' and that
a lease be substituted for the improper sale. The report
added that the buyer 'has consented to accept such lease
... and to concur, as far as he is able in completing the
arrangements we have proposed.' (26)

When the inquiry reached Hartlepool it found a critical
situation in the school trust. By a deed of 1795, there

had been seven trustees, but 'of these trustees, William
Sedgwick was in October 1828 the only survivor, except
Timothy Johnson, who had been for ten years a pauper in
the workhouse.... We suggested that another trustee should
be nominated in the room of Timothy Johnson, who declared
his readiness to assign over his interest in the premises.' (27)   There was certainly no place for a pauper in
managing the affairs of the poor.

Under old procedure, when a group of trustees had dissolved, a clumsy, time-consuming process was required to
re-establish the trust.   The court would order a search
for all heirs (of trustees, and the original donor). When
all parties were located or proven dead, the court could
set about composing a new trust, supervising the conveyances and drawing new deeds, etc.   The procedure was long
and costly, and as a rule completely beyond the means of
a small trust income.   There were some minor changes in
the law affecting this procedure between 1819 and 1830 (28)
but a major reform was first proposed in 1831.   In March
a bill was introduced, at the same time as renewal. Both
measures were held up as a result of dissolution in April.
The renewal bill passed in the Fall, but the bill for new
powers was delayed, and only introduced a week before the
issuance of the new Commission in December.   The bill
became law in January 1832, extending the powers of certification and adding a special provision for Commissioners
petitioning the court when trustees had disappeared.   But
the most innovative clause said

Whenever it shall appear to the said Commissioners ...
that the property belonging to any charity consists of
only one or more annuities or rent charges ... not
exceeding in the whole the yearly sum of twenty pounds,
and that there are no existing trustees or persons
legally qualified to receive and give an effectual
discharge for such annuity or rent charge ... it shall
and may be lawful for any Five of the said Commissioners, by writing under their hands and seals, to empower
the resident minister and the churchwardens or the
chapelwardens for the time being ... to receive the
said annuity or rent charge, annuities or rent charges
or any arrears thereof and to apply the same according
to the purposes of the charitable donations or bequests
thereof ... to remain in force until the trustees of
the said charity duly appointed shall appear and claim
the administration of the funds thereof, or until the
trustees of the said charity shall be appointed by the
Court of Chancery or the Court of Exchequer. (29)

The impact of the rent charge powers was very limited.
First, it could only apply to that thirty per cent of

charitable trusts which had not already been investigated
in the twenty-four reports preceding the 1831 Commission.
Next, of course, was its own limitation, to annuities or
rent charges, and to those of less than £20 value (later
raised to £50). These limits were not as severe as they
might seem, for the rent charge was a popular form of
bequest, and it was generally of small value, and its
value did not increase with inflation or other improvements.

But the statutory limitations on rent charge powers
were toughened somewhat by the Commissioners themselves.
In February 1833, they resolved that the power would be
used only where a Commissioner 'who shall have so inquired
shall think the granting of such power expedient for enforcing the payment or due application of the rent charge
or rent charges or for any other particular reason.' (30)
This may or may not have been a serious obstruction, as it
put the matter in the discretion of individuals. In among
the Commission papers there is one folder with nine
duplicates of powers for parishes in Buckingham which was
transcribed: 'The within powers were not granted, the
Commrs having on 9 Feby 1833 resolved to confine the
granting of such powers to cases where special reasons
could be assigned for doing so.' (31) Surely if the
latter wording was followed, very few powers might have
been issued. And as the bulk of duplicates surviving bear
the dates 1836 and 1837, it seems plausible that the Commissioners only used this power rather sparingly prior to
the last stage, when over 600 of the powers were actually
issued.

IV

The principal statutory function of the Commission was to
compile its reports on the state of charitable trusts. It
was these reports which were to be both a register of the
trusts and a revelation of their mistreatment. And of
course, the latter was supposed, in the minds of reformers,
to be sufficient to ignite further indignant and righteous
reform. As we have seen, reform was quite adequately inspired by simple necessity during the inquiry. But what
of the reports and their performance? First, we need to
understand how a report was made, then how they were produced and circulated, and finally, what steps were taken
to collate the information in them.

The report which every Commissioner tried to file on a
trust was built around a document of foundation, a
sequence of trust deeds, and a current account. When any

of these elements existed, it was sufficient to form
the basis of a report; when none of them existed, the
Commissioners could only proceed with some other tangible
evidence of a trust. In short, Commissioners had to be
informed of trusts, they could not literally discover
(except by accident) trusts which had been terminated or
had lapsed.

The actual unearthing of documents and construction of
a 'history' of each charitable trust was reasonably good
by legal standards of the day, though not always by standards of contemporary historians or antiquarians. (32)
Few trusts had unbroken histories, most had large lacunae.
Of course to all concerned, the main importance was the
current working of a facsimile of an earlier trust. Commissioners could not be fastidious about how much earlier
If an old deed or lease were found, confirming a trust
which corresponded approximately to current memory or
fact, it would be cited and hopefully accepted. A wide
range of dubious documents were used, and a fair amount
of information was based on tradition. Further, and again
in keeping with Chancery usage and practice, most information was in affadavit form. It was physically and eco-
nomically impossible for Commissioners to take evidence
in more direct fashion. Thus the reports were fallible.

Whatever the defects of composition may have been, we
must add an estimate of circulation to our account.
Brougham said in 1828 that 'many hundreds of copies of the
Commissioners' Reports had been spread all over the country.' (33) According to Luke Hansard, testifying before
the Select Committee on Public Documents in 1833, some
2,500 copies of each report had been printed. He also
conceded that he had 'many copies of those in hand' and
'the accumulation' of twenty-six Reports was 'very large.'
(34) In 1835, Joseph Parkes, Secretary to the Municipal
Corporations Commission, testified that his employers
found local reports 'in all the corporate towns in the
Kingdom' where the Charity Commissioners had investigated. (35)

To assist circulation, and to inform local authorities,
the Commissioners resolved in 1821 'that extracts from the
printed reports of this Commission shall be sent, if the
same can be conveniently done, to the Minister or Churchwardens of the different parishes of which the charities
are therein reported, as far as related to the charities
of each parish respectively.' (36) How completely this
was done is not clear, and evidently it did not become an
automatic procedure. While insufficient staff and funds
prevented full implementation, there were many cases where
extracts were sent, either on request or in the course of
correspondence.

Brougham commented on another form of circulation when
he said that 'in various places, portions of those reports
had been reprinted, to make all mankind acquainted with
the contents.' (37)   Allowing for Brougham's rhetorical
excess, it is certain that reprinting enhanced the
reports' impact.   It seems that such activity was un-
planned, and Brougham stated that 'he considered the reprinting of parts of the reports a very judicious proceeding, and was desirous that some plan be devised for
doing it more frequently.' (38)   No such plan seems to
have been devised and certainly none was implemented.
Still a large amount of reprinting was done, by Commissioners themselves, or with their consent, or by independent investigators.   In 1835, Parkes said that 'there is
hardly a single town of considerable population in the
kingdom in which the reports are not locally reprinted.'
(39)   Between direct reprints and indirect reproduction,
the Commission reports dominated charity literature in
the early 19th century. (40)

What was the impact of the original and the copied
reports?   In the simplest terms, the reports did only what
the publications of the 18th century had done - they
registered charitable trusts, more thoroughly and widely
than ever, and perhaps more cheaply, if Brougham was right
that 'the cheapest mode of registration was by means of
the press.'   But that was all the printed word could do.

On the other hand, there was much that could be done
with the reports in the way of summarizing their contents.
This had been recognized along the way, and in fact early
Digests of the reports had been made in 1832 and 1835 by
Daniel Finch, and he thus had had experience with the
process when he set about making the Digest of the whole
series. (41)   The plan of the Digest was actually quite
simple.   The counties were all summarized in alphabetical
order of parishes, and under each the donor's name/gift/
purpose/income/and observations were recorded.   There was
also a separate section added for General Charities, those
trusts which were not restricted in distribution to a
single locality.

Such a Digest was an extremely useful guide, but in
addition there was produced, at the conclusion, a 'Summary
of the Reports made by the Commissioners of Inquiry into
Charities.'   This was a two-part tabulation, with a
'Summary of Land and Principal Sums' and a 'Summary of
Income.'   In these one could see the county totals of
(1) acreage, three per cent stock, three and a half per cent
stock, four per cent stock, five per cent, Bank and India
stock and other mortgages, personal loans, turnpike investments, etc. as well as (2) rent, rent-charges, inter-

est, and educational income divided into: grammar schools, other schools, and charities given for or applied to education.

The Analytical Digest which comprised the 'final' results of the Commission, was compiled on the order of the House of Commons, of 31 March 1840. (42)   By this date, and more so by the date of publication of the Digest (1842), the matters raised by the Commission had passed into that limbo which they occupied for sixteen years after the expiration.   Therefore little was immediately done with the evidence thus presented.   But what was the picture of the charitable trust which emerged (if un-noticed) from the work of the inquiry?

The inquiry showed that the suspected scandals of trust were few and far between.   Indeed, Commissioners had spotted this very early in their work.   We can tell this from a paragraph which was deleted from the draft of the first introductory report:

> The Commn have to add that so far as they have hitherto extended their enquiries, after making allowance for some irregularities and errors which may have arisen in some few cases, they have no reason to think that (with the exception of - (if any cases) any instances of corrupt mismanagement in the conduct of these charities are to be found; and they have also reason to think that of late years more attention has been paid to the management and good conduct of these charities than was perhaps the case in former times. (43)

This impression, which may have been that of one of the minority hostile to the inquiry, was suppressed here, and did not appear in any subsequent report.   Nevertheless, it seems valid in the light of the collected evidence.   Some 400 certifications and about 2,100 renovations out of about 29,000 trusts means that over ninety per cent got a clean bill of health.   Of course the latter could have been the result of concealment, or whitewash, or incom-petence - or it could have been the true state of the trusts.   We can never know how much of the work of the inquiry was defective.   The later General Digest of 1871 suggested that the Commissioners overlooked about ten per cent of the trusts in their jurisdiction, which estimate constitutes the only simple external check on the veracity or competence of the Commission.   The general impression of the reports was that the work of the inquiry could not have been easily subverted or diverted.   Trust deeds which might have quietly vanished before 1818, steadily became more durable.

A sad postscript must be added here, for no reports and no recommendations, for that matter, no 'remedial powers' were going to retrieve those foundations which were so completely lost to memory that only a chance recollection or documentary trace remained. Actually, the Commissioners investigated a great many of these foundations, but all that showed in their reports was a brief line or listing to the effect that nothing had been found in way of proof. These losses were literally incalculable. The Commissioners may have only touched the top layer of a sunken mass. But as their basic method was to trace foundations through existing local evidence, they were stymied. Unless they could have planned a thorough combing of all registries, and integrated that with local follow up, they could not hope to do better.

Many leads of different kinds were pursued: where a gift was known, say through the Gilbert Returns, or a parish church tablet, but was no longer in evidence; where a parish or other trustee dispensed with a known gift, and no original document survived; or where only a rumour of a donation had survived. Many a parish report contained the forlorn heading 'Lost Charities,' for which there was no hope of recovery, regardless of remedial powers.

The Commission of Inquiry was clearly a valuable, economical, and productive enterprise, whatever the actual state of the trusts. Of course the inquiry rather awkwardly sliced across the body of trusts, leaving out a wealthy sector, and jaggedly cutting across a twenty-year span of time. These factors helped to give the reports their sprawling and incoherent quality. Keeping in mind that this was the first full survey, and thus naturally limited in what it could tell us about the trust situation, the result of the inquiry was indeed impressive.

COUNTING CHARITIES

It would seem that the reports of the Charity Commission should lend themselves to some form of quantitative analysis. Some tabulation of charities and income along the lines pursued by W.K. Jordan for Tudor and Stuart charity ought to be possible. (44) However, close examination shows that the attractive prospect hides treacherous pitfalls and raises serious questions about any work of this kind. There are two possible routes to follow: counting money values or counting units of charity. Both are unworkable when applied to the reports of the Charity Commission.

If one sets out to assess the monetary value of charitable trusts, there are six connected and concrete

obstacles. First, the valuation of property often was not
given in the deeds of trust.   There may or may not be a
description, which may or may not be precise, and the
proportion of property left in trust may itself be doubtful: residual amounts after the sale of estate were often
bequeathed. The first obstacle then is the case of total
absence of specified value. This can only be surmounted
by inspired guessing.

The second obstacle is in taking any bequest value as
it stands. We are usually not told about legacy duty,
land tax, rates, or other assessments. Were they part of
the gift, or should they (or some of them) be deducted?
Under this heading may be put those exciting but misleading cases where a bequest was not in fact available
after settlement of the estate.

The third obstacle is introduced by selection of a
tabular system, basing entries either on income or total
value. All must be rendered into one version, by some
uniform rate of conversion, for purposes of computation.
But ratios between property and income, whatever else we
know about them, can be safely described as fluid.   The
ratio will be relatively more stable (say from 1660 to
1760) at some times, but the widely-used five per cent or
twenty-years' purchase has to do violence to some properties. And for gifts of rent charges, for example, there
was no standard ratio. Finally, where the ratio is known
to deviate from the standard, say four per cent stock in
a system using a five per cent conversion, it is possible
to recompute the principal, but is it satisfactory?

The fifth obstacle is the worst of all, the bane of
commercial stability, inflation. As monetary values,
expressed in rents, wages, or prices, are subject to
change, any sequential calculation of these values must
take account of this change. Yet the incidence and
duration of price or other fluctuation was highly local-
ized and poorly recorded before the 20th century. Any
serious reconstruction of a comprehensive index seems
hopeless in the best circumstances. But much of the
period of industrialization, urbanization, enclosures and
war, was far from normal. If the effect of inflation
cannot be accurately calculated, we may either use an
estimated index, or we may ignore it as Professor Jordan
did. Either method leaves us with artificial figures. (45)

Finally, there are no adequate measurements of the
losses of charitable trusts to balance against foundations,
for a fair accounting. Before 1818, outside of local
surveys, Gilbert's Act, and Romilly's Act, there was only
one uniform charitable trust accounting - filing, enrolment or registry of deeds or wills, or other documents of

trust. In such circumstances, the principal exposure will
fall upon founding documents. In the pursuit of 'social
aspirations' such as Jordan's, it is easy to ignore later
losses. Yet it is unsatisfactory to use any such figures
for current assessments of philanthropic assets. Only
when a more thorough current accounting was instituted
(1818 -) could there be a better picture of losses. Of
course this accounting was instituted to impede losses,
and we have every reason to believe that they occurred.
But we can have no record or even general idea of the
earlier rate of loss. Jordan seems to have rashly minimized the effect. (46) Certainly the Charity Commission
reports dispute his view. In any case, to ignore the loss
question is irresponsible; to calculate its effect is
impossible.

Given these problems, one might be forgiven for
suggesting that it is hopeless to try to count charitable
trust values at foundation. But surely it should still
be possible to count the trusts themselves. This decept-
ively simple proposition falls on some of the same grounds
as its predecessor, and on others as well. The foremost
difficulty is defining the unit of measurement. What is a
charitable trust? A single gift? What about a subsequent
gift to a functioning trust? What about a multiple gift?
These and other instances force the definition to the
lowest common denominator: any gift of value, which constitutes a legally-binding trust. Even this is not the
end of the problem.

Once the liberal definition is given, the next question
is, gift to whom? What is a single gift? A grant to 'four
widows?' a dole to three parishes, a school to serve one
township and a nearby chapelry? These are difficult but
not insurmountable questions. But in surmounting them, we
will necessarily do some violence to the entities created
by the donors.

This distortion extends to the geography of charitable
trusts. What is to be done about inter-county trusts,
assuming that tabulation is on a county basis? Should
charity be counted in the donor's or the recipient's
community? Or should a separate 'general' category contain all of these?

A fourth problem for this 'simple' accounting comes
from the mixture of subscriptions and traditional endowments, a merger which occurred with growing frequency in
the later 18th century. If a subscription school is later
endowed, that may make it an endowed school from the date
of the bequest. But what if a collection is taken, and
that in turn is held in trust? What of a donor who leaves
his estate in trust to be distributed to subscription

charities? What of a school run concurrently on endowment
and subscription?

The Charity Commission survey was anything but comprehensive. That being the case, knowing that the
universities, some old schools and voluntary subscriptions
were left out, the uncomfortable fact is that the reports
represent one thing only: the status of selected institutions as described to the Charity Commission.

Bearing in mind that the Commissioners did not do the
kind of calculation we are considering, we may decide
that the inquiry was not made for statistical uses at
all. Instead, we may see that it was simply a tally of
charitable trust assets and income, only comparable at
the time of the inquiry. And even here, it must be noted
that the 'time of the inquiry' was a period of nineteen
years!

Establishment of the Charity Commission

There is a general belief that the Charity Commission
inquiry 'led to' the formation of the permanent Board of
Commissioners. This belief has no foundation outside of
a romantic myth about inquiries in general. Even so, the
belief has a fair pedigree, reaching from the Select Committee on the Charitable Trusts Acts (1884) to the Nathan
Committee (1952). (1) The actual history of the aftermath
shows that in only the least direct sense did the inquiry
'lead' to anything, especially the events of 1853.

The aftermath of the charity inquiry was about as
prolonged as the inquiry itself, and its tortuous un-
folding formed a fascinating epilogue to the inquiry, as
well as an intriguing introduction to the modern Commission. The conclusion of actual inquiring was not followed
by any positive legislative action. This was the consequence of internal weaknesses in the ranks of charity
reform aupporters. In the first place, we have already
seen how the chief architect of the Commission had over-
reached himself in 1837; he continued to promote his
'Education and Charities' bill through 1839. In the
second place, the Charity Commission was already behaving
in some respects like an office of government, perhaps
making it difficult to believe that it was not; this
fantasy persisted until 1841. Thirdly, the reform of
charitable trusts inevitably intersected with (or infringed upon) several other reforms: poor law, municipal
corporations, and Chancery reform in particular. This
fact (or combination) which had earlier sped the inquiry's
foundation, now stalled its continuation.

No lurking establishment dragons threatened the foundation of the Charity Commission at first. Only when some
serious developments looked like happening, from the mid-
1840s, were the elderly monsters aroused against charitable trust reform. The church, the universities, the

corporations and the companies were stout opponents, many of whom had sore toes from the earlier investigations - and all of whom were or had been experiencing one form or another of the commission of inquiry. The reform attempts of 1844-53 returned to and even intensified the experience of 1816-18. New scandals appeared, committees followed, as did another Commission. These triggered another string of Bills, finally culminating in the Charitable Trusts Act of 1853. This measure, however much it might resemble earlier schemes, was the product of the more recent reform endeavours. While the inquiry of 1818-37 was a vital preliminary, in no way did it lead to the established board.

We need to be cautious in defining the success represented by the initial establishment. The new board, more than anything else, was a bureaucratised agency of inquiry. While the Charity Commissioners did a small and growing share of actual management of trusts, the first large-scale undertaking of the new Board was a new inquiry to update the original. From 1861-75 the Commissioners collected, collated and published data. Their findings were a substantial confirmation of the original effort; moreover, they underlined the nature of what had been done in 1818-37: an inquiry was merely an exercise in data-collection. Others had to examine, assess, and act upon that collection.

I

In characteristically paradoxical fashion, the Charity Commission office in Great George Street stayed in business from 1837-41, some time after efforts to establish the Commissioners failed. The proponents and proposals for establishment were themselves largely to blame: the bills of Brougham which wedded educational and charity reform and administration; the schemes of others, including James Hine, which united Chancery and charity reform; and the occasional confluence of charity with the work of other reform bodies threatened to disrupt the already fragile efforts.

The last payment from the Treasury to the account of the Charity Commission was made on 26 June 1841. (2) The last publication under the aegis of the Commissioners was the Analytical Digest in 1842, (3) and nearly a hundred suits brought in the name of the Commissioners in Chancery were pending in 1852. (4) Between 1837 and 1841 over $14,000 was expended in arrears of salaries and in the same period, six volumes of reports, plus the Digest and

Index were printed. Even more interesting, however, were the legal proceedings. Some 110 informations and 28 petitions were brought in the name of the Commissioners after 1837. (See Table 6.)

In one sense, it is quite wrong to refer to these matters as after the Commission, for they were the clerical or legal consequences thereof; or the bureaucratic hangover therefrom. In order to do this business, the office remained in place and Secretary Hine was available at least part time. Correspondence was kept up at least through 1838, with ex-Commissioners and with the general public. (5) The work of compiling the last reports crept along, until part VI of the thirty-second report was submitted to the Home Office on 21 June 1841.

By the end of this period, it was clear that the Commission would not be perpetuated. But that had not been the appearance of the early months. We have already seen that Brougham's measure for a permanent Commission was stimulating hopes of establishment in 1837. As it turned out, his idea of a Commission of Public Instruction was not at all popular, though Brougham either could not or would not see this. He presented essentially the same Bill four times, between 1835 and 1839. In no case did the measure get any support in the Lords, and it never appeared in the Commons. The Bills only succeeded in pre-empting the field of general charitable trust legislation, and doing a bad job of it.

In these circumstances, when the true end of the Commission's existence came, Secretary James Hine wrote a long pamphlet in support of the permanent establishment of the Charity Commission. (6) Packed with documented cases and a selection of official reports, it was Hine's parting effort, a last desperate attempt to establish the Commission's findings. Hine's 'Observations' were neither well-organized nor well-designed to capture the public imagination. The pamphlet was a thoroughly competent, documented, and even moving account of the plight of charitable trusts, which having received all the attention of the Commissioners, were now to be abandoned to Chancery once more. The force of Hine's essay was dissipated by its cumbersome prose and its awkward structure, both in the main narrative and in the relegation of his cases to an Appendix where they could repose unread, alongside extracts of Select Committee and Charity Commission reports. No flourishes or flaunted scandalous extracts for Mr Hine. Rather, he squarely laid the argument on two questions. In a passage typical of his style, he said:

The necessity of a legislative measure for the super-

intendance and regulation of charities will be evinced,
if, as I believe, the two following propositions can be
incontrovertibly established:

1. That, as the Court of Chancery is the only tribunal which can at present be resorted to for the protection and regulation of property devoted to charitable purposes, a vast number of charities, which,
though of immense aggregate, are of small individual
amount, are, in consequence of the expense unavoidably
attendant on Equity proceedings, left, for all practical purposes, without a remedy for the inconveniences
and losses to which they are exposed.

2. That, as many proceedings which are instituted in
Chancery relative to charities originate in motives
more or less objectionable, and are not directed *bona
fide*, to the benefit of endowments; as such proceedings,
in numerous instances, are languidly conducted during
their progress, and often abandoned before they have
produced any useful result; and as, whether they are
prosecuted to a close or left incomplete, the funds of
the charities are often greatly impaired, and sometimes
wholly exhausted by the large amount of expenses incurred, an effectual control over the institution of
such proceedings, and a superintendance of them during
their progress are imperatively required. (7)

Under the verbiage, Hine was making a rather startling
assertion. The man who was one of those closest to the
process, as Solicitor and then Secretary (1821-41), was
saying that the process of suits, presumably not those of
Commissioners, was utterly corrupt. And the court was
utterly incapable of correcting the corruption: 'It is
perfectly consistent with a deep reverence for the Court
of Chancery to remark, that it acts only on the impulse of
the parties, and can scarcely ever, by a movement of its
own, accelerate the progress of a suit.' Nor could it
'discover motives' or the presence of 'combining to mis-
lead the Court,' for all evidence was on affadavit,
'unquestionably the worst form in which evidence can be
adduced.' Having said all this, Hine did not presume to
say that Chancery should be reformed, but only that a
Board of Charity Commissioners should be established 'for
purposes purely administrative.' (8)

Hine's proposed Board was specifically not to interfere
with Chancery, but to take over administrative questions,
and matters affecting small trusts 'such as from their
amount, never can be brought before the court.' Appeals
would lie to the Master of the Rolls or the Vice Chancellor, so conceivably the small charities would (if they
dared) get to be 'brought before the court.' The form and

details of Hine's plan were not very different from the
proposals he had made in 1834. The changes were the
addition of 'a limited number of assistant commissioners,'
a revised proposal for a treasurer of charities, and a
number of details on proceedings.

The striking thing about Hine's 'Observations' was
that his critique of Chancery (presumably a product of
his experience), had become more sour than ever. Yet his
solution still placed a new body under that court's
control, subject to its jurisdiction. He gave the Charity
Commission authority to screen all cases, to certify those
it thought fit, and to keep tabs on those that went in.
But Hine had to leave loopholes: the Court could grant
leave to petition (in spite of the Board) and the suitor
could appeal any order of the Board to the Master of the
Rolls or the Vice Chancellor. There were clear signs
that a Board so constituted would have become just another
layer of Chancery encrustation. But Hine's propositions
were even less successful than Brougham's Bills.

What we can see clearly in James Hine's 'Observations'
was the central obstacle to implementation of the Charity
Commission's recommendations: what to do about Chancery?
The court would apparently defy efforts to evade it à la
Brougham, and surely it would devour efforts to encroach
à la Hine. But Chancery, as we know, had been under surveillance since the beginning of the century, and by the
1840s it was showing signs of change. The reform of
Chancery was a constant, if submerged theme in the writing
and analysis of charitable trust reform, but major Chancery reform was not achieved until 1852, after a long
examination and preparation (1810-30) and three periods of
alteration (1831-3, 1841-2, 1852). As charitable trusts
remained in Chancery jurisdiction, therefore, any reform
of trust administration was bound to be intimately related
to the court, or reforms thereto. This is not the place
for a history of court reform, though it is a project
waiting for a hardy volunteer. But the phases of court
reform suggest a guide to the fortunes of charitable trust
administration. In the first wave of real reform, 1831-2,
Brougham was doing well to rid the court of accumulated
arrears and to initiate some staff reforms. It was not
until 1841-2 that the first major structural change came
with the abolition of the Six Clerks' Office. And the
third wave of reform in 1852 brought the abolition of the
Masters in Chancery. Therefore, by 1852, it was far
easier to envisage the kind of Chancery jurisdiction
'loss' implicit in the establishment of a permanent Charity Commission. Also, by that time the reforms in Bankruptcy, Lunacy, and the County Courts, had completely

altered the perspective on Chancery and its place in the legal system.

The Charity Commissioners' inquiry also stumbled across the path of new bodies and was diverted and delayed as a result. The reform of the Poor Law and of Municipal Corporations in different ways intersected with the Charity Commission and impeded the effort to institute a charity board. In the case of the Poor Law Commission, the problem was an overlap of jurisdiction. The Poor Law Commissioners were made honorary Charity Commissioners, but there was little sign of their participation, and they never signed a Charity report. In fact there soon was evidence of friction, when Poor Law Commissioners began to authorize the sale of parish properties, which in some cases turned out to be held in trust. After several cases where the two bodies came into direct conflict, meetings were held at the working level, and formal communication was begun. Hereafter, the Poor Law Commissioners obtained clearances from the Charity Commission in doubtful cases. (9) It is difficult to gauge the real significance of this overlap, beyond the obvious fact that it made more work for the Poor Law Commissioners, and it certainly was of no benefit to the Charity Commission.

The entanglement with the reform of municipal corporations was a more direct and complex case of conflict and resultant delay. The issue here was the corporation charities, and this class had some of the largest and some of the most corrupt trusts found by the Charity Commissioners. In 1835, since no disposition had been reached on charitable trusts generally, the Municipal Corporations Act (5 and 6 Will. IV, c. 76 sec 71) kept existing trustees in office until 1 August 1836, pending further legislation. That legislation never came, and meanwhile the Lord Chancellor was empowered by the Act to make orders for the administration of estates. According to Hine's 'Observations,' there were still many of these trusts unsettled in 1842.

The legal proceedings were involved in some confusion, as Hine explained to Rev. Christopher Napier of Morpeth Grammar School (19 November 1838)

No provision having been made by Parlt for these cases previously to Aug 1836 applications were in many instances made by petn to the Ld Chr on which his Lordship made references to a Master to approve of proper persons to be Trustees accy.

Doubts, I understand afterwards arose whether such appointments had the effect of vesting the legal estate in the property in the new trustees: and I find by a Return (1837.XLIV.1) lately made to Parlt that it has

now been made a question whether the Chr had the power
so to appoint them; in order to decide this, an appeal
in the case of the Norwich charities has been made to
the Ho. of Lords and is now pending. Till this is
decided, it appears by the return, that proceedings in
sevl suits relating to charities are suspended. (10)

Much of the delay was a political matter; a complicated
series of legislative moves only frustrated a clear solution. In the midst of these moves was the Brougham
proposal on Education and Charities. In 1835, his Bill
was put off on the issue of the municipal corporations.
In 1836, a sizeable dispute blew up over a proposal to
elect the new trustees. When a Bill on this subject
reached the House of Lords, it was dropped on the pretext
that the Peers were waiting for Brougham's Bill! (11)

There was no action in 1837, but in 1838 Lord Portman
offered a Bill to settle the smaller corporation charities,
and Hine said this was withdrawn 'in the expectation, it
is believed, of the adoption of a general measure for the
regulation of charities.' (12) We know what became of
those expectations, but in fact Brougham's Bill on Education and Charities in 1839 did have a new section specifically covering corporation charities. (13) By this point,
neither issue was able to force the measure beyond a first
reading.

In 1841 a measure offering to 'facilitate the transfer
of trust property' was presented, in hopes of settling
some of the corporate trusts. (14) This failed on its
second reading in the Lords. In 1843 a Bill passed the
Commons but did not reach the Lords, for appointing corporation trustees. The issue was only going to be settled
in the Charitable Trusts Act of 1853. Meanwhile, corporation trusts had gotten a sort of vengeance on the Charity
Commission.

One field where cooperation or rivalry might have been
expected, but apparently did not develop, was in the work
of the Committee of Council on Education, which from 1833
was administering grants ('in aid of private subscriptions') to schools through the National Society and the
British and Foreign School Society. (15) The Treasury
had decided, in setting rules for the grants, that 'due
inquiries should also be made ... whether there may not
be charitable funds, or public and private endowments
that might render any further grants inexpedient or unnecessary.' (16) The Charity Commission papers do not
indicate any contact with the Committee, and it is possible that the printed reports and early Digests were taken
as a satisfactory means of verification. On the other
hand, while Commissioners found many endowments for

education, there were certainly few communities where
additional funds would be 'inexpedient or unnecessary.'
Finally, a deeper reason for lack of contact was the fact
that the Committee was engaged in providing new facilities
for 'poor scholars,' whereas the Commission was looking
at older foundations. In any case, the Committee of
Council seems to have had little or no influence on the
charity inquiry, and we have no evidence that it was
instrumental in preventing the establishment of a permanent Commission.

Of course the Committee, and nearly everyone else, must
have shuddered at Lord Brougham's Commission of Public
Instruction. Probably such a measure could not have
passed either house at any time in the 19th century. But
certainly when the Chancery relation was unresolved, and
when new authorities were sources of distraction and not
support, there was little hope for a permanent board,
especially one with any degree of independence.

II

The pursuit of charitable trust reform was not only prolonged by internal confusion and friendly frustration.
It became clear, when the moves toward reform grew more
serious in the mid-1840s, that there was still very powerful residual establishment opposition. The Church, the
courts, the companies and the universities were chief
opponents. The Commissioners of Inquiry may have covered
the countryside and terrorized tiny trustees, but the big
powers were still relatively safe, and the big question
remained unanswered: would the state impose either a
regulatory power or a reformatory agency on charitable
trusts?

In the decade from 1844 to 1853, this question was
thrashed out at great length. One might be excused for
thinking that nothing had ever been done on the subject
of charity reform, for basic arguments as to abuses,
property rights, charitable duties, mortmain and the law
of inheritance all were rehearsed at very great length.
A spate of scandals appeared on schedule. A dozen bills
dealing directly with charitable trust regulation were
introduced, two Select Committees on Mortmain were conducted, and a further Commission of Inquiry was created
'to examine the cases reported but not certified' by the
old Commissioners.

The mere existence of prolonged debate was subject to
more than one interpretation. Perhaps this was 'the
usual period ... to arrive at maturity' and that 'fuller

and riper deliberation' were indeed the reason. (17) The
reform campaign was really a matter of finding an accept-
able formula for the administration of charitable trusts
- one which would bring some order to trust management
with the least disturbance to existing institutions.
The general direction of the campaign was one of pro-
gressively watering down measures: first an independent
judicial commission, then a commission to existing judges,
then an administrative commission under existing courts.
The last was enacted in 1853. It was a modified version
of the proposals of 1833 and 1834, and not quite as
advanced as the Select Committee plan of 1835.

The first phase of this search for a solution was
opened in 1844. Lord Chancellor Lyndhurst brought in a
Bill in June 'for securing the due administration of
charitable trusts.' (18) This would have given the
Secretary of State power to appoint two Commissioners,
two inspectors, a secretary, solicitor and clerks. The
Commission would have made and enforced regulations for
charitable trusts, or at least for those of up to £100
annual value (some eighty to ninety per cent). With
powers including direction and removal of trustees and
authority to make new schemes, this Commission did not
survive its second reading in the Lords.

Meanwhile, a Select Committee in the Commons had been
looking into the law of Mortmain, and its report found
that 'the operation of the laws is most unsatisfactory'
since litigation was complicated and the avowed object of
mortmain legislation was not aided. (19) The report did
not go as far as some witnesses who supported abolition,
but the tenor was clear: the restrictive law (9 Geo. II
c. 36) was wrong, was evaded, and was therefore pernicious.
While this action was indirectly related to charitable
trusts, it surely focused attention on anomalies in that
field. And this was sustained when, in 1845, 1846 and
1847 Bills were introduced for the abolition of the
'Mortmain Act,' as well as general liberalization of
bequests, and of powers of the Lord Chancellor (marshall-
ing assets), and of trustees (variance in restricted
cases). However, these Bills obtained little support,
and none reached committee stage.

The Lyndhurst Bill was resumed in 1845. This time it
came up in April, received the full attention of a Lords
Select Committee, and passed to the Commons on 1 July.
There the Bill met twenty-eight hostile petitions from
City companies, and was allowed to expire. The third and
last attempt by Lyndhurst was introduced in 19 February
1846. The new version called for three Commissioners,
the Master of the Rolls, a Master in Chancery, and a

Barrister of twelve years' standing. They were to have
the same powers as before, plus an income from a 'charity
administration fund,' i.e. a tax on trusts, similar to the
old idea of the 'salvage fee.' On 18 May, on the second
reading in the Lords, postponed since March, the Bill was
defeated by two votes. Lord Campbell admitted later that
the Whigs had 'very factiously' combined with Protection-
ists to embarrass the government. Indeed, he considered
it 'the death warrant of Sir Robert Peel's administration.'
(20) Be that as it may, the defeat was unquestionably the
death warrant for aggressive charitable trust administration.

  With the change of government, the new Lord Chancellor,
Lord Cottenham, tried to obtain a different form of
charitable trust regulation. His scheme was basically a
less bureaucratic and more judicially-oriented plan, which
came before Parliament in four different versions, 1847-51.
The first of these was presented 8 July 1847, but not
printed as the session ended (23 July). The essence was
to give the new county courts a role as registrars and
'bare' trustees. (21) An enlarged version of Cottenham's
Bill was brought in on 13 July 1848. (22) This provided
charitable trust regulation authority (for trusts of up
to £30 income) for county court judges; the Bill passed
the Lords, but arrived in the Commons in August, too late
for passage. In the following Spring, a similar Bill was
introduced in the House of Commons, adding administration
powers for charities in the income range of £30-100 for
a Master in Chancery. (23) This Bill was dropped after
the report stage in the Commons. In all probability, that
interruption was due to Joseph Hume's motion (20 June
1849) for an address to the crown. His target was the
Hospital of St Cross, Winchester, and his aim was to
direct the intervention of the Attorney-General. As Hume
had a list of twenty more cases, it was thought wise to
anticipate further motions by the creation of a Commission
(by royal warrant) to inquire into cases (like St Cross)
'reported but not certified.' (24)

  A fourth and final Cottenham Bill was introduced in
1850, passed the Commons, but failed its second reading
in the Lords. (25) This was a more elaborate plan still,
to make complex adjustments of judicial machinery for the
task of trust administration. While this Bill was still
in Committee in the Commons, the First Report of the 1849
Commission came out. (26) The research of this Commission,
through collected material from the first Commission, confirmed the suspicion that lack of an administrative
solution had allowed scandalous practice to continue.
They strongly urged a permanent board on the basis of the

1835 Committee's Report. The Commissioners drafted a
Bill which inaugurated a new phase in the search for an
administrative solution.

In 1851, Lord Chancellor Truro introduced the Com-
mission-inspired Bill, which recommended five Commissioners, two of them paid. The Commissioners would not be
judges, but they would be a board of inquiry, without a
judicial function. (27) The Bill went through careful
deliberation in the Lords, passed on 31 July, but only
got one reading in the Commons. The following year the
measure began in the Commons. An excellent speech by
Frederic Thesiger, the Attorney-General, reviewed the
history of inaction but was not effective enough to secure
passage. (28)

After another change of government in December 1852,
a Bill was brought in the Spring of 1853 by Lord Cranworth,
lately elevated to the woolsack. This proposal began its
three-month passage through the Lords as a prestigious
though powerless 'Board of Public Charities.' The members
were to be the Lord Chancellor, Lord President of the
Council, First Lord of the Treasury, Chancellor of the
Exchequer, Secretary of State for the Home Department,
three Privy Councillors, and two barristers of twelve
years' standing. The Board would have been able to
appoint inspectors, and it would approve schemes for
charities, subject to veto by resolution of either House.
(29) The Lords Committee threw out the luminaries and
substituted a Board of four Commissioners, three paid and
one honorary. It also stipulated that schemes made by
the Board would require the approval of an Act of Parliament. The Charity Commission was thus to be a Board of
Examiners, not unlike the original Commissioners. But at
last a permanent board was able to gain the majority
support of both houses. After its long passage through
the Lords, the Bill took five weeks to clear the Commons.
(30) It did not meet serious or sustained opposition
along the way. The Act received the Royal Assent on 20
August, the thirty-fifth anniversary of the original Commission.

J.P. Fearon was certainly right when he commented that
'it cannot be said that the legislation has been hasty.'
He added the further sound observation that 'it is probably true that it is still incomplete.' (31) Incomplete
or not, the Act of 1853 was an achievement, at least of
endurance. The fuller meaning of the new Commission would
only become clear when it began to operate.

III

The Charitable Trusts Act of 1853 created an innocuous
Board of Commissioners, a kind of permanent inquiry,
permanently understaffed, ignored, and isolated. That
Board proceeded to chip away at its task while it duti-
fully evolved a bureaucratic barony. By 1860, Parliament
augmented the Commission's authority and solidified its
mandate. As if in celebration, or commemoration, the
Board began a new charity inquiry in 1861. It is at this
point, with a glance at the results of the new inquiry,
that we may conclude our narrative.

The Board which emerged in 1853 'fell very short of the
recommendations of the Committee of 1835.' (32) The Commissioners were able to inquire, report, certify - and
they later added the administrative duties of an Official
Treasurer and Official Trustee. Fearon said, with some
aggravation, 'there is scarcely anything which the Commissioners have power themselves to do.' (33) All actions
were taken on the petition of others, and most acts were
under the jurisdiction of either the District Bankruptcy
Courts or the County Courts (for trusts of £30 or less
income) or the Vice Chancellor or Master of the Rolls.
Any suggested modification of a charitable trust had to
go to Chancery or to Parliament. So in statutory terms
there appeared to be no progress on the legal situation as
it had been before 1818. But just as the travelling
inquiry had become more than its statutory image, so the
permanent Board would become, by bureaucratic osmosis,
much more than its blueprint implied. The Commissioners
were able to assist and give the colour of legality to
innumerable arrangements made ad hoc in the days before
reform; what the Board did not have was a fundamental
shift of power to itself.

In order to accommodate the tasks which it had acquired,
the Charity Commission evolved a considerable bureaucratic
apparatus. In their first two months, the Commissioners
drafted 'regulations and instructions concerning applications,' which included detailed rules and a set of sixteen (16) printed forms for application to, notice from,
or inquiry by the Board. (34) This procedure was necessitated (or thought to be) by the fact that the Board was
expected to do most of its business by correspondence,
with investigation being reserved for the difficult cases.
They might have been reminded of the testimony of their
predecessor William Grant in 1835: 'We have a good deal of
correspondence ... and nothing is so unsatisfactory as the
information that we get by that mode, and I should be
unwilling to trust to it.' (35)

In all likelihood, the new Commissioners soon lost
their trust as well. The Board hoped to have 40,000
returns by March 1854. (36)   But they experienced the
greatest difficulty in getting simple returns. The Board
received accounts of 2,336 trusts in 1853; by 1855 this
was up to 8,499; it took a decade to reach 14,000.   Thus
it was simply impossible, without some added enforcement
power, to get a regular check on trusts.   The Board's
other major correspondence was in the requests or applications for aid.   These are shown, as reported, in Table 8.
As one of the old Commissioners might have observed, there
was no place to report the time and effort that went into
the compilation of the figures.

Table 8 does reflect the major developments in the
Board's power in the first decade. In 1855, the Secretary was designated as the 'Official Trustee' and as such
was empowered to hold lands on behalf of charitable foundations. (37)

TABLE 8   Charity Commission business, 1853-64

	Applications	Transfer Orders	Total Orders
1853	340	---	---
1854	1,100	---	---
1855	864	26	608
1856	1,007	181	999
1857	958	337	1,034
1858	1,289	403	1,281
1859	1,091	515	1,508
1860	1,094	529	1,556
1861	1,179	518	1,326
1862	1,234	616	1,440
1863	1,303	610	1,612
1864	1,369	671	1,728

Source: Charity Commission, Annual Reports.

This innovation brought an obvious measure of security to
many small trusts for whom the periodic necessity of conveyances and new deeds had posed a significant financial
threat. Of course the new power meant a major addition to
the correspondence and other routine duties of the Board.
The orders for transfers of property to the Official
Trustee quickly became the largest single class of orders
given by the Board. Along with this growth of course, the
funds in the custody of the Official Trustee rose from
the first reported figure of £145,603 (31 December 1856)

to £2,085,281 (31 December 1864). The Commissioners
issued orders on a wide range of other items, too broad
and diffuse to list in detail. Until 1860 the great bulk
of orders related to the actions taken in court, allowing
or directing a case or requesting an order. The author-
izations for sales were the next largest group. But when
the Commission was reformed in 1860 - allowing the Board
to issue orders in its own right without court approval -
the composition of orders shifted (and later recovered
from a slight slump in numbers). The number of orders
related to court action dropped to less than ten per cent,
and the orders of direct jurisdiction became paramount.
Now there were many things which the Commissioners did
'have power themselves to do.'

By the early 1860s the Charity Commission had reached
a point where the need was felt for a general digest.
The annual returns had failed to come in satisfactorily,
and the original Commission's reports were by now more
than twenty years old. The first published note of the
plan was in the ninth annual report in 1861.

> Our attention has been directed to the importance of
> endeavouring to supply the existing want of a General
> Digest ... of all Endowed Charities under our juris-
> diction, showing the present value, and the purposes
> and the application of their endowments, which may be
> of considerable interest and importance, and we have
> been accordingly engaged on the labour of collecting
> and arranging the materials for such a Digest, but the
> undertaking is of difficulty and magnitude, and will
> necessarily occupy a considerable period in its com-
> pletion. The result also can only be approximately
> complete, though perhaps little less important on that
> account. The annual returns made to our office are far
> too imperfect to afford the means of framing such a
> Digest, and the present value of the endowments, and
> the application, and even the number of the existing
> Charities, would be very incompletely represented by
> the existing Parliamentary Reports. It is necessary
> to found, on the information derived from these sources,
> extended inquiries, to be conducted principally by
> correspondence, by the local investigations which can
> be instituted by our inspectors, and by reference to
> documents sent for other purposes to our office, and
> to other accidental sources of information. (38)

The difficulty of the project was plain - as was the
reflection it cast over the preceding half-century's work.
The 'digesting' of charitable trusts was a much more complicated business than the successive plans for reform had
envisaged, and its completion was perhaps only a will o'

the wisp. Inquiry, it seemed, had no end. The Digest
mentioned here was regularly promised and its difficulty
was regularly cited over the following years, until its
'final' form in 1876 (the last of a series of installments,
published periodically since 1868!).

The new Digest was a great advance over its predecessor.
It was far more detailed and sophisticated, and as such
it came closer to the modern objective of inquiry: to
provide information which would be the basis for general
assessment and legislation. But even so, the matter of
charities still remained tangled with education and other
questions. The vision of a survey which would eradicate
abuse and point to a reform solution proved to be an
apparition. This suggests that inquiry remained overrated,
that its conduct and conclusions were hard to see and to
summarize at the time of its completion, a task not made
any easier by the fact that the makers of the inquiry
were now permanently established.

Commissions of Inquiry
and the Age of Reform

The experience of the Charity Commissioners in their
inquiry and its sequel ought to be an adequate warning to
those seeking a facile explanation of reform in general,
or of commissions of inquiry in particular. The Charity
Commission was a landmark - a renovative reform with a
renovated instrument; its value to philanthropy and
welfare has been known, if incompletely understood, and
now its historical importance may be clearer: a commission
of inquiry, early but no pioneer, socially-conscious but
conservative, unfulfilled but no failure. It was a
reform quite outside the range of explanation afforded by
our conventional assumptions.

Moreover, the Charity Commission experience contains
positive suggestions for the future study of commissions
and reforms. When we put the clues of the Charity Commission in the context of the Age of Reform, we can see
the need for a more careful assessment of commissions of
inquiry individually and collectively: the motives behind
them, how they were created, who composed them, how they
operated, and what they accomplished. For the commission
of inquiry remains a surprisingly dim and little-studied
phenomenon, even for the particularly popular ventures
into the poor law, the factories, and the municipal corporations. The initial inquiries here as elsewhere have
received little notice. (1) A study of commissions in
this critical period will encounter many of different
shape and scope than the Charity Commission, most of them
a great deal shorter and cheaper. But that body nevertheless can be used as a guide to the general form and
some of the specific problems which a commission study
must solve. And probably a series of individual studies
is needed before a satisfactory general analysis can be
attempted.

I

It takes very little imagination to divine the presence
of a major influence in the 160-odd royal commissions
of inquiry which were spawned between 1780 and 1850.
It takes a great deal of charity to condone the minimal
attention paid to this phenomenon by historians. The
Charity Commission may have been atypical, but then no
one has bothered to develop the type. As a device for
relating the Charity Commission to its context, and as an
illustration of the potential value of commission studies,
we may sketch some of the principal questions raised by
any inquiry and compare the 'answers' given by the Charity
Commission with those of some of its contemporaries.

The first obvious question is 'why?'. The motives were
a compound of both visible and invisible urges. On the
face of it, every inquiry was ipso facto a search for
facts - facts to aid decisions. But facts and acts have
always had several possible relationships. First, an
inquiry might be a genuine search for truth, with action
consistently based upon the answers; second, it might be
a self-serving quest for justification (possibly the
truth) for a decision already taken; or third, it might
be a sham search, with hopes of disguising a plan of
inaction.

In the dawn of the age of inquiry, it was easy to
believe that the first, or ideal, type was the norm.
The Charity Commission appeared to be close to this ideal
version, though some critics saw in it the telltale signs
of the two illegitimate types. The answer was that the
Charity Commission might have been a self-serving exercise
but for Brougham's 'divorce' in 1818; it could have been
a sham also, but the government was not sufficiently
smart or cynical - and it was not threatened by the reform
of charitable trusts. So by default, the only thing left
for the Charity Commission was the straight pattern. An
interesting confirmation of that status was seen in the
exposure of Commissioner Warren's diffidence (or carelessness) on the questions put by the 1828 Finance Committee.
These interested but uncommitted views were echoed in the
circulated questions and answers in the Commission's
papers (above, pp.160-1).

The motivation for inquiry varied, and there probably
was no pattern in the variation. In the early twenties
the government faced a crescendo of criticism on the
delays and costs of Chancery. Having already resorted
to a number of inquiries in this field, it was but a small
step to establish a Commission of Inquiry. (2) This particular Commission went to a group of judges and Chancery

barristers headed by the Lord Chancellor. As Bentham remarked, Lord Chancellor Eldon had advised the King 'to commission Lord Eldon to report on Lord Eldon.' (3) The Commission produced 'an apology for all the abuses of the court,' but it also gave a long and detailed set of proposals for revision of Chancery procedure. (4) The Chancery Commission was probably a 'sham' in design, even if it failed to be one in practice.

In some fine research on the Poor Law inquiry, Mark Blaug took the trouble to read the Reports and Appendices, and he concluded that the findings and recommendations did not match. (5) It was a clear case of a self-serving inquiry. Ideas and plans took precedence over actual findings. In each of these cases, there was a gap between motive and report which could lead to serious misunderstanding.

Our next step in exploring commissions takes us into the corridors of power, or at least into the closets of clerks, and the parade of parchment which constituted government action. Issuing a commission under the Great Seal in 1800 was yet a process of some pomp if little circumstance. Between 1780 and 1830, the process became perceptibly more routine and less awesome. Where once only a statute had been sufficient to initiate an inquiry, by 1820 there were several modes, the most prevalent being that of direct ministerial authorization. This direct process preceded and no doubt accelerated the drastic simplification of the clerical minuet in the third quarter of the 19th century. (6) Meanwhile, the ancient route persisted: a draft bill (with the sign manual and ministerial countersignature) went to the clerk of the Signet Office; the smooth bill made there (and re-signed) went to the Clerk of the Privy Seal; he issued a writ which was sent to the Clerk of the Crown in Chancery, who ordered the drafting and issue of the Commission under the Great Seal.

The shift to simplified ministerial authorization did not occur openly or abruptly, or for that matter with any keen sense of innovation. (7) The royal prerogative, 1688 notwithstanding, was theoretically capable of commanding any number of inquiries. But ministers seemed at first unwilling to use the power directly, and instead wanted parliamentary sanction. That (statutory) control was phased out, as the direct control of the sovereign was reduced. In the early 19th century a number of cases occurred where the Address of the House of Commons, or in one or two cases, reports of parliamentary committees, were taken as the basis for issuing a commission. Of course the essential power was still that of the pre-

rogative; once that power was no longer feared, and its
free use by ministers was accepted, the issue by means of
a warrant only became the dominant source of the commission of inquiry. This change was one important reflection
of the fundamental constitutional shift being confirmed
in this period - from a ruling sovereign to ministerial
rule.

The Charity Commission was actually old-fashioned in
this context. In its case, statute was required in part
because the initial proposal was made by a member of the
opposition. Also, the institutions affected, the size
and cost of the project, and the public interest in such
an inquiry all seemed to dictate the formal approval of
the legislature.

But most of the Charity Commission's contemporaries
were not statutory. What of them? The Courts Inquiry
(1815), the Customs and Excise Inquiry (1817) the Weights
and Measures Inquiry (1819) were the closest in point of
time, and none were statutory. The Common Law (1828) Real
Property Law (1829), Ecclesiastical Courts (1830), and
Public Accounts (1831) Commissions were likewise without
statutes. So were the better-known Poor Law (1832),
Factory (1833), and Municipal Corporation (1833) inquiries. About half of the foregoing list were initiated
by an Address, the remainder by warrant.

Given the significantly changing creation of commissions, we might expect a change in the composition of the
inquiries. Yet the selection process apparently was quite
consistent. The choice of commissioners was and remained
a ministerial one. The criteria, so far as they were
visible, were whether the commissioner should be an
office-holder, whether he should be paid, and whether (and
how) he was qualified.

The first two criteria were linked, in that for political reasons it was not possible to appoint a paid,
office-holding commissioner; for economic reasons it was
not possible to appoint an unpaid commissioner with no
other means of support. It is difficult to discern any
pattern in regard to salary. Certainly none is apparent
in Table 9, unless it is that staff were always paid. (8)
The mixed commission was a novelty at the time of the
Charity Commission, but became fairly regular thereafter.
Yet the picture in this area was really one of variety
and little else.

Most troublesome was the variable of 'qualification'.
This subjective measure has been much discussed in the
context of the so-called 'administrative revolution.'
In fact the commissioners were very hard to classify on
this basis. First, we have no reliable universal standard.

TABLE 9 Selected Royal Commissions of Inquiry, 1819-50

Title	Origin (a)	Term	Pay (b)	Initial report
Weights and Measures	W	1819-21	S	1819.XI.307.
Department of Stamps (c)	A	1821	O	1821.X.271.
Revenue, Irish and British	P	1821-5	CS	1822.XII,XIII.
Process of Courts of Law (S)	P	1823	S	1824.X.1.
Court of Chancery (E)	W	1824-6	S	1826.XV.1.
Common Law	A	1828-34	MS	1829.IX.1
Real Property Law	A	1828-33	CS	1829.X.1
Ecclesiastical Courts (EW)	W	1830	S	1831-2.XXIV.1.
Public Accounts	R	1831	S	1831.X.1.
Poor Laws (EW)	W	1832-4	MS	1834.XXVII.1.
Ecclesiastical Revenue (E)	W	1832-5	S	1834.XXIII.1.
Employment of Children in Factories (EWS)	A	1833-4	CS	1833.XX,XXI.
Municipal Corporations (E)	A	1833-7	CS	1835.XXIII.1.
Law Digest	W	1833-9	S	1834.XXVI.105.
State of Registers	W	1836-8	S	1837-8.XXVII. 377.
Handloom Weavers	A	1837-41	MS	1841.X.273
Employment of Children	A	1840-3	CS	1842.XV.1.
Health of Towns	W	1843-8	MS	1844.XVII.1.
Land Registration	R	1847-54	S	1850.XXXII.1.
Oxford University	W	1850-2	S	1852.XXII.1.
Cambridge University	W	1850-2	S	1852-3.XLIV.1.
Chancery (E)	W	1850-6	S	1852.XXI.1.

Source: Reports (as listed); Returns on Commissions-1834.
XLI.349; 1836.XXXVIII.491; 1837-8.XXXVI.191;
1842.XXVI.373; 1846.XXV.299; 1856.XXXVIII.395.

(a) P - Act of Parliament W - Warrant
A - Address R - Report

(b) O - no salary C - all commissioners salaried

S - staff salaried M - some commissioners salaried

(c) This Commission was issued by the Lords of the Treasury, and reports were made to them, not the crown. The initiating act was a resolution of the Committee of Supply (8 June 1819, 'CJ' LXXIV,509).

To fall back on general social background is to beg the question. Indeed, the most hopeful prospect lies in detailed study of the work done in the various commissions. Even here, there will be difficulties. For example, in the records of the Charity Commission it is possible to identify the authors of most reports, even before those reports were signed (by using itineraries, correspondence, and other records). However, the form of the individual reports varied so slightly over the years, and that form was so well set by its traditional legal requirements, that very little individual talent (or lack of it) shows through.

In their varied fields of action, commissions of inquiry were given very consistent powers. This did not necessarily mean they operated in the same manner, for of course they might act very differently within, and sometimes outside, the strict limits of their official powers. Thus, we need a careful analysis of what commissions' powers were, and how they were used. In every case, commissions of inquiry exercised quasi-judicial powers, summoning witnesses, calling for documents, administering oaths (backed by legal sanctions against perjury), and usually having access to courts. All commissions furthermore were expected to make reports to the crown, within a period and under conditions laid down in their founding document. Beyond these basic outlines, there was ample latitude for the Commissioners.

The variation in powers was probably greatest in areas outside the prescribed limits of a given commission. In the course of inquiry, commissioners were apt to extend or extrapolate from their mandated powers. The Charity Commissioners were perhaps an extreme example of this tendency. Where they encountered malpractice, their job was strictly to report it, and to add suggestions (in the report) for correction. But it seemed obvious and unavoidable to them, in the actual local situations, that they should 'animadvert' with the local authorities. This in turn led to involvement in local reform, and that involvement gradually edged the Commissioners along the line between inquiry and administration. The movement was facilitated by the peculiar power given to Commissioners in the form of certification to Chancery. Wielding such an instrument, the Charity Commissioners often tended to behave as prosecutors. Surely some had seen the law in this light: Brougham had said 'abuses were not properly denounced;' but the Commission's real task was an inquiry, with the prosecuting power added (and applied) for the small minority of transgressors.

What happened to other commissions? Only a full and

careful comparison of mandates and actions can answer
this. All of the commissions in Table 9 had the same
basic powers of inquiry and reporting. Only the Chancery
Commission of 1824 had other prescribed powers - in that
case, to 'make regulations' for the reform of Chancery
procedure. But equally important, if not moreso, would be
a comparison of these commissions' prescribed powers and
their actual performance. How many exceeded their nominal
capacity, and in what ways? This can only be established
by extensive examination and by detailed explanation of
what each commission of inquiry actually did.

One measure of our ignorance about commissions is the
confusion about what they did, or what they led to. There
are connections of some sort between commissions and their
reports, their agency successors, and larger reforms in
the respective fields of inquiry. But these connections
have only been poorly explored in separate cases, let
alone collectively. We tend to assume that a report or
action was a simple product of an inquiry. More dangerously, we tend to use such 'products' as indicators of
what reformers, or commissions, or their contemporaries
intended from the start. A much fairer general scheme
should study inquiries in their context, through their
actual proceedings, and thence to their alleged results.

The Charity Commission's performance was a combination
of scandal hunting, trust registration, and administrative
recommendation. To review what it did, we need to examine
its acts with each of these levels in mind; then we need
to add a review of the areas outside the mandate, and the
acts subsequent to the inquiry. The Charity Commission
led to an extended debate and produced a factual foundation (possibly ill-used) for that debate. The Commission
did not produce its bureaucratic successor. Confusions
within reform leadership, lack of distinct objectives
(including a failure to find great masses of scandal and,
ironically, fair success in reforming innocent error)
marred the 'fruition' of the Charity Commission.

Even in cases where swift action followed inquiry, e.g.
the Municipal Corporation, Poor Law, and Children's
Employment (Factories) inquiries, the action may once
again be of questionable relation, for speed was frequently the clear characteristic of the self-serving inquiry:
what was produced was ordained before the evidence was
taken. And of course, 'results' of the sham inquiries
must be challenged, though on obviously different grounds.

On the face of it, an inquiry was passive. Its evidence was to be pursued or implemented in some way, and
the decision as to what that action would be lay with the
government of the day. The real test of a particular

inquiry's result, has to be a careful narrative of the conduct, supplemented by a full review of reports and recommendations, ending with an examination of the action which followed. We may reasonably expect a variety of relations and responsibility between commission findings and ultimate events. But whatever we do, the results of commissions of inquiry and their role in the Age of Reform can no longer be dominated by the old assumptions.

II

The foregoing sketch indicates the gaps which need to be filled to give us a comprehensive picture of reform commissions. That such a picture is long overdue should have been demonstrated by our account of the Charity Commission. It remains here only to summarize the insights which the story of the Charity Commission has allowed into that nebulous entity, 'the age of reform.' Never a term of great precision, the 'age' has been thought to fall somewhere in the century after the American Revolution. The 'reform' has been taken (according to fashion) as primarily electoral, industrial, or administrative, with subordinate themes in each general category. Each approach has sought to answer the same question: how and why did modern society emerge? If instead of asking this question through the old spectrum, we look through the reconstructed prism of the Charity Commission, some heretical visions appear.

The first heresy has to do with the democratic or popular content of reform. There are three parts to the problem: conception, execution, and results. What truly egalitarian concept prompted a reform? Slavery (abolition) perhaps, but few if any others. Which reforms were made by egalitarian acts? Strictly speaking, none. All reforms were made by, and in the name of, property owners. What reforms had a democratic product? The census, the register of births and other apolitical reforms alone. This does not mean that reform was of, and for, and by the elite. However, that would be closer to the truth than to say that reforms were for 'the people.'

The second heresy is that reform was always a governmental act. Individuals and movements and parties certainly expounded, campaigned, and 'fought' for reforms. They fought to induce the government to act. For the government act was the reform. The symbiosis between reformer and government tends to be obscured by the hostilities of verbal campaigns, and by the heroic style of their chronicles. The result has been a romanticisation of reform.

A third heresy stems from the second. The positive
government interest in reform has been shrouded.   There
was indeed a strong interest in reinforcement and preservation of the power structure, which added up to reform.
The conservative approach to reform has been seriously
shortchanged by progressive historiography. Yet it has
always been known that major reforms owed a great deal to
conservative impulses. The whole story of the early 19th
century law reform movement (one which is poorly and
rarely narrated) was basically conservative. That preservation should be rechristened 'progress' may be natural,
but it is historically and politically misleading.

The next, more orthodox point is that many progressive
changes were merely the stripping away of medieval
apparatus, a form of 'progress' which included enclosure
of common land, commutation of tithes, and renovation of
patronage and office-holding. The common action in all
of these cases was the pragmatic removal of encumbering
arrangements (usually as to property), to clear the ground
for economic and social modernization.

Finally, reform was often a continuing (even cyclical)
process. Patterns varied widely in different areas of
law and society, but one thing was common: the existence
of reform was well-known before the 'age of reform.'
This truism is often forgotten, but it must be remembered
in trying to comprehend the reform activity of our period.

The Charity Commission inquiry was a remarkable application of the tool of the royal commission. That powerful
engine was being turned to the shakeup and ventilation of
government. That was the principal 'revolutionary' change
in inquiry (inspired by empirical as well as by political
motives). The main function of inquiry had always been
judicial (claims, frauds, impeachments) and that function
would continue. Now however, what we would call 'claims'
of modern society were being laid against the established
institutions, and to meet the claims, those institutions
paid in the currency of reform. Modern investigations
were at first directed to renovation, chiefly in the area
of office-holding and revenue. The aiming of an inquiry
at a social institution was novel, but less so than it
appears to us. The trusts were legal property, and as
such they might be seen as liable to inquiry as fees,
accounts, or other public expenditures.

The inquiry into charitable trusts was not like its
commissioned antecedents. It set to work along the lines
of many other legal inquiries. But its work in local com-
communities converted it into a reformatory commission.
Charities were venerable institutions with vulnerable
features. To the lawyer-commissioners, the restoration

of original terms of trust was a marginally proper task;
at the same time, of course, their acts were administrative reforms.   The work of the Charity Commissioners mixed
judicial and administrative roles, not through any careful
plan, but rather because there was no plan.   Yet this
combined form was impractical, and later commissions of
inquiry, with more certain direction from the outset, were
usually confined more carefully to inquiry, with specific
(and separate) authority for administration.   The Charity
Commission straddled a transitional period.   It began its
life in one era, and ended it in another.   As such, the
inquiry was not embodied promptly in a permanent agency,
and thence its history went astray.

Appendix A

◇◇

Charity Commission Reports

◇◇

No.	Date	Paper
1	2 Mar. 1819	1819.X(A)
2	5 July 1819	1819.X(B)
3	15 Jan. 1820	1820.IV.
4	8 July 1820	1820.V
5	16 Jan. 1821	1821.XII.
6	30 June 1821	1822.IX.
7	28 Jan. 1822	1822.X.
8	13 July 1822	1823.VIII.
9	23 Jan. 1823	1823.IX.
10	28 June 1823	1824.XIII.
11	24 Jan. 1824	1824.XIV.
12	9 July 1824	1825.X.
13	22 Jan. 1825	1825.XI.
14	2 July 1825	1826.XII.
15	23 Jan. 1826	1826.XIII.
16	24 June 1826	1826-7.IX.
17	27 Jan. 1827	1826-7.X.
18	7 July 1827	1828.X.
19	26 Jan. 1828	1828.XI.
20	12 July 1828	1829.VII
21	31 Jan. 1829	1829.VIII.
22	11 July 1829	1830.XII.
23	30 Jan. 1830	1830.XII.327
24	26 June 1830	1831.XI.
25	10 July 1832	1833.XVIII.
26	10 Jan. 1833	1833.XIX
27	10 July 1833	1834.XXI.
28	10 Jan. 1834	1834.XXII.
29i	19 July 1834	1835.XXI(i)
29ii	19 July 1834	1835.XXI(ii)
30	26 Nov. 1836	1837.XXIII.
31	4 Feb. 1837	1837-8.XXIV.

```
32i      30 June 1837    1837-8.XXV.
32ii     30 June 1837    1837-8.XXVI.
32iii    30 June 1837    1837-8.XXVII.
32iv     30 June 1837    1839.XIV.
32v      30 June 1837    1839.XV.
32vi     30 June 1837    1840.XIX(i).
```

Related volumes

General Index (Reports 1-14)	1826-7.VIII.
Analytical Digest (Reports 1-24)	1831-2.XXIX.
Analytical Digest (Reports 25-9)	1835.XL.
Index to Reports (complete)	1840.XIX(ii)
Analytical Digest (complete)	1843.XVI,XVII.
Digest of Schools, etc.	1843.XVIII.

Appendix B

◇◇

Charity Commissioners

◇◇

The Commissioners are listed alphabetically under their respective dates of appointment. Their legal training is indicated (under 'Bar') with the notation of the Inn and the year in which they were called to the bar (GI - Gray's Inn, IT - Inner Temple, LI - Lincoln's Inn, MT - Middle Temple). If one was a student not called to the bar, then the date of admission ('adm') is given. All Commissioners probably had other positions of some importance, but what is listed below are those posts which may have had some bearing on the appointment or performance of the individual Commissioner (some standard and peculiar abbreviations are used: PC - privy councillor; CJ - chief justice; J - judge; KC - king's counsel; MP - member of parliament; C - chairman; AC - assistant commissioner; Cn - commission member). Commissioners ended their service either by resignation or termination of the commission. In addition there were a number of Honorary Commissioners whose non-attendance may have been tantamount to resignation. If a Commissioner ceased to participate actively, the terminal date given is that of the last signed report. If the Commissioner participated but signed no reports, the 'terminal' date is written '1834(O).' If service as a stipendiary was ended by promotion, the entry is written 'P1831.' Otherwise, dates given are those at which a formal termination or severance was made. For those whose service continued until the final expiration in 1837, there is a '---'.

(1) HONORARY

Name	Bar	Other positions	Left
1818			
Grant, Sir William (1752-1832)	LI/1774	Master of the Rolls, 1801-17	1831
Luxmore, John (1756-1830)		Bishop, St Asaph, 1815-30	1826
Parsons, John (1761-1819)		Bishop, Peterborough, 1813-19	1819
Scott, William (Lord Stowell) (1745-1836)	MT/1780	J, Admiralty, 1798-1828	1828
Sutton, Charles Manners (1780-1845)	LI/1806	Speaker, 1817-35	1834
Yorke, Charles Philip	LI/1787	PC, 1801; MP (1790-1810); Home Secretary (1803-4)	1821
1819			
Burton, Francis (1744-1830)	LI adm 1761	MP (1780-1812)	1820
Gibbs, Sir Vicary (1751-1820)	LI/1783	CJ, Common Pleas, 1814-18	1820
Legge, Edward (1767-1827)		Bishop, Oxford, 1815-27	1824
Leycester, Hugh (1750-1836)	MT/1775	KC; CJ Anglesea Great Sessions	1821
Nicholl, Sir John (1759-1838) (1821)	MT/1793	J, Prerogative Court Canterbury	1829
Russell, Sir Henry (1751-1836) (1827)	LI/1783	CJ, Supreme Court, Bengal, 1807-13; PC,1816	1826
Const, Francis (1 (1751-1839)	MT/1783	C, Middlesex Quarter Sessions; Westminster Sessions, 1835	1838
1831 Blomfield, Charles J. (1786-1857)		Bishop, London, 1828-56; Poor Law Cn, 1832; Ecclesiastical Cn, 1836	1834 (O)
Brougham, Henry P. (1778-1868)	LI/1808	MP; Lord Chancellor, 1830-4	----
Copley, John (Lord Lyndhurst) (1772-1863)	LI/1804	MP; Attorney-General; Lord Chancellor (1827-30, etc.,) Chief Baron, Court of Exchequer, 1831-4	1834 (O)

Name	Bar	Other positions	Left
Lushington, Stephen (1782-1873)	IT/1806	MP; J Consistory Court, 1828-38; Admiralty Court 1836-67; Ecclesiastical Revenue Cn, 1832	1834 (O)

1835

Name	Bar	Other positions	Left
Eden, Rev. Robert, 2d Baron Henley (1789-1841)	LI/1814	Master in Chancery, 1826-40	----
Lewis, Thomas Frankland (1780-1855)		MP, Irish Revenue Cn Irish Education Cn, 1825; C- Poor Law Board, 1834	----
Milman, Rev. Henry Hart (1791-1868)		Rector, St Margaret's Westminster, 1835	----
Nicholls, George (1781-1865)		Poor Law Board, 1834	---- (O)
Shaw, Lefevre, John G. (1797-1879)	IT/1825	Boundary Cn, 1832 Australia Cn, 1834; Poor Law Board, 1834	---- (O)
Sugden, Edward B. (1781-1875)	LI/1807	Solicitor General, England, 1829-30; Lord Chancellor, Ireland, 1834-5	----
Warre, John Ashley (1787-1860)		MP	----

(2) STIPENDIARY

1818

Name	Bar	Other positions	Left
Finch, Daniel (1789-1868)	IT/1814		----
Grant, William (1779-1840)	MT/1805	Irish Education Cn, 1826	----
Holbech, Henry H. (1779-1835)	LI/1804	Recorder of Warwick	P1831
McMahon, James (1782-1861)	LI/1814		P1831
Marsham, Robert B. (1786-1880)	LI/1813	Warden, Merton College, 1826-80	1831
Mathews, Wilkinson (1784-1866)	LI/1810	QC; Bencher	P1831
Roberts, William (1767-1849)	MT/1806	Secretary, Ecclesiastical Revenue Cn, 1832	P1831

Name	Bar	Other positions	Left
Warren, John W. (1771-)	IT/1798		P1831
1819			
Burnaby, Sherrard B. (1772-1848)	LLD, 1801	Advocate, Court of Arches, 1801-; Commissary, Canterbury, 1834	1830
Daniell, George (1758-1833)	MT/1782	Bencher, 1824, Reader 1826	1830
1831			
Cameron, Charles H. (1795-1880)	LI/1820	Poor Law Cn, 1832	1834
Carlisle, Nicholas (1771-1847)		Sec. to Commission, 1818-31; Poor Law Cn, 1832	P1835
Macaulay, Zachary (1768-1838)			1834
MacDonnell, Sir Alexander (1794-1875)	LI/1824		1834
Miller, John ( )	LI/1811	KC; Bencher; Author	1834
Romilly, Cuthbert ( )	GI/1815	Equity draftsman	1834
Smith Samuel (1795-1880)	LI/1820		----
Wrottesley, Sir John (1798-1867)	LI/1823		
1835			
Clark, Edmund (1804-)			----
Fellows, John M. ( )			----
Gunning, Henry B. ( )	MT/1834		----
Hume, James ( )	IT/1832		----
Humfrey, Charles ( )	LI/1834		----
Johnston, Patrick F. ( )	MT/1831	Poor Law Cn, 1832	----
Long, George (1780-1868)	GI/1811	Police magistrate; Municipal Corporation Cn 1835	----

Name	Bar	Other positions	Left
MacKintosh, Robert (1807-)	LI/1833	Factory Cn 1833	----
MacQueen, John (1803-)	LI adm 1832		----
Martin, Francis O. (1805-1878)	LI/1829	Tithe Commission, AC 1836; Charity Commissioner, 1872-8	----
Miles, William A. (1797-1878)	LI adm 1818	MP and author	----
Pennington, George J. (1795-1850)	IT adm 1813	Auditor of Civil List, 1835; Boundary Cn, 1835	1836
Peter, William (1785-1853)	LI/1813	MP	
Romilly, Edward (1804-70)	LI adm 1827	MP; Auditor Public Accounts, 1837-66	1836
Sedgwick, James (1775-1851)	MT/1801	C, Board of Stamps	----
Walsham, Sir John J.G. ( ) (Dec. 1835)		Poor Law Board AC, 1835	Pl836
Eagle, Francis K. (1784-1856)	MT/1809	Bencher, 1839, Reader 1843	----
1836			
Buller, Arthur W. (1808-69) (1836)	LI/1834		----
Lennard, George B. (1796-1870)	IT/1822	Boundary Cn 1835	----
Whishaw, James (1808-79)	GI/1832	Law writer	----

Notes

INTRODUCTION: HISTORIANS AND THE AGE OF REFORM

1 See for example, A. Aspinall and E. Anthony Smith (eds), 'English Historical Documents, 1783-1832' (vol. XI. London, 1971). In their introduction, they note: 'The reaction that set in against the excesses of the French revolution, and the avalanche of reformist legislation that followed the great act of 1832, have tended to obscure the fact that the period covered here was itself an Age of Reform.'

2 E. Halévy, 'England in 1815' (A History of the English People in the Nineteenth Century; vol. I, London, 1913), p. 20.

3 J. Brewer, 'Party Ideology and Popular Politics at the Accession of George III' (Cambridge, 1976) offers an excellent analysis of what he regards as the first stage of popular politics in the 1760s; P. Hollis (ed.), 'Pressure From Without' (London, 1974) has collected a group of essays generally following a more traditional interpretation.

4 London, 1905.

5 Ibid., pp. 10, 70, 95, 103.

6 J.B. Brebner, Laissez Faire and State Intervention in Nineteenth Century Britain, 'Journal of Economic History' (1948), supp. 8, 59-73; O. MacDonagh, The Nineteenth Century Revolution in Government: A Reappraisal, 'Historical Journal', I (1958) 52-67, H. Parris, The Nineteenth Century Revolution in Government: A Reappraisal Reappraised, 'Historical Journal,' III (1960), 17-37; Parris, 'Constitutional Bureaucracy' (London, 1969), esp., pp. 258-66; J. Hart, Nineteenth Century Social Reform: A Tory Interpretation of History, 'Past and Present,' no. 31 (1965), 39-61; V. Cromwell, Interpretations of Nineteenth Century Administration: An Analysis, 'Victorian Studies,' IX

(1966), 245-55; G. Himmelfarb, The Writing of Social
History: Recent Studies of 19th Century England,
'Journal of British Studies,' XI (1971), 148-70.

7   'Genesis of Parliamentary Reform' (London, 1913;
reprint, 1965).

8   Ibid., pp. 23, 350, 355.

9   'English Radicalism, 1832-1852' (London, 1935) pp. 7-8.

10   'Temporal Pillars: Queen Anne's Bounty, The Ecclesiastical Commissioners and the Church of England'
(Cambridge, 1964), pp. 240-1.

11   Peel to Croker, 23 March 1820, 'Croker Papers' (ed.)
L.J. Jennings, 2 vols (New York, 1884), I, pp. 155-6.

12   'James Mill and the Art of Revolution' (New Haven,
1963), p. 271.

13   Brebner (Laissez Faire and State Intervention) concluded that Dicey could not have read or understood
Bentham. He surely did not analyse Bentham's contacts
with contemporaries.

14   Jeremy Bentham and the Victorian Administrative State,
'Victorian Studies,' II (1959), 210. For this view,
Roberts has been taken to task, and Jenifer Hart has
argued that Benthamite influence did not depend upon
direct and exact tutelage in the master's ideas:
'ideas can influence people who are unconscious of
their origin, by becoming part of the general climate
of opinion.... If they cannot, there would be few
thinkers who could be shown to have any practical
influence at all.' (Nineteenth Century Social Reform,
p. 45). Of course this brings us full circle: opinion
causes influence which produces opinion. Recently,
another scholar has concluded that 'it seems likely
that to understand the genesis of Victorian reform,
one must look to the words and actions of moderate
Whig and Tory ministers, even minor ministers, rather
than to bureaucratic spectres - Benthamite or pragmatic - lurking in the background.' D.G. Paz,
Working-Class Education and the State, 1839-1849:
The Sources of Government Policy, 'Journal of British
Studies,' XVI (1976), 152.

15   'The Treasury' (New York, 1969), p. 148.

16   'James Mill and the Art of Revolution,' pp. 272-3

17   Oliver MacDonagh (19th Century Revolution in Government) made the fourth stage of his reform model the
shift from what he called static to dynamic administration. Yet in his introduction, he recognized that
generally 'administration may be, so to speak, creative and self-generating.... It may gather its own
momentum; it may turn unexpectedly in new directions;
it may reach beyond the control or comprehension of
anyone in particular,' (p. 53).

18   Roseveare, 'The Treasury,' pp. 153, 161
19   Aspinall and Smith, discussing the shape of party
     alignments in the early 19th century, pointed out an
     estimate that an opposition of 173 members 'if well
     managed and supported by public opinion (in other
     words, by the votes of the independent country gentle-
     men) was strong enough to turn out any government.'
     ('English Historical Documents, 1783-1832,' p.23).
20   'England in 1815,' p. 20.
21   'Tory Radical: The Life of Richard Oastler' (New York
     1946), pp.111-12.
22   W.O. Aydelotte, The Conservative and Radical Inter-
     pretations of Early Victorian Social Legislation,
     'Victorian Studies,' vol. XI (1967), 225-36, shows
     absence of party cohesion on selected issues in the
     1840s, which in all probability was true of earlier
     periods as well.
23   'The Making of the English Working Class' (New York,
     1963), pp. 603-49.
24   'The Origins of Modern English Society, 1780-1880'
     (London, 1969), p. 212.
25   Association, Convention and Anti-Parliament in British
     Radical Politics, 1771-1848, 'English Historical
     Review,' 88 (1973), 504-33.
26   'Victorian Origins of the British Welfare State' (New
     Haven, 1960), p. 27.
27   'Life and Times of Edwin Chadwick' (London, 1952),
     pp. 33-4.
28   'Making of the English Working Class,' p. 626.
29   'Life and Times of Edwin Chadwick,' p. 22.
30   'The Making of the English Working Class,' pp. 485,493.
31   Joel H. Weiner, 'The War of the Unstamped' (Ithaca,
     1969).
32   'Genesis of Parliamentary Reform,' p. 345.
33   For examples of this type, see above, pp. 22-6.
34   'The Making of Victorian England' (New York, 1967),
     pp. 3, 9.
35   This may also be a problem with official sources. The
     best example is probably Mark Blaug's research on the
     inquiry into the poor law: The Myth of the Old Poor
     Law and the Making of the New, 'Journal of Economic
     History,' 23 (1963) 151-89; and The Poor Law Report
     Reexamined, ibid., 24 (1964), 229-45. Other examples
     may be found in the movement for legal reform, the
     work of evangelicals, and in connection with political
     unions.
36   'The Anti-Corn Law League' (London, 1958), p. 208.
37   D.C. Moore, The Other Face of Reform, 'Victorian
     Studies,' V (1961), 7-34, discusses a wide range of

issues which brought together a majority for the Bill. Also see Aspinall and Smith (eds.), 'English Historical Documents, 1783-1832,' pp. 19-20.

38 33 Geo. III c. 54.

39 Poor Returns, 1803-4. XIII.715.

40 P.H.J.H. Gosden, 'The Friendly Societies in England, 1815-1875' (Manchester, 1961), pp. 6-7.

41 For unions, 5 Geo. IV c. 95; cooperatives, 4 & 5 Will. IV c. 40.

42 'Age of Improvement, 1784-1867' (London, 1959), p. 65.

43 'A Plan for Rendering the Poor Independent of Public Contributions' (Exeter, 1786).

44 'Society and Pauperism: English Ideas on Poor Relief, 1795-1834' (London, 1969), p. 38.

45 42 Geo. III c. 73.

46 B.L. Hutchins and A. Harrison, 'A History of Factory Legislation,' 3rd edn (London, 1926), p.2.

47 Ibid.

48 Ibid., pp. 16-17.

49 48 Geo. III c. 151.

50 Brian Abel-Smith and Robert Stevens, 'Lawyers and the Courts: A Sociological Study of the English Legal System, 1750-1965' (London, 1967), pp. 17, 29.

51 'Chronological Table of the Statutes' (London, 1954); this includes only acts dealing specifically with courts (not criminal law, mutiny acts, or specific legal penalties).

52 'Scotch Reform: considered with reference to the plan proposed in the late Parliament for the regulation of the courts and the administration of Justice in Scotland' (1808) in 'Works,' (ed.) John Bowring, vol. 5, pp. 48-53. The matter of authorship is unclear; Bentham addressed himself in these letters to Lord Grenville, and characterized him as 'patron and introducer' of the measure (p. 3). In fact, part of Bentham's argument on this Bill, amid an array of criticism, was an assertion that Eldon could not have written it, but might conceivably have delegated the task to a clerk.

53 1810.IX.53, 93, 115.

54 See speech by Samuel Romilly, May 18 1808 (11 Hansard 395).

55 Norman Gash, 'Mr. Secretary Peel' (Cambridge Mass., 1961) p. 330.

56 6 Geo. IV c. 50.

57 Among the innovations in the Jury Act were the transfer of juror lists from the responsibility of constables to that of churchwardens and overseers, better definition of jurors' qualifications, appeals on

method for selecting special juries. Gash, 'Mr.
Secretary Peel,' p. 335.

58   March 9 1825 (12 n.s. Hansard 970) and May 20 1825
(13 n.s. Hansard 800-1).

59   'The Whig Interpretation of History' (London, 1931).

60   'English Local Government: Statutory Authorities for
Special Purposes' (London, 1922), p. 353.

61   'Royal Commissions of Inquiry: The Significance of
Investigations in British Politics'(Stanford, 1937).

62   Ibid., v-vi, 54-69. In Table 1, they claim to list
some sixty commissions before 1832, but a number of
those listed were committees or other ad hoc bodies,
and some commissions were not listed.

63   Ibid., chapter VI Contemporary Decline, pp. 191-217.

64   Roberts, 'Victorian Origins,' pp. 315-16.

65   'A Pattern of Government Growth, 1800-1860: The
Passenger Acts and their Enforcement' (London, 1961).

66   'Oxford English Dictionary,' VIII, 347-8.

67   'The Age of Improvement,' p. 9.

68   'The Age of Reform, 1815-1870,' 2nd edn (Oxford, 1962),
p. 40.

69   Roger Anstey, 'The Atlantic Slave Trade and British
Abolition, 1760-1810' (London, 1975),pp. 250-1. For
further background, see David Brion Davis, 'The
Problem of Slavery in Western Culture' (Ithaca, 1966).

70   Briggs, 'Age of Improvement,' pp. 70-1.

71   Dale H. Porter, 'The Abolition of the Slave Trade in
England, 1784-1807' (New Haven, 1970), p. 143.

72   'Origins of Modern English Society,' pp. 183 ff.

73   'The Making of the English Working Class,' pp. 733-4.

74   'Society and Pauperism,' p. 310.

75   Brian Abel-Smith and Robert Stevens, 'Lawyers and the
Courts;' Henry Parris, 'Constitutional Bureaucracy;'
R.R. Nelson, 'The Home Office, 1782-1801' (Chapel
Hill, 1969); J.C. Sainty, comp. 'Office-Holders in
Modern Britain,' 5 vols. (London, 1972-5).

76   'Parliamentary Reform, 1640-1832' (London, 1973).

77   'Party Ideology and Popular Politics at the Accession
of George III.'

78   Two complete works have treated the Commission:
Nicholas Carlisle, 'An Historical Account of the
Origin of the Commission, appointed to inquire concerning charities in England and Wales' (London, 1828);
and James Hine, 'Observations on the Necessity of a
Legislative Measure for the Protection and Superintendance of Endowed Public Charities' (London, 1842).
Modern scholarship has provided no full-length
treatment.

1   THE STATE OF INQUIRY: EMPIRICISM AND POLITICS

1   Frederick Pollock and F.W. Maitland, 'History of
    English Law before the Time of Edward I,' 2 vols
    (Cambridge, 1898), I, pp. 93, 140-3; II, pp. 604 and
    n. 1.   Though the authors belittle the connections,
    perhaps doomsmen, tithings and the custom of 'frank-
    pledge' were relatives of the jury.   Later scholar-
    ship has devalued the Norman contribution: Henry G.
    Richardson and George O. Sayles, 'Law and Legislation
    from Aethelberht to Magna Carta' (Edinburgh, 1966),
    ch. 2.
2   There was no institutional break, although a number of
    individual justices did resign.   See G.E. Aylmer, 'The
    State's Servants' (London, 1973), pp. 29-33.   The pro-
    ceedings of the period were expressly confirmed at
    the restoration by 12 Chas II, c. 12. For a negative
    view of this episode in legal history, see Alan
    Harding, 'A Social History of English Law' (Harmonds-
    worth, 1966), pp. 265-7.
3   Sir William S. Holdsworth, 'A History of English Law,'
    7th edn, A.L. Goodhart and H.G. Hanbury (eds.) 16
    vols (London, 1956-66), IX, p. 126.
4   Ibid., V, p. 355 and nn.
5   This thesis has been lucidly elaborated in J.G.A.
    Pocock, 'The Ancient Constitution and the Feudal Law'
    (Cambridge, 1957).   Evidence is offered for most of
    western Europe, and the central point for our analysis
    would seem to be the adaptability of the legal system;
    for the lawyers' cultivation of their sources was not
    only a vital basis for historical scholarship, it was
    an affirmation of a habit of mind with far wider
    implications.
6   (Ed.), Charles N. Gray (Chicago, 1971), p. 41.
7   A good brief introduction may be found in S.L. Ollard
    and P.C. Walker, 'Archbishop Herring's Visitation
    Returns, 1743,' vol. 1. (Yorkshire Archaeological
    Society Record Series, vol. 71, 1928).
8   Anthony R. Wagner, 'Heralds and Heraldry in the Middle
    Ages,' 2nd edn (London, 1956).
9   Cromwell's original order is in PRO State Papers, 6/3
    (1).   The text is printed in J.C. Cox, 'The Parish
    Registers of England' (London, 1910) pp. 2-3.   The
    register was indirectly made a statutory requirement
    by several laws, and Rose's Parish Register Act in
    1812 settled the legal position (52 Geo. III c. 146).
    See D.J. Steel, 'National Index of Parish Registers,'
    vol. I (London, 1968).
10 Several registries of deeds, conveyances and wills

were established in the early 18th century (in Yorkshire, the West Riding - 1705, East Riding - 1708 and
North Riding - 1735; and in Middlesex - 1709). In
each case, the statutes referred to earlier provision
for enrolment of freehold transactions in 27 Hen. VIII
c. 16. According to Holdsworth, Henry's Act in its
original form would have established a general system
of registration ('History of English Law,' IV, p.457).
On the other hand, a Scottish system of registration
had been in existence for centuries (ibid. XI, p.17).

11 William Letwin, 'The Origins of Scientific Economics'
(New York, 1964) offers the best discussion of this
subject, especially of the work of William Petty.
However, the author's abrupt dismissal of political
arithmetic, implying that Swift satirized it to death
(pp. 149-51), differs from the explanation offered
here.

12 Graunt was a member of the Common Council of the City
of London. His publication apparently was the basis
for election as a fellow of the Royal Society.
'Natural and Political Observations mentioned in a
following index, and made upon the Bills of Mortality'
(London, 1662). See Major Greenwood, 'Medical Statistics from Graunt to Farr' (Cambridge, 1948).

13 Ibid., pp. 72 74.

14 'Political Arithmetick' (London, 1690), pp. xii-xiii.

15 (Ed.), George Chalmers.

16 D.V. Glass, Gregory King's Estimate of the Population
of England and Wales, 1695, 'Population Studies,' II
(1950), 338-74.

17 D. Waddell, Charles Davenant - A Biographical Sketch,
'Economic History Review,' 2nd series, XI (1958), 279.

18 'Political Arithmetic,' p. (xiv).

19 'Political Arithmetic' (London, 1774), pp. ix-x.

20 'An Estimate of the Comparative Strength of Britain
during the present and four preceding reigns: and of
the losses of her trade from every war since the
Revolution' (London, 1782).

21 Ibid., pp. iii, iv, 45-6.

22 'An Examination of Dr. Price's Essay on the Population
of England and Wales' (Maidstone, 1781). For official
returns, see 'CJ,' XXXVI, 804-6 (for 1777) and 50
Lambert 1 (for 1781). Chalmers's comments are on pp.
150-71.

23 7th edition, p. 585; see table on p. 587.

24 Sinclair was twice President of the Board of Agriculture (1793-8 and 1806-13) and he was an excise commissioner in 1811. In the 1790s he was also involved
in the movement to develop planned villages in Scot-

land. T.C. Smout, The Landowner and the Planned
Village in Scotland, in 'Scotland in the Age of
Improvement' (eds), N.T. Phillipson and R. Mitchison
(Edinburgh, 1970).

25   41 Geo. III c. 15.
26   M. Dorothy George, 'London Life in the Eighteenth
     Century' (London, 1925), pp. 42-7.
27   See Leona Baumgartner, 'John Howard, 1726-1790. Hosp-
     ital and Prison Reformer. A Bibliography' (London,
     1939).
28   For example, the reform of gaol fees, 14 Geo. III
     c. 20.
29   'An Essay on the Slavery and Commerce of the Human
     Species.'
30   'History of the ... Abolition of the African Slave
     Trade,' 2 vols (London 1808), I, p. 470.
31   Dolben's Act (28 Geo. III, c. 54).
32   Porter, 'The Abolition of the Slave Trade,' p. 51.
33   For a sketch of committees and their shortcomings, see
     Sheila Lambert, 'House of Commons Sessional Papers of
     the Eighteenth Century,' Introduction, vol. I, pp.
     45-8. Also P.D.G. Thomas, 'The House of Commons in
     the Eighteenth Century' (Oxford, 1971), pp. 264-8.
34   Roseveare, 'The Treasury,' p. 120. The act was 20
     Geo. III c. 54. Also see J.E.D. Binney, 'British
     Public Finance and Administration, 1774-1792'
     (Oxford, 1958).
35   41 Lambert 55.
36   25 Geo. III c. 19; 26 Geo. III c. 87; 29 Geo. III
     c. 64.
37   The Record Commission was instituted in reply to an
     Address of the House of Commons of 11 July 1800;
     the Irish education commission was by statute (46 Geo.
     III c. 122) as was the Justice Commission (48 Geo.
     III c. 151-Scotland).
38   The same phenomenon was seen in the 19th-century
     evolution of bureaucracy. 'Everyone was used to the
     idea that a new task meant a new board. In particular,
     temporary commissions were an immemorial tool of
     government.' Henry Parris, 'Constitutional Bureau-
     cracy,' p. 42.

2   THE STATE OF CHARITY: AUTONOMY OR ANARCHY?

 1   Leonard Shelford, 'The Law of Mortmain' (1836),
     pp. 117-266; see also the testimony before the Select
     Committee on Mortmain, 1844.X.507.
 2   The most remarkable event in this twilight era was a

near-miss at institutionalization through the creation
of a national 'mortmain fund.' The Bill for this
purpose was introduced in 1773. It stated that a
general fund should be established into which property
held by corporate bodies and trustees could be invested, in the form of shares of government stock. The
Bill claimed that 'too large dispositions of land to
uses in mortmain' were 'contrary to sound policy,
highly detrimental to the state' and if such a fund
were established, all parties would benefit. Moreover, the fund would take over the assets of Queen
Anne's Bounty, the Accountant-General of Chancery,
and the Deputy Remembrancer of the Exchequer. All
these assets would be vested in 'trustees of the mortmain fund,' to be appointed by the Lord Treasurer.
The Bill failed to pass even though it was sponsored
by the Solicitor-General and other members of government ('CJ' XXXIV, 245, 249, 291, 301, 310; 23 Lambert
387, 397). The Mortmain Fund Bill demonstrated, aside
from its radical solution, that mortmain remained
mingled in the public (and official) mind with charitable trusts, and with evil effects on land dealing.
But most of all, the Bill clearly showed an intent to
remodel and remove the traditional structure of mortmain.

3 'CJ,' XV, 60.
4 'CJ,' XXV.464.
5 21 Lambert 19, 43.
6 28 Geo. II c. 38.
7 11 Geo. III c. 14.
8 Chichester (26 Geo. II c. 99) and Southampton (13
Geo. III c. 50) received powers over specific trust
properties. Shrewsbury (24 Geo. III c. 15) and Hamp-
stead (39 & 40 Geo. III c. 35) obtained wider powers
over charitable trusts. On the other hand, a number
of local poor relief Acts specifically prohibited
incorporated Guardians from asserting any authority
over trust property (e.g., 2 Geo. III c. 45; 4 Geo.
III c. 57; 5 Geo. III c. 97).
9 This case was described in the 4th Report of the
Commissioners to Inquire Concerning Charities in
England and Wales, p. 72. Hereafter the form of
citation will be 4 R 72. A list of the Commissioners'
Reports with their respective dates of completion and
location in Sessional Papers will be found in Appendix
A.
10 32 (II) R 57 (emphasis added).
11 The redemption of the land tax was begun in 1798
(38 Geo. III c. 60). The first provision made with

regard to charitable trusts was in 1802 (42 Geo. III c. 116). The special exemptions were first provided in 1806 (46 Geo. III c. 133); extended by 54 Geo. III c. 173 and 57 Geo. III c. 100). The exercise of this legislation is indicated in Report of the Commissioners for the Redemption of the Land Tax, 1814-15, XII. 525, which lists 200 charitable trusts whose land tax had been redeemed; but the report did not list or record the trusts exonerated.

Also in 1806 an exemption was provided from Property (income) tax by 46 Geo. III c. 65 (amending 43 Geo. III c. 122 and repealing 45 Geo. III c. 49). Detailed returns of the exemptions claimed under this statute were made in 1820; a return of the rents and profits and a return of the stock or dividends - both for those trusts claiming exemption during the year ending 5 April 1815, 1820, VI.1.161. On tax liability in general, see Shelford, 'Law of Mortmain,' pp. 773-97.

12 'CJ,' LIII, 176.

13 A motion to exempt charitable trusts from legacy duty was defeated in 1812. 'CJ,' LXVII, 68.

14 George Bramwell, 'Analytical Table of the Private Statutes, 1727-1812' (1833) tabulated acts from 1760-1812 on a classified basis. He found at least 65 which dealt with 'charitable institutions' (a few may have escaped into some of his other headings). This would overlook the few acts which were elevated (at extra expense) to the dignity of a public Act. For verification of this general impression, 'Local and Personal Acts (Charitable Trusts) 1800-1837' (Charity Commission Library) contains a total of 81 acts.

15 The best modern authority is still Holdsworth, 'History of English Law' (see vol. I, pp. 395-476). The best contemporary was Joseph Parkes, 'History of the Court of Chancery' (1828). See also F.W. Maitland, 'Equity: A Course of Lectures' (Rev. John Brunyate, 1936), Sir Henry Maxwell-Lyte, 'Historical Notes on the Use of the Great Seal' (1926), and a good brief record survey in 'Guide to the Contents of the Public Record Office' (1963), I, pp. 7-10.

16 8 R 466.

17 The decline of commissions of charitable uses has been discussed in George Jeremy, 'Treatise on the Equity Jurisdiction of the High Court of Chancery' (1828), p. 246; Gareth Jones, 'History of the Law of Charity' (1969), p. 56; and R.S. Tompson, 'Classics or Charity? The Dilemma of the 18th-Century Grammar School' (1971), pp. 105-7. A further possible reason for the decline

of these commissions, not mentioned in any of the
foregoing accounts, was that the process of 'country
Commissions' for taking routine affadavits became
more widespread and reliable from the late 17th
century, and this reduced the need for special commissions.

18 Jeremy Bentham, 'An Introductory View of the Rationale
of Evidence' (in 'Works,' (ed.) Bowring, VI, p. 43.
The criticism of the court often strayed from the
constitution of the tribunal to the conduct of its
officers. This became a favourite tactic of the
critics of Lord Eldon (see Brougham's speech, 3 June
1818; 38 Hansard 1222-3). But most delays were simply
the product of antique procedure and a growing caseload. See also, Joseph Harrison, 'The Accomplish'd
Practiser in the High Court of Chancery' (1767), anon.,
'Costs in the Court of Chancery' (1791), and anon.,
'Observations on the Judges of the Court of Chancery'
(1823).

19 2 R 8.

20 1 R 217.

21 See testimony of Samuel Romilly to Select Committee
on Education of the Lower Orders, 12 June 1816 (1816.
IV. 245). See also reports of the Commission on
Duties and Salaries in Courts of Law (England) 1816.
VII.91, 1818.VII.255.

22 6 R 587.

23 11 R 358.

24 3 R 71.

25 12 Geo. I, c. 32. The Lord Chancellor had ordered
the Masters to give over their accounts in the Bank to
one central account. The statute confirmed this order
and created the post of Accountant General to
administer it.

26 12 Geo. II c. 24; 4 Geo. III. c. 32; 5 Geo. III c. 28;
9 Geo. III c. 19; 14 Geo. III c. 43; 17 Geo. III 3. 59;
20 Geo. III c. 33; 32 Geo. III c. 42.

27 1812-13.XIII.67. There were a number of other papers
on Chancery process at the same period (1810-11.III.
295; 1812.II.343) and slightly later (1816.IV.483 and
1816.VIII.91 and 1818.Vii.255), the last two being
reports of the 'Duties and Salaries' Commission.

28 The Six Clerks Office made this report, and in making
it asserted that there was no way to distinguish the
charity cases from the rest: 1818.XV.305.

29 We can only estimate and infer from very rough contemporary guides, but the inference seems clear enough.
For example, in 1819 there were nearly 20,000 unendowed schools, and slightly more than 4,000 endowed

(1819.IX). Patrick Colquhoun ('Treatise on the Police of the Metropolis,' (1796, p. 382) estimated that in London there was an income of £300,000 from endowments, and £205,000 from unendowed sources, not including friendly societies and missionary societies. Later he guessed ('Treatise on Indigence,' 1806, p. 61) that £400,000 in endowed income was compared with a national figure of 'public and private charity' (?) of £3.3 million. In 1850, Sampson Low ('Charities of London,' p. 452) listed voluntary contributions at £1,022,864 and 'secured income' at £741,869.

30 F.K. Brown, 'Fathers of the Victorians' (1961), esp. pp. 329-40.
31 David Owen, 'English Philanthropy, 1660-1960' (Cambridge, Mass., 1964), pp. 97-133.
32 18 R 30.
33 20 R 40.
34 20 R 115.
35 20 R 75.
36 20 R 161.
37 12 R 403; Reynolds ordered that none of his trustees could be clergy, lawyers, doctors or officers of other trusts; he also gave detailed directions on the meetings, investments and disbursements of funds. One is tempted to guess that Reynolds himself had some substantial trustee experience which dictated all of these stipulations.
38 William Grant told the Select Committee of the Commons in 1835 'I have known £100 paid for preparing and settling a trust deed.' 1835.VII.652.
39 23 R 42.
40 4 R 21.
41 12 R 140.
42 4 R 93.
43 12 R 379.
44 6 R 380.
45 13 R 142.
46 11 R 435.

3 CHARITY AND INQUIRY

1 'An Account of certain charities ... in Tyndale Ward in the County of Northumberland' (Newcastle, 1713), p. 55. Apparently the commission which Ritschel sought was never issued, however, his book was used extensively by the Charity Commissioners when they visited Hexham. 23 R 805-14.

2   'An Account of the Many and Great Loans, Benefactions,
     and Charities belonging to the City of Coventry'
     (1733), p. xi.
3   'An Alphabetical Register of divers persons, who ...
     have given tenements, rents, annuities, and monies,
     towards the relief of the Poor of the County of Devon
     and city and county of Exon' (1736), pp. 8, 13, 39.
4   'An Account of the Gifts and Legacies that have been
     given and bequeathed to Charitable Uses in the Town of
     Ipswich' (1747). Some other examples of local com-
     mittees were Bristol in 1737 (6 R 486), Much Woolton,
     Lancashire, in 1748 (20 R 89), and Burscough, Lanc-
     ashire, in 1774 (20 R 125).
5   Watts, 'A Black Scene ...' (1749), p. 31.
6   Rouse, 'A Collection of the Charities ... Market
     Harborough' (1768), quoting 'Lloyd's Evening Post,'
     28 March 1763, pp. xiii-xiv.
7   Samuel Mitchell, 'A Catalogue of Charitable Gifts ...
     Enfield,' (1709).
8   'The History of the Rise and Progress of the Charit-
     able Foundations at Church Langton' (1767).
9   'Account of the Hospitals ... Bristol' (1775).
10   22 R 311.
11   23 R 7.
12   For example, separate accounts such as Robert Loder,
     'Statutes and Ordinances of Woodbridge Priory' (1792)
     and 'Constitutions and Directions, to be Observed, for
     and concerning, the Free School in Woodbridge,' 2nd edn
     (1796); or local and county histories, e.g. Edward
     Hasted, 'History and Topographical Survey of the County of
     Kent,' 4 vols (1778) who spoke of the need to preserve
     accounts of 'many public foundations ... many endowments
     for the education of youth ... and many offices of trust
     and emolument ... confined to kindred by their founders
     and benefactors' (vol. I, p. vii); or collected works such
     as Antony Highmore, 'Pietas Londinensis,' 2 vols (1810),
     or Nicholas Carlisle, 'Description of the Endowed
     Grammar Schools of England and Wales,' 2 vols. (1818).
13   3 Geo. III c. 18 (Irish)
14   40 Geo. III c. 75 (Irish).
15   28 Geo. III c. 15 (Irish), continued by 30 Geo. III
     c. 34 and 31 Geo. III c. 41 (to 1796 and thence to
     the end of the session).
16   46 Geo. III c. 122. The reports of the Commission were
     reprinted in series in 1813-14.V.1.
17   1813-14.V.327. The alteration was apparently made in
     1811 in response to communication from the Principal
     Secretary, William Wellesley Pole.
18   53 Geo. III c. 107. This body was followed by still

another inquiry in 1825, and that in turn by a new Commission of Education in 1834.

19   28 Lambert 129.
20   (1777) 'CJ,' XXXVI, 309, 420, 525; (1786) 26 Geo. III c. 58 (Charitable Donations) and 26 Geo. III c. 56 (Overseers' Returns).
21   They were reprinted, 1816.XVI.A-B.
22   First Series, vol. IX, p. 543.
23   'A Plan to Prevent All Charitable Donations ... from Loss, Embezzlement' (1807).
24   'Letter to Sir Samuel Romilly, on the necessity of an immediate inquiry into the causes of delay in Chancery proceedings' (1810), p. 39.
25   The review was in vol. II (1807), col. 225; the society proposal was discussed in vol. VII (1810), cols 906-8.
26   Thomas Blore, 'An Account of the Public Schools, Hospitals, and other charitable foundations in the Borough of Stanford' (sic) (1813), p. 366.
27   Zachary Clark, 'An Account of the different charities belonging to the poor of the county of Norfolk' (1811) The preface to this volume was written by the anti-slavery crusader, Thomas Clarkson.
28   43 Eliz. c. 2 was the basic authority.
29   This practice was of course abetted by the reforms of the 1760s for the infant poor. At the same time, the earliest efforts at registration of the parish apprentice were being made (7 Geo. III c. 39).
30   42 Geo. III c. 46.
31   'Report of the Select Committee to examine into the number and state of parish apprentices bound into the country ...' 1814-15.V.1567.
32   56 Geo. III c. 139.
33   1814-15.V.1569.
34   14 Geo. III c. 49; see Sir George Clark, 'A History of the Royal College of Physicians of London,' 2 vols (Oxford, 1966), II, p. 584-87; and see Kathleen Jones, 'Lunacy, Law and Conscience' (London, 1955).
35   1807.II.69.
36   40 Geo. III c. 94.
37   48 Geo. III c. 96. According to a return made in 1834, fifteen counties reported an expenditure of £545,000 for the construction of asylums. 1834.LI.53.
38   1814-15.IV.801. In this testimony there is an interesting early example of medical statistics given by Dr Richard Powell. For a commentary, see Ida Macalpine and Richard Hunter, 'George III and the Mad Business' (New York, 1969), pp. 291-3.
39   55 Geo. III c. 69; 57 Geo. III c. 106.

40   59 Geo. III c. 127 and 9 Geo. IV c. 41.
41   17 Geo. II c. 5.
42   1814-15.III.231.
43   1816.V.391.
44   Ibid., pp. 402-6.
45   1809.I.283; 'CJ,' LXIV, 258.
46   1810.II.255.
47   Beckwith, 'Letter to Romilly,' p. 40.
48   2 vols (1810); 'Observations on the Amended Bill ...'
     (Jan. 1810); 'A Letter to William Wilberforce' (March
     1810).
49   1814-15.XII.1.3.5.
50   1818.XV.303.
51   1829.XX.19.
52   Jeremy, 'A Treatise on the Equity Jurisdiction of the
     High Court of Chancery,' p. 247.
53   38 Hansard 976 (27 May 1818). Also see Jones, 'Law
     of Charity.'
54   Third Report, 1816.IV.245-46.
55   32(i) R 67.
56   'CJ,' LXVIII; 1812-13.II.1387.
57   'CJ,' LXX, 444; 1814-15.II.909.
58   1816.XVI.A-B.
59   'CJ,' LXXI, 324; 1816.I.477.

4   ENACTMENT OF THE CHARITY COMMISSION

1   Lord Campbell's acerbic comment was suggestive if
    severe:
        It may be conceived in what a state of repletion
        Brougham was after a retention which had endured
        nearly four consecutive years. Writing frequent
        pamphlets and countless articles for reviews,
        magazines, and newspapers, had brought him some
        occasional relief, aided by after-dinner speeches,
        and copious ebullitions of rhetoric at public
        meetings; but there remained an immense conglom-
        eration of ideas in his mind, which could only be
        vomited forth in the House of Commons. 'Lives of
        the Lord Chancellors,' VIII, p. 283.
2   'Edinburgh Review,' no. 37 (Nov. 1811); 2 Hansard
    49-91 (28 June 1820) and the education bill, 1820.I.
    471.
3   He spoke of the Irish schools as 'a model' when pro-
    posing the Select Committee (21 May 1816; 34 Hansard
    636); the Scottish system was favourably described on
    8 May 1818 (38 Hansard 593).
4   Wrottesley spoke (20 June) of receiving, in connect-

ion with the charitable donations bill, 'a variety of
letters from respectable clergymen in different parts
of the country, stating abuses which, to their knowledge, existed in charitable foundations in education'
(34 Hansard 1234).

5   The committee did print some data, quite uncontro-
versial in nature, on trusts in the counties of
Middlesex, Surrey, Bedford, Berkshire, and Kent,
received from the Poor Return Office. 1816.IV.314.

6   1816.IV.3.

7   34 Hansard 1230 ff.

8   1817.III.81.

9   Charles Tower to Brougham, 14 July 1817 (Brougham
MSS. 25,535).

10 37 Hansard 818; the Brentwood case went on through
prolonged discussion and debate, was certified by
the Charity Commissioners to Chancery and heard on
26 March 1828 (1828.XXI.18) and settled on 4 March
1833 against the defendants (1833.XXXI.286), by Lord
Chancellor Brougham.

11 37 Hansard 818.

12 1819.IX (i-iii). The General Tables from the Digest
were also printed in 1820.XII.341-360.

13 37 Hansard 440.

14 Ibid., 338, 820.

15 Ibid., 773.

16 According to Creevey, there was a more sinister
possibility: 'He has always some game or underplot
out of sight - some mysterious correspondence - some
extraordinary connection with persons quite opposite
to himself' ('Creevey Papers,' vol. I, p. 172).

17 The Lords title was 'for appointing commissioners to
inquire concerning charities in England (and Wales)
for the Education of the poor.' The Commons title:
'for appointing a commission to inquire into the
abuses in charities connected with the education of
the poor ...' But speakers and/or Hansard, noting
the provenance of the Bill, shortened it to 'education of the poor.'

18 The tactical plan seems to be verified by a statement
in the 'Edinburgh Review' in March, 1819, after the
Commission was an established reality: 'The radical
question is about the Education of the Poor ... the
incidental and accessary question is about the abuse
and perversion of charitable endowments,' vol. 31,
p. 547.

19 38 Hansard 596; see also, 'The Speech of Henry
Brougham ... on the Education of the Poor and Charitable Abuses' (1818).

20   38 Hansard 976 (27 May, 1818).
21   The only other substantial debate on commission-
     composition and powers was in connection with the
     Naval Inquiry, December 1802 ('Parliamentary History,'
     vol. 36, cols 1139-46).
22   18 May 1818 (38 Hansard 763).
23   8 May 1818 (38 Hansard 612-13).
24   8 May 1818 (38 Hansard 609).
25   3 June 1818 (38 Hansard 1218).
26   'CJ,' LXIII, 347.
27   'CJ,' LXXIV, 528.
28   'CJ,' LXXV, 117, 467 (1820); 'LJ,' LV, 576 (1822).
29   8 May 1818 (38 Hansard 605).
30   The exact circumstances around the last days of the
     Bill are something of a mystery. Brougham spoke of
     a meeting 'in another place' in alluding to the
     revisions which enabled him to renew support for the
     Bill. But there is no record of a conference on the
     Bill; somehow amendments which were voted by the Lords
     on 1 June were gone by the final version of 3 June.
     Draft amendments: 1 & 2 June, House of Lords, 'Main
     Papers,' 20 May, 1818 295 a-d; final version, 'CJ,'
     LXXIII, 415 (3 June 1818).
31   The preface was dated 20 August; the 'Quarterly Review'
     said it was published in September. There were event-
     ually eleven editions.
32   'Letter to Romilly,' pp. 57-64.
33   'Letter to the Rt. Hon. Sir William Scott in answer
     to Mr. Brougham's Letter to Sir Samuel Romilly upon
     the Abuse of Charities' (1818). The author of this
     tract has been identified as a lawyer named Holt
     (G.F.A. Best, 'Temporal Pillars' (1964), p. 181).
     'Quarterly Review,' December, 1818 vol. XIX, 492-569.
34   'Letter to Scott,' pp. 38-50.
35   'Extracts from Mr. Fleming's Letter' (1819).
36   3 R 5 and App. pp. 517-80; certified 4 February 1820
     (C2/456/1); decree 24 January 1827 (1828.XXI.14).
37   'Letter to Henry Brougham' (1818).
38   31 R 867.
39   'Letter to Romilly,' p. 17.
40   The phrase is from Wykeham's statutes for Winchester.
     It was recurrent in this and several other forms in
     most early school statutes. See a discussion of the
     point in A.F. Leach, The True Meaning of Free Schools,
     'Journal of Education,' XXX (1908) 378-80, 495-7.
41   See Croydon and Brentwood among those mentioned here.
     Free schools had been (re)started in each case, but
     citizens wanted a higher school.
42   William Bowles, 'Vindiciae Wykehamicae' (1818);

Liscombe Clarke, 'A Letter to Henry Brougham (1818);
and (C.H. Ker) 'A Vindication of the Enquiry ...'
(1819).

43   'Edinburgh Review,' 32 (July 1819),110.
44   anon., 'Remarks upon an Address to Sir William Scott'
      (1818), p.1.
45   'Edinburgh Review,'32 (July 1819), 90.
46   23 June 1819 (40 Hansard 1300).
47   The new Commission (59 Geo. III c. 81).was empowered
      by the Equity Facilities Act (59 Geo. III c. 91).

5   ORGANIZATION

1   In series, the enabling (or extending) Acts were:
     58 Geo. III c. 91; 59 Geo. III c. 81; (5 Geo. IV c.
     58); (10 Geo. IV c. 57); 1 & 2 Will. IV c. 34; 5 & 6
     Will. IV c. 71; (7 Will. IV c. 4).
2   59 Geo. III c. 91 gave the access to equity courts.
     This was extended and confirmed by 2 & 3 Will. IV c.
     57, under which rent charges could be vested in
     parochial authorities.
3   See complete list of Honorary Commissioners, Appendix
     B.
4   Attendance was regularly recorded in General Minute
     Books (Strong Room, Charity Commission). The early
     minutes indicate that the bishops and Charles Yorke
     never attended in the first five months, and rarely
     thereafter.
5   Holbech to Brougham, 6 November 1831 (Brougham MSS.
     2994).
6   See list, Appendix B.
7   Only two were without legal training; twenty eight
     were members of the bar, three were students (at
     least), and one was DCL.
8   Five were of unknown age.
9   The latter places were apparently never filled: '...
     as no such officers had been appd under a similar
     authy given by the former acts, the Commn did not
     think proper to make any further appointmt.' Draft
     reply, Hine to Charles Sharp, 19 November 1835
     (C2/438/1).
10   For the last sixteen months only £10,000 was appro-
     priated in Committee of Supply, 31 May 1836 ('CJ,'
     XCI, 413).
11   Assistant Librarian, King's Library, 1812; Secretary
     of Society of Antiquaries, 1807-. 'Topographical
     Dictionary,' 4 vols (1808-13) and other works. The
     DNB (Richard Garnett) uncharitably noted 'an amiable

and worthy man, whose abilities were by no means commensurate with his industry.'

12 Hine to Treasury, 9 June 1832 (C2/432/1).
13 1830-31.XIV.18.
14 Miles to Hine, February 1836 (C2/439/2).
15 The travelling commissioner was in various respects a familiar figure. Surely the enclosure movement had seen to that. On the experiences of that process, see M.W. Beresford, Commissioners of Enclosure, 'Economic History Review,' XVI (1946) 130.
16 Country depositions have been classed separately before 1714 (Chancery papers C. 21, 22). Since that date, they have been deposited in proceedings of the several divisions (C. 5-13).
17 W.S. Holdsworth, 'History of English Law,' I, p. 470; C.P. Cooper, 'Observations on ... Chancery' (1832); Bankruptcy reform: J.H. Brady, 'Laws Relating to Bankruptcy and Insolvents' (1832); E.E. Deacon, 'Law and Practice of Bankruptcy,' 2 vols(1864).
18 Metropolitan commissioners were established by 2 & 3 Will. IV c. 107; for the commission of inquiry on lunacy, see 3 & 4 Will. IV c. 36.
19 Another influence may have been the assize circuits; most commissioners had some experience on circuit, and the practice had some value, though as Warren testified, there was no real link between such service and 'the investigation in those counties where they were in the habit of proceeding periodically on the circuits.' 1835.VII.655.
20 Actually the pair-system was in effect from 1819 to 1834; the first year there were three to a unit; at the end commissioners worked singly.
21 Even the extreme plan of all working on the same county would have been subject to dislocations by delay, change of terms of commission, or extraordinary problems.
22 1835.VII.635.
23 5 June 1829 (21 Hansard 1759).
24 1835.VII.672.
25 10 September 1818; draft, C2/423; final, Minute Book 1, p. 5.
26 Ibid., p. 178.
27 1830-31.XIV.17.
28 Minute Book 3, p. 220, emphasis added.
29 Minute Book 4, p. 8, emphasis added.
30 Minute Book 5, p. 7.
31 Ibid., p. 187 (1 April 1837).
32 Ibid.
33 Minute Book 4, pp. 5-8.

34   Minute Book 5, pp. 10-11.
35   Ibid., p. 12.
36   See Minute Book 5, passim.
37   See Chapter 8, where the evaluation of performance
     bears out this conclusion.
38   Filed in forty-eight bundles in C2/429-431.
39   C2/438/1.
40   Ibid.
41   Humfrey, C2/441/2; Butler, C2/441/1; also letters from
     Johnston (C2/438/1), Finch (C2/438/2), Eagle (C2/439/1).
42   2 & 3 Will. IV c. 57.
43   The request is in Minute Book 4, p. 75. The Summary
     is in C2/426.
44   The Commissioners' demurrer was recorded following the
     Lord Chancellor's request (ibid.). About 540 copies
     of questionnaires were returned to the Home Office,
     and filed in C2/424-425. No record survives of the
     number sent.

6   PROCEDURE

1   There may be no way to tell the exact total number of
    sittings. There are three types of record: (1) actual
    counts of sittings, in Returns to Parliament, covering
    the period 1832-6 (1836.XXXVII.495); (2) Minute Books
    of Commissioners, some of which are known to be
    missing (C2/417-19); and detailed papers of local in-
    vestigations (C2/1-368).
2   The Commissioners adopted a method which began with
    existing trusts. It was not practicable to trace
    all documents down to trusts, but only to find trusts
    and then look for documents. There was no evidence
    that the other plan was ever suggested.
3   Samples of this form abound in county papers along
    with replies (C2/1-368), and out-letter lists are in
    C2/432/2.
4   1835.VII.657.
5   Long (1836) C2/439/2; Gunning (2 March 1836) C2/439/1;
    Eagle (1836) C2/439/3; See a detailed chart of York-
    shire returns from 1824, C2/436/3.
6   1819.IX (i-iii).
7   16 November, 9 December 1818 (C2/420/ pp. 53-63).
8   Miles (1836) C2/439/2; Eagle (1836) C2/439/3;
    Johnston (1836) C2/439/4.
9   13, 30 November 1818. C2/420/pp. 52, 59.
10 1835.VII.655.
11 John Wade, 'An Account of the Public Charities in
    England and Wales' (1828), p. 201.

12 C2/420/p. 65.
13 The precept went through several minor variations;
    see C2/434/1, 434/2, 441/1. Copies also throughout
    C2/1-368.
14 Finch to Hine, 10 October 1836 (C2/440/1).
15 Minute Book 1, p. 81; C2/432.
16 One Commissioner (Edmund Clark) observed belatedly in
    1836 that parish authorities were indeed required to
    'furnish evidence against themselves.' But the prin-
    ciple did not apply to public service (C2/439/1).
17 1835.VII.650.
18 Further evidence of Commissioner's preparation can be
    seen in the (only?) individual group of papers (James
    McMahon, C2/437/4) and also in county papers, passim
    C2/1-368.
19 1835.VII.677.
20 1830-31.XIV.16
21 See Finch to Hine 24 January 1836 (C2/439/1).
22 1835.VII.655.
23 Hume to Hine, 3 May 1836 (C2/439/3).
24 1835.VII.656.
25 Martin to Hine, 1 February 1836 (C2/439/2). There
    was no record of such a decision in any of the general
    minute books for the early months of the 1835 Com-
    mission.
26 Thomas Love Peacock, 'Crochet Castle' (1831), p. 107.
27 Requests for surveyors: Eagle to Hine, 9 March 1836
    (C2/439/1), MacQueen to Hine, 23 July 1836 (C2/439/4);
    other correspondence in county papers.
28 1830-31.XIV.19.
29 1835.VII.672.
30 25 R 250.
31 19 R 133.
32 4 R 195.
33 12 R 307.
34 12 R 345.
35 3 R 131.
36 19 R 243.
37 Letter to Hine, 31 July 1836 (C2/439/4).
38 32iii R 343.
39 Letter 1 September 1836 (C2/440/2). Emphasis in
    original.
40 32iv R 62.
41 2 R 57.
42 12 R 534.
43 19 R 246.
44 25 R 129.
45 1835.VII.691.
46 5 R 248.

47   3 R 91.
48   12 R 368; the rent increase was from £5 10s. to
     £31 10s.
49   Clark to Hine 17, 26, 31 March 1836 (C2/439/1).
50   Sir John Deane's Grammar School, Witton (31 R 438).
51   25 R 129.
52   Commission to Alan Hutchinson, 1 May 1828 (C2/432/3).
53   Commission to Isaac Robinson, 25 August 1829 (C2/432/3).
54   Minute Book 2, pp. 156, 215, 217, 225, 246; Minute
     Book 3, pp. 6, 46, 54, 107, 115, 220, 245; Minute
     Book 4, p. 69.
55   32 (I) R 207.
56   18 R 533.
57   25 R 65.
58   32(II) R 395.
59   32(I) R 195.
60   32(I) R 251.
61   32(I) R 297.
62   3 R 199.
63   1830-31.XIV.16.
64   1830-31.XIV.15-19; 1835.VII.647-654.
65   19 December 1836 (C2/436/2).
66   C2/1-368.
67   18 July 1836 (C2/440/2).
68   25 July 1836 (C2/439/3).
69   18 April 1836 (C2/439/4).
70   17 November 1836 (C2/440/1).
71   C2/440/1.
72   Ibid.
73   C2/441/1.
74   Ibid.
75   1 R 3.
76   Minute Book, C2/420, pp. 16-17.
77   2 & 3 Will. IV, c. 57; see above, p. 129.
78   Minute Book 4, p. 54.
79   C2/459-62.
80   Carlisle to Treasury 27 April 1829 (C2/435/3).
81   C2/443-8.
82   Minute Book 2, p. 88.
83   Carlisle to Hine, 18 June 1836 (C2/439/3).

7   INTERRUPTIONS

1   C2/435/3. Hobhouse was permanent under secretary in
    the Home Office from 1817 to 1827.
2   The bulk of the information from Carlisle's report
    was printed in 1824.XVIII.43.
3   5 Geo. IV c. 58.

4   Completed 'counties' were, Bedford, Cumberland, Devon, Oxford, Rutland, Westminster, and Bristol.

5   1826-27.XX.499. See Table 4, p. 181 below.

6   Actually the 1807 figure only included five commissions, whereas in 1826 there were twelve, the high having been sixteen in 1824.

7   1786-1863; solicitor, journalist, and politician. Eldest son of an Essex merchant, Harvey was articled and became a country solicitor. From 1808-18 he was on the London Common Council; he entered the Inner Temple in 1819, but was refused admission to the bar on alleged grounds of fraud and theft, later cleared by a Commons committee (1834.XVIII.327). Harvey was a member for Colchester, 1818-35, and for Southwark, 1835-40. He also ran the 'Sunday Times' and the 'True Sun.'

8   17 Hansard 981.

9   Harvey was accused by members of the Commission of picking up charities from the reports and indiscriminately bringing them into court. See below, pp. 168-9.

10 7 March 1828 (18 Hansard 1056).

11 Letter from Hobhouse 15 March 1828 (C2/435/4); reply 29 May 1828 (Minute Book 3, p. 98; C2/432/1); and returns printed in 1828.XXI.7.31.

12 Apparently copies of this testimony and the accompanying return were requested by the House on 22 June 1829 ('CJ,' LXXXIV, 411) and presented on 24 June, at which time the renewal bill had already passed. The testimony was printed in 1830-31.XIV.15.

13 C2/435/4.

14 Ibid.

15 Ibid.

16 The papers are incomplete but are plainly remnants of exchanges between the Audit Office and the Commission and the Commissioners of Public Accounts and the Commission. Among the papers are cover letters and draft replies to detailed queries (not here) which referred to a report on accounts by Carlisle (also not here). C2/464.

17 Minute Book 3, p. 114.

18 See below, on Bills of 1835-9, pp. 172-4.

19 5 June 1829 (21 Hansard 1758).

20 'CJ,' LXXXV, 559.

21 'Mirror of Parliament' (1830), p. 2402.

22 1831-32.XXVII.674 ff.

23 1830.III.259; 1830-31.I.301; 1831-32.I.315.

24 1830.II.233; 1830-31.I.323.

25 Ecclesiastical Courts Commission (28 January 1830) Ecclesiastical Revenues Commission (25 June 1832).

26   1826-27.I.235.275; II.525; 1829.I.4O1; 183O.I.61.69.
     77. As to orders made by Lyndhurst, see S. Atkinson,
     'Complete Chancery Orders and Statutes' (1833). Also
     Holdsworth, 'English Law,' XVI, pp. 6, 7, 16, 17.
27   For official returns, see 1834.XLVIII.2O1.
28   27 September 1831 (7 Hansard 7O1).
29   29 December 1833 (Brougham MSS. 46,747).
3O   'Cy pres' was the legal term for the limited doctrine
     of the court's ability to authorize deviation from a
     founder's will: namely, when strict performance would
     be harmful to the charity: virtually what this section
     itself says, only of course this proposal would have
     the Lord Chancellor sharing that power with Commis-
     sioners.
31   Brougham MSS. 46,904.
32   Returns: 1829.XXI.63/183O.XXIX.263/1831-32.XXVI.5O1/
     1834.XLI.349.
33   Harvey to Brougham, 4 October 1835 (Brougham MSS 3167).
34   Harvey to Brougham, 16 January 1831 (Brougham MSS
     3OO8)
35   Brougham MSS. 3167.
36   Brougham to Russell, September 1835 (Brougham MSS
     BL 267).
37   Smith to LeMarchant,'Hints' (Brougham MSS. 46,747).
38   Martin to Hine, January-February 1836 (C2/439/2).
39   11 June,1835, 'CJ,' XC, 330.
4O   11 June 1835 (29 Hansard 675-8).
41   'Report,' 1835.VII.631.
42   1835.VII.677-760.
43   (L) 1835.I.487.
44   3 September 1835 ('Mirror of Parliament
45   Brougham to Russell, September 1835 (Brougham MSS. BL
     267).
46   'Early Correspondence of Lord John Russell,' (ed.),
     Rollo Russell, 2 vols (1913) vol. II, p. 126.
47   (L) 1835.I.487, 1837.II.277.
48   (L) 1837-8. No. 27, 1839.II.179. For the former,
     see also 'LJ,' LXX, 27, and 39 Hansard 425-66
     (1 December, 1837).
49   4 February 1837 (Brougham MSS 1806).
5O   28 March 1837 (Brougham MSS 15,937).
51   25 March 1837 (C2/441/3).
52   15 February 1837 (C2/441/4).
53   19 February 1837 (C2/441/2).
54   22 February (C2/441/2).
55   On 20 February 1837 Hine received the following pro-
     test from Arthur Buller: 'My dear Sir, Is no remon-
     strance to be made by the Commissioners against this
     shabby cunning of Lord John's. Let us all unite and

tell him that we will be blowed if we work without
pay - Really it won't do. Pray let me know whether
the rest mean quietly to acquiesce in this tyranny.
If they do they are a pack of ——' (C2/441/1).

56 'LJ,' LXIX, 500.
57 C2/436.
58 Minute Book 5, p. 209.
59 Minute Book 5, pp. 213-15.
60 The non-signers were, after Brougham, Eden, Milman,
    and Sugden: Carlisle, Lewis, McMahon, Nicholls,
    ShawLefevre, Walsham, and Warre.
61 1837.XXV. (32i R 3-6) '30 June.'

8   EVALUATION

1   Regular estimates of total printing costs (votes,
    journals, and a catchall category of bills, reports,
    etc.) are in sessional papers; also see Expenses of
    Printing, 1829-31 (1833.XII.118); Expenses of Papers
    printed ... by Order (1839.XLVII.493); Returns of
    printing, 1837-41 (1842.XXVI.657).
2   A full analysis of the cost of all printing in the
    session of 1844 is available: 1844.XXXVIII.345.
3   11 June 1835 (29 Hansard 678). The total number of
    volumes included thirty seven volumes of reports, two
    index volumes, and three digests (in five volumes).
4   1856.XXXIX.713.
5   1842.XXVI.657.
6   1850.XX.15, 1851.XXII.303.
7   The best contemporary authority estimates that the
    Commissioners lost only three or four cases in all.
    J.P. Fearon, 'The Endowed Charities' (London, 1855),
    p. 35.
8   26 March 1852 (120 Hansard 214).
9   'Endowed Charities,' p. 23.
10 1830-31.XIV.19.
11 Brougham MSS. 46,747.
12 Ibid.
13 3 R 216.
14 4 R 113.
15 4 R 207.
16 3 R 32.
17 19 R 124.
18 12 R 399.
19 C2/439/3.
20 32(ii) R 28.
21 20 R 63.
22 24 R 371.

23   Hine to Singleton, 30 September 1836 (C2/440/2).
24   Singleton to Hine, 20 October 1836 (C2/440/2).
25   20 R 145.
26   23 R 22.
27   23 R 91.
28   59 Geo. III c. 91, and 1 & 2 Geo. IV c. 92 which
     empowered Bishops to appoint temporary trustees where
     none could be found.
29   2 & 3 Will. IV c. 57.
30   Minute Book 4, p. 51.
31   C2/459/3.
32   See Wade, 'Account of Public Charities,' p. 3;
     Shelford, 'Law of Mortmain,' pp. 300-21; and note
     Nicholas Carlisle's subtitle: 'An Historical Account
     of the Origin of the Commission appointed to inquire
     concerning Charities in England and Wales, and an
     illustration of several old customs and words which
     occur in the reports.'
33   7 March 1828 (18 Hansard 1057).
34   1833.XII.98.
35   1835.VII.746. Parkes also told the Select Committee
     on the Charity Commission that the inquirers 'have
     not reported anything like the extent of abuses of
     charities,' but surely his Corporation Commission
     experience had not given Parkes a balanced sample.
36   20 June 1821 (Minute Book 2, p. 88).
37   18 Hansard 1057.
38   Ibid.
39   1835.VII.746.
40   Anthony Highmore, 'Philanthropia Metropolitana'
     (London, 1822); Adele Du Thon, 'An Account of the
     Principal Charitable Institutions of St. Marylebone'
     (London, 1823); anon., 'An Inquiry into the Revenues
     and Abuses of the Free Grammar School at Brentwood'
     (London, 1823); anon., 'Brentwood Free Grammar School.
     Report of the Commissioners of Inquiry, with Notes and
     Observations' (Chelmsford, 1825); Robert Clutterbuck,
     'An Account of the Benefactions to the Parish of
     Watford, in the County of Hertford' (Watford, 1828);
     Ralph B. Hankin, 'An Account of the Public Charities of
     the Town of Bedford' (Bedford, 1828); John Landale,
     'A Collection and Abstract of all the Material Deeds,
     Wills, Leases, and Legal Documents, Relating to the
     Several Donations and Benefactions to the Church and
     Poor of the Parish of Dartford' (London, 1829); T.J.
     Manchee, 'The Bristol Charities, being the Report of
     the Commissioners so far as relates to the Charitable
     Institutions in Bristol,' 2 vols (Bristol, 1831);
     anon., 'An Account of the Hitchin Charities. Extracted

from the further Report of the Commissioners' (Hitchin, 1836); William Grant, 'Charity and Trust Estates of Hinckley' (London, 1839); James Whishaw, 'An Account of the Endowed Charities on Herefordshire' (London, 1839); Edmund Clark, 'Hereford City Charity Reports' (London, 1840); Francis O. Martin, 'An Account of the Bethlehem Hospital abridged from the Report of the late Charity Commissioners' (London, 1853).

An interesting variation was Richard Gilbert, 'The Parent's School, and College Guide,' 2nd edn (London, 1843) which dealt with scholastic exhibitions and other endowments, drawn to a large extent from the Reports.

41   1831-1832.XXIX.1; 1835.XL.1; 1843.XVI.XVII.
42   'CJ,' XCV.236.
43   C2/421.
44   W.K. Jordan, 'Philanthropy in England' (1959).
45   W.G. Bittle and R.T. Lane, Inflation and Philanthropy in England: A reassessment of W.K. Jordan's Data, 'Economic History Review,' XXIX (1976), 203.
46   'Philanthropy in England,' p. 119.

9   ESTABLISHMENT OF THE CHARITY COMMISSION

1   1884.IX.3; 1952-53.VIII.5.
2   1846.XXV.279.
3   1843.XVI-XVII.
4   1852.XXXVIII.361.
5   C2/442.
6   'Observations on the Necessity of a Legislative Measure for the Protection and Superintendance of Endowed Public Charities' (1842); sent to Brougham; see Hine to Brougham, 4 November 1842 (Brougham MSS 3455).
7   Ibid., pp. 6-7.
8   Ibid., pp. 19-20.
9   Correspondence (1836-9) in C2/443-8.
10   Draft letter, C2/442/3.
11   30 Hansard 479; 34 Hansard 201; 35 Hansard 314, 585, 638, 676, 891; Bills 1836.I.569, (L) 1836.III.589.
12   (L) 1837-38.II.335.339.343.   Hine, 'Observations,' p. 38.
13   (L) 1839.II.179.
14   1841.I.237.239.243, (L) 1841.II.303.
15   J. Alexander and D.G. Paz, The Treasury Grants, 1833-1839, 'British Journal of Educational Studies,' XXII (1974), 78.
16   Treasury Minute, 30 August 1833. 1834.XLII.527.

17   'The Times,' 22 July and 4 August 1853.
18   (L) 1844.II.207.
19   1844.X.507.
20   Campbell, 'Lives of the Lord Chancellors,' VIII, 160, 542.
21   Fearon, 'Endowed Charities,'p. 31.
22   1847-48.II.31 (L) 1847-48.III.471.487.491.
23   1849.II.15.35.
24   Warrant dated 18 September 1849; Commission papers are in C2/466-9; see Fearon, 'Endowed Charities,' pp. 34-5.
25   1850.I.247,267; (L) 1850.III.423.
26   1850.XX.15.
27   1851.I.227, (L) 1851.III.229,275.
28   1852.I.141; speech 26 March 1852 (120 Hansard 208); bill withdrawn 21 May 1852 ('CJ,' CVII, 233).
29   (L)1852-52.III.391,419,449,479.
30   1852-53.I263.293; 16 & 17 Vict. c. 137.
31   'Endowed Charities,' p. 46.
32   Select Committee on Charitable Trust Acts, 'Report,' 1884.IX.1.
33   'Endowed Charities,' p. 53.
34   First Report, Charity Commissioners. 1854.XIX.79 (Appendix 2.)
35   1835.VII.658.
36   1854.XIX.79.
37   18 & 19 Vict. c. 124.
38   1862.XIX.189 (Reprinted 1877.LXVI.15).

10   COMMISSIONS OF INQUIRY AND THE AGE OF REFORM

1   The only general work is Clokie and Robinson, 'Royal Commissions of Inquiry.' Its perspective is not historical and it is particularly weak on the early 19th century. Nevertheless, others have had to rely on it (see Holdsworth, 'History of English Law,' XIII, pp. 270-4).
     Some recent studies have dealt more fully and successfully with specific commissions. The best effort was by Mark Blang, The Myth of the Old Poor Law and the Making of the New, and The Poor Law Report Re-examined. Other recent studies include G. Finlayson, The Municipal Corporation Commission and Report, 1833-35, 'Bulletin of the Institute for Historical Research,' XXXVI (1963), 36 and The Politics of Municipal Reform, 1835, 'English Historical Review,' LXXI (1966), 673.
2   Warrant 26 April 1824, 1826.XV.3.
3   'Indications Respecting Lord Eldon' (1825), p. 28.
4   Holdsworth, 'English Law,' I, 443, 1816.XV.1; XVI.571.

5 The Poor Law Report Re-Examined, 'Journal of Economic
   History,' XXIV (June, 1964), 229-45.

6 The Offices of Clerks of the Signet and Clerks of the
   Privy Seal were abolished in 1851 (14 & 15 Vict. c.
   82). The Privy Seal Office was abolished in 1884 (47
   & 48 Vict. c. 30).

7 The passing of warrants for the Great Seal was in the
   power of the royal council, or individual ministers,
   from as early as the 13th century (Maxwell-Lyte, 'The
   Great Seal,' pp. 179, 200). The formalization of the
   processes at various times inhibited but did not
   eradicate this possibility (e.g., Thomas Cromwell, as
   explained in G.R. Elton, 'Tudor Revolution in Government' (Cambridge, 1953), p. 279.

8 One possible ground of differentiation lies in the
   objects of the inquiries; briefly, most of those
   dealing with old institutions were unpaid and ex
   officio, most of those dealing with newer, social
   issues were paid and 'professional'. However, there
   is too small a sample in Table 9 on which to base an
   assertion of this kind.

Bibliography

PRIMARY SOURCES

a. Manuscripts

The principal official sources for commissioners of inquiry will be the standard printed series of parliamentary papers. More detailed information on legislative proceedings may be found in printed and edited Bills and other material in the Main Papers, House of Lords Record Office. The work of a commission might generate sizeable quantities of minutes memoranda and correspondence. For the Charity Commissioners, these are found in PRO class 'Charity 2' and in the original Minute Books in the offices of the Commission. Other official documents may be found among the papers of government agencies which had business with the inquiry or in its area of interest. Useful in this manner are the papers of the Court of Chancery, particularly Commissions of Charitable Uses (C.90-93, 192); and the Home Office papers, especially papers of Expired Commissions (H.O. 73) and the general series of Royal Warrants (H.O. 38).

Private papers relating to the Charity Commission are relatively rare. The Brougham Manuscripts in the Library of University College, London, are the largest single source. These scattered letters between Brougham and the Commissioners and others are concentrated in the years of his Chancellorship, with little material on this subject in the years before 1830. No other active commissioner had significant papers, nor did any other major collection contain more than isolated references to the charity inquiry.

b. Printed works

ANON., 'An Account of the Gifts and Legacies that have been Given and Bequeathed to Charitable Uses in the Town of Ipswich,' 1747.
ANON., 'An Account of the Hitchin Charities. Extracted from the further Report of the Commissioners,' Hitchin, 1836.
ANON., 'An Account of the Hospitals, Alms-houses and Public Schools in Bristol,' Bristol, 1775.
ANON., 'An Account of the Many and Great Loans, Benefactions and Charities belonging to the City of Coventry,' 1733.
ACLAND, JOHN, 'A Plan for Rendering the Poor Independent of Public Contribution; founded on the Basis of the Friendly Societies,' Exeter, 1786.
'The Annual Subscription Charities and Public Societies in London,' London, 1823.
A BARRISTER, 'A Letter to Samuel Compton Cox, Esq., One of the Masters of the Court of Chancery,' London, 1824.
BARTON, CHARLES, 'An Historical Treatise of a Suit in Equity,' London, 1796.
BECKWITH, WILLIAM, 'A Letter to Sir Samuel Romilly, on the Necessity of an Immediate Inquiry into the Causes of Delay in Chancery Proceedings; and of Arrears of Appeals in the House of Lords,' London, 1810.
BECKWITH, WILLIAM, 'A Plan to Prevent all Charitable Donations, for the Benefit of Poor Persons, in the Several Parishes of England and Wales, from Loss, Embezzlement, and Abuse in Future,' London, 1807.
BENTHAM, JEREMY, 'Indications Respecting Lord Eldon, including History of the Pending Judges' Salary-Raising Measure,' London, 1825.
BENTHAM, JEREMY, 'An Introductory View of the Rationale of Evidence,' London, 1810.
BENTHAM, JEREMY, 'Scotch Reform; Considered, with Reference to the Plan, Proposed in the late Parliament, for the Regulation of the Courts, and the Administration of Justice, in Scotland: with Illustrations from English Non-Reform,' London, 1808.
BLORE, THOMAS, 'An Account of the Public Schools, Hospitals, and other Charitable Foundations in the Borough of Stanford,' London, 1813.
BOWLES, WILLIAM, 'Vindiciae Wykehamicae,' London, 1818.
BOYLE, WILLIAM R.A., 'Practical Treatise on the Law of Charities,' London, 1837.
BRADY, J.H., 'Laws Relating to Bankruptcy and Insolvents,' London, 1832.
ANON., 'Brentwood Free Grammar School. Report of the Commissioners of Inquiry, with Notes and Observations,' Chelmsford, 1825.

BROUGHAM, HENRY PETER, 'Brougham and His Early Friends, 1798-1809,' London, 1908.

BROUGHAM, HENRY PETER, 'A Letter on National Education, to the Duke of Bedford,' Edinburgh, 1839.

BROUGHAM, HENRY PETER, 'A Letter to Sir Samuel Romilly upon the Abuse of Charities,' London, 1818.

BROUGHAM, HENRY PETER, 'The Life and Times of Henry Lord Brougham, written by Himself,' 3 vols, Edinburgh, 1871.

BROUGHAM, HENRY PETER, 'Practical Observations upon the Education of the People,' 6th edn, London, 1825.

BROUGHAM, HENRY PETER, 'The Speech of Henry Brougham on the Education of the Poor and Charitable Abuses,' London, 1818.

BURDETT, FRANCES, 'Annals of Banks for Savings,' London, 1818.

CARLISLE, NICHOLAS, 'Description of the Endowed Grammar Schools of England and Wales,' 2 vols, London, 1818.

CARLISLE, NICHOLAS, 'An Historical Account of the Origin of the Commission, Appointed to Inquire concerning Charities in England and Wales,' London, 1828.

CHALMERS, GEORGE, 'An Estimate of the Comparative Strength of Britain During the Present and Four Preceding Reigns; and of the Losses of Her Trade from Every War since the Revolution,' London, 1782.

CLARK, EDMUND, 'Hereford City Charity Reports,' London, 1840.

CLARK, ZACHARY, 'An Account of the Charities Belonging to the Poor of the County of Norfolk abridged from the Returns under Gilbert's Act, to the House of Commons in 1786, and from the Terriers in the Office of the Bishop of Norwich,' Bury St Edmunds, 1811.

CLARKE, LISCOMBE, 'A Letter to H. Brougham, Esq., M.P., F.R.S. in reply to the Strictures on Winchester College, contained in his Letter to Sir Samuel Romilly, M.P.,' London, 1818.

CLARKSON, THOMAS, 'An Essay on the Slavery and Commerce of the Human Species,' London, 1786.

CLARKSON, THOMAS, 'The History of the Rise, Progress and Accomplishment of the Abolition of the African Slave Trade by the British Parliament,' 2 vols, London, 1808.

CLUTTERBUCK, ROBERT, 'An Account of the Benefactions to the Parish of Watford, in the County of Hertford,' Watford, 1828.

COLQUHOUN, PATRICK, 'A Treatise on Indigence,' London, 1806.

COLQUHOUN, PATRICK, 'A Treatise on the Police of the Metropolis,' London, 1796.

COLQUHOUN, PATRICK, 'A Treatise on the Wealth, Power, and Resources of the British Empire,' London, 1814.

COOPER, CHARLES P., 'Observations on the Calendar of the Proceedings in Chancery,' London, 1832.

ANON., 'Costs in the Court of Chancery, with Practical Directions and Remarks,' London, 1791.

CREEVEY, THOMAS, 'The Creevey Papers' (ed.), Sir Herbert Maxwell, 2 vols, London, 1903.

CROKER, JOHN WILSON, 'The Croker Papers' (ed.), L.J. Jennings, 2 vols, New York, 1884.

DUKE, GEORGE, 'The Law of Charitable Uses' (rev.), R.W. Bridgman, London, 1805.

DU THON, ADELE, 'An Account of the Principal Charitable Institutions of St. Marylebone,' London, 1823.

EDEN, SIR FREDERICK M., 'The State of the Poor,' 3 vols, London, 1797.

'EDINBURGH REVIEW.'

FEARON, JOHN P., 'The Endowed Charities; with some Suggestions for further Legislation Regarding Them,' London, 1855.

FLEMING, JOHN, 'Extracts from Mr. Fleming's Letter to Mr. Brougham,' Kendal, 1819.

GILBERT, RICHARD, 'The Parent's School and College Guide,' 2nd edn, London, 1843.

GRANT, WILLIAM, 'Charity and Trust Estates of Hinckley,' London, 1839.

GRAUNT, JOHN, 'Natural and Political Observations mentioned in a Following Index, and made upon the Bills of Mortality,' London, 1662.

HALE, SIR MATTHEW, 'A History of the Common Law,' (ed.), Charles Gray, Chicago, 1971.

HANBURY, WILLIAM, 'The History of the Rise and Progress of the Charitable Foundations at Church Langton,' London, 1767.

HANKIN, RALPH B., 'An Account of the Public Charities of the Town of Bedford,' Bedford, 1828.

HARRISON, JOSEPH, 'The Accomplish'd Practiser in the High Court of Chancery,' London, 1767.

HASTED, EDWARD, 'History and Topographical Survey of the County of Kent,' 4 vols, Canterbury, 1778-99.

HIGHMORE, ANTHONY, 'A Letter to William Wilberforce, Esq., M.P. relative to the Second Bill introduced by Him ... for Registering Charitable Donations,' London, 1810.

HIGHMORE, ANTHONY, 'Observations on the Amended Bill now depending in the House of Commons "for the registering and securing of charitable donations for the benefit of poor persons in England."' London, 1810.

HIGHMORE, ANTHONY, 'Philanthropia Metropolitana,' London, 1822.

HIGHMORE, ANTHONY, 'Pietas Londinensis,' 2 vols, London, 1810.

HINE, JAMES, 'Observations on the Necessity of a Legis-
lative Measure for the Protection and Superintendance of
Endowed Public Charities,' London, 1842.
HOWARD, JOHN, 'The State of the Prisons,' London, 1777.
HOWLETT, JOHN, 'An Examination of Dr. Price's Essay on the
Population of England and Wales,' Maidstone, 1781.
ANON, 'An Inquiry into the Causes of Delay attending Pro-
ceedings in the Court of Chancery,' London, 1824.
ANON., 'An Inquiry into the Revenues and Abuses of the
Free Grammar School at Brentwood,' London, 1823.
IRELAND, JOHN, 'Letter to Henry Brougham,' London, 1818
IZACKE, RICHARD, 'An Alphabetical Register of divers
Persons, who ... have given Tenements, Rents, Annuities,
and Monies, towards the Relief of the Poor of the County
of Devon and City and County of Exon.,' London, 1736.
JEREMY, GEORGE, 'A Treatise on the Equity Jurisdiction of
the High Court of Chancery,' London, 1828.
KER, C.H., 'A Vindication of the Enquiry into Charitable
Abuses, with an Exposure of the Misrepresentations con-
tained in the Quarterly Review,' London, 1819.
KING, GREGORY, 'Natural and Political Observations and
Conclusions upon the State and Condition of England, 1696,'
(ed.), George Chalmers, London, 1804.
LANDALE, JOHN, 'A Collection and Abstract of all the
Material Deeds, Wills, Leases, and Legal Documents,
relating to the several Donations and Benefactions to the
Church and Poor of the Parish of Dartford,' London, 1829.
ANON., 'Letter to the Rt. Hon. Sir William Scott in Answer
to Mr. Brougham's Letter to Sir Samuel Romilly upon the
Abuse of Charities,' London, 1818.
'LITERARY PANORAMA.'
LODER, ROBERT, 'Constitutions and Directions, to be
Observed, for and Concerning the Free School in Wood-
bridge,' 2nd edn, Woodbridge, 1796.
LODER, ROBERT, 'Statutes and Ordinances of Woodbridge
Priory,' Woodbridge, 1792.
LOW, Sampson Jr., 'The Charities of London,' London, 1850.
MADDOCK, HENRY, 'A Treatise on the Principles and Practice
of the High Court of Chancery,' 2 vols, London, 1815.
MANCHEE, T.J., 'The Bristol Charities, being the Report of
the Commissioners so far as relates to the Charitable
Institutions in Bristol,' 2 vols, Bristol, 1831.
MARTIN, FRANCIS O., 'An Account of the Bethlehem Hospital
abridged from the Report of the Late Charity Commissioners,'
London, 1853.
MILLER, JOHN, 'An Inquiry into the Present State of the
Civil Law of England,' London, 1825.
MITCHELL, SAMUEL, 'A Catalogue of the Charitable Gifts,
Rents, and Revenues belonging to the Parish of Enfield,'
London, 1709.

NEWLAND, JOHN, 'The Practice of the High Court of Chancery,' London, 1813.

OASTLER, RICHARD, 'Brougham versus Brougham on the New Poor Law,' London, 1847.

PAUL, JOHN, 'The Law of Tythes,' London, 1781.

PEACOCK, THOMAS LOVE, 'Crochet Castle,' London, 1831.

PETTY, WILLIAM, 'Political Arithmetick,' London, 1690.

'QUARTERLY REVIEW.'

REEVES, JOHN, 'History of the English Law,' 4 vols, London, 1787.

ANON., 'Observations on the Judges of the Court of Chancery and the Practice and Delays Complained of in that Court,' London, 1823.

ANON., 'Remarks upon an Address to Sir William Scott,' London, 1818.

ANON., 'A Reveiw of the Delays and Abuses Occasioned by the Constitution and Present Practice of the Court of Chancery with Practical Hints as to the Remedy: in a Letter to the Commissioners of Inquiry,' London, 1825.

RITSCHEL, GEORGE, 'An Account of Certain Charities ... in Tyndale Ward in the County of Northumberland,' Newcastle, 1713.

ROMILLY, SIR SAMUEL, 'The Life of Sir Samuel Romilly, written by Himself,' 2 vols, London, 1842.

ROUSE, ROWLAND, 'A Collection of the Charities and Donations given ... to the Town of Market-Harborough,' Market-Harborough, 1768.

RUSSELL, LORD JOHN, 'Early Correspondence of Lord John Russell' (ed.), Rollo Russell, 2 vols, London, 1913.

SHELFORD, LEONARD, 'A Practical Treatise of the Law of Mortmain, and Charitable Uses and Trusts,' London, 1836.

SINCLAIR, SIR JOHN, 'The History of the Public Revenue of the British Empire,' 3 vols, London, 1785-90.

SINCLAIR, SIR JOHN, 'The Statistical Account of Scotland,' 21 vols, Edinburgh, 1791-9.

SMITH, JOSHUA T., 'Government by Commissions, Illegal and Pernicious,' London, 1849.

WADE, JOHN, 'An Account of the Public Charities in England and Wales, abridged from the Reports of His Majesty's Commissioners on Charitable Foundations,' London, 1828.

WATTS, JOHN, 'A Black Scene Open'd: Being the True State of Mr. John Kendrick's Gift to the Town of Reading,' Reading, 1749.

WHISHAW, JAMES, 'An Account of the Endowed Charities in Herefordshire,' London, 1839.

WHISHAW, JAMES, 'A Synopsis of the Members of the English Bar,' London, 1835.

YOUNG, ARTHUR, 'Political Arithmetic, containing Observations on the Present State of Great Britain,' London, 1774.

SECONDARY SOURCES

ABEL-SMITH, BRIAN, and ROBERT STEVENS, 'Lawyers and the
Courts: A Sociological Study of the English Legal System,
1750-1965,' Cambridge, Mass., 1967.
ALEXANDER, J., and D.G. Paz, The Treasury Grants, 1833-39,
'British Journal of Educational Studies,' XXII (1974),
82-9.
ARMYTAGE, W.H.G., 'Heavens Below: Utopian Experiments in
England, 1560-1960,' London, 1961.
ASPINALL, A., and E. Anthony Smith (eds), 'English
Historical Documents, 1783-1832,' vol. XI of 'English
Historical Documents (ed.), D.C. Douglas, London, 1971.
ATLAY, J.B., 'The Victorian Chancellors,' 2 vols,
London, 1906-8.
ANSTEY, ROGER, 'The Atlantic Slave Trade and British
Abolition, 1760-1810,' London, 1975.
AYDELOTTE, W.O., Conservative and Radical Interpretations
of Early Victorian Social Legislation, 'Victorian Studies,'
XI (1967), 225-36.
AYLMER, G.E., 'The State's Servants,' London, 1973.
BAUMGARTNER, LEONA, 'John Howard, 1726-1790, Hospital and
Prison Reformer. A Bibliography,' London, 1939.
BERESFORD, M.W., Commissioners of Enclosure, 'Economic
History Review,' XVI (1946), 130-40.
BEST, G.F.A., 'Temporal Pillars: Queen Anne's Bounty, the
Ecclesiastical Commissioners, and the Church of England,'
Cambridge, 1964.
BINNEY, J.E.D., 'British Public Finance and Administration,
1774-1792,' Oxford, 1958.
BITTLE, W.G. and R.T. LANE, Inflation and Philanthropy in
England: A Reassessment of W.K. Jordan's Data, 'Economic
History Review,' XXIX (1976), 203-10.
BLAUG, Mark, The Myth of the Old Poor Law and the Making
of the New, 'Journal of Economic History,' XXIII (1963),
151-84.
BLAUG, MARK, The Poor Law Report Re-examined, 'Journal of
Economic History,' XXIV (1964), 229-45.
BOND, MAURICE F., 'Guide to the Records of Parliament,'
London, 1971.
BRAMWELL, GEORGE, 'An Analytical Table of the Private
Statutes, 1727-1812,' London, 1813.
BREBNER, J.B., Laissez-faire and State Intervention in
Nineteenth-Century Britain, 'Journal of Economic History,'
supp. VIII (1948), 59-73.
BREWER, JOHN, 'Party Ideology and Popular Politics at the
Accession of George III,' Cambridge, 1976.
BRIGGS, ASA, 'The Age of Improvement, 1784-1867,' London,
1959.

BROWN, FORD K., 'Fathers of the Victorians,' Cambridge, 1961.

BUTTERFIELD, HERBERT, 'The Whig Interpretation of History,' London, 1931.

CAMPBELL, JOHN CAMPBELL, BARON, 'Lives of Lord Lyndhurst and Lord Brougham,' London, 1869.

CAMPBELL, JOHN CAMPBELL, BARON, 'The Lives of the Lord Chancellors and Keepers of the Great Seal of England,' 8 vols, London, 1845-7.

CANNON, JOHN, 'Parliamentary Reform, 1640-1832,' London, 1973.

CLARK, SIR GEORGE, 'A History of the Royal College of Physicians of London,' 2 vols, Oxford, 1966.

CLARK, GEORGE KITSON, 'The Making of Victorian England,' New York, 1967.

CLOKIE, HUGH and J.W. ROBINSON, 'Royal Commissions of Inquiry,' Stanford, 1937.

CROMWELL, VALERIE, Interpretations of Nineteenth Century Administration - An Analysis, 'Victorian Studies,' IX (1966), 245-55.

DICEY, ALBERT VENN, 'Lectures on the Relation between Law and Public Opinion in England during the Nineteenth Century,' London, 1905.

DRIVER, CECIL, 'Tory Radical: The Life of Richard Oastler,' New York, 1946.

FINER, Samuel E., 'The Life and Times of Sir Edwin Chadwick,' London, 1952.

GASH, NORMAN, 'Mr. Secretary Peel,' Cambridge, Mass. 1961.

GEORGE, M. DOROTHY, 'London Life in the Eighteenth Century,' London, 1925.

GLASS, D.V., Gregory King's Estimate of the Population of England and Wales, 1695, 'Population Studies,' II (1950), 338-74.

GOSDEN, P.H.J.H., 'The Friendly Societies in England, 1815-1875,' Manchester, 1961.

GRAY, BENJAMIN K., 'A History of English Philanthropy,' London, 1905.

GRAY, BENJAMIN, K., 'Philanthropy and the State, or Social Politics,' London, 1908.

GREAVES, HAROLD R.G., 'The Civil Service in the Changing State,' London, 1947.

GREENWOOD, MAJOR, 'Medical Statistics from Graunt to Farr,' Cambridge, 1948.

GRETTON, R.H., 'The King's Government: A Study in the Growth of the Central Administration,' London, 1913.

HALEVY, ELIE, 'England in 1815.' A History of the English People in the Nineteenth Century, vol. I, London, 1913.

HAMBURGER, JOSEPH, 'James Mill and the Art of Revolution,' New Haven, 1963.

HARDING, ALAN, 'A Social History of English Law,'
Harmondsworth, 1966.
HARRISON, BRIAN, Philanthropy and the Victorians,
'Victorian Studies,' IX (1966), 353-74.
HART, JENIFER, Nineteenth-Century Social Reform: A Tory
Interpretation of History, 'Past & Present,' XXXI (1965),
39-61.
HIMMELFARB, GERTRUDE, The Writing of Social History:
Recent Studies of 19th Century England, 'Journal of
British Studies,' XI (1971), 148-70.
HOLDSWORTH, SIR WILLIAM S., 'A History of English Law,'
7th edn (eds), A.L. Goodhart and H.G. Hanbury, 16 vols,
London, 1956-66.
HOLLIS, PATRICIA, (ed.), 'Pressure from Without,' London,
1974.
HUTCHINS, B.L., 'Public Health Agitation, 1833-1848.'
London, 1909.
HUTCHINS, B.L. and A. HARRISON, 'A History of Factory
Legislation,' 3rd edn, London, 1926.
JONES, GARETH, 'History of the Law of Charity, 1532-1827,'
Cambridge, 1969.
JONES, KATHLEEN, 'Lunacy, Law and Conscience, 1744-1845,'
London, 1955.
JONES, M. GWLADYS, 'The Charity School Movement,'
Cambridge, 1938.
JORDAN, WILBUR K., 'The Charities of London, 1480-1660,'
London, 1960.
JORDAN, WILBUR K., 'The Charities of Rural England, 1480-
1660,' London, 1961.
JORDAN, WILBUR, K., 'Philanthropy in England, 1480-1660,'
London, 1959.
KEETON, GEORGE W., 'The Modern Law of Charities,' London,
1962.
LAMBERT, SHEILA, 'Bills and Acts: Legislative Procedure
in Eighteenth Century England,' Cambridge, 1971.
LETWIN, WILLIAM, 'The Origins of Scientific Economics,'
New York, 1964.
LUBENOW, WILLIAM C., 'The Politics of Government Growth,'
Newton Abbot, 1971.
MACALPINE, IDA, and RICHARD HUNTER, 'George III and the
Mad Business,' New York, 1969.
MACCOBY, SIMON, 'English Radicalism, 1832-1852,' London,
1935.
McCORD, NORMAN, 'The Anti-Corn Law League,' London, 1958.
MACDONAGH, OLIVER, The Nineteenth Century Revolution in
Government: A Reappraisal, 'Historical Journal,' I (1958),
52-67.
MACDONAGH, OLIVER, 'A Pattern of Government Growth, 1800-
1860: The Passenger Acts and their Enforcement,' London,
1961.

MAITLAND, FREDERIC W., 'Equity: A Course of Lectures,'
(rev.) John Brunyate, Cambridge, 1936.
LYTE, SIR H.C.M., 'Historical Notes on the Use of the
Great Seal of England,' London, 1926.
MOORE, D.C., The Other Face of Reform, 'Victorian Studies,'
V (1961), 7-34.
NEW, CHESTER, 'Life of Henry Brougham to 1830,' Oxford,
1961.
OWEN, DAVID E., 'English Philanthropy, 1660-1960,'
Cambridge, Mass., 1964.
PARRIS, HENRY, The Nineteenth-Century Revolution in
Government: A Reappraisal Reappraised, 'Historical
Journal,' III (1960), 17-37.
PARRIS, HENRY, 'Constitutional Bureaucracy,' London, 1969.
PARSSINEN, T.M., Association, Convention and Anti-
Parliament in British Radical Politics, 1771-1848, 'Eng-
lish Historical Review,' LXXXVIII (1973), 504-33.
PAZ, D.G., Working-Class Education and the State, 1839-
1849: The Sources of Government Policy, 'Journal of
British Studies,' XVI (1976), 129-52.
PERKIN, HAROLD, 'The Origins of Modern English Society,
1780-1880,' London, 1969.
POCOCK, J.G.A., 'The Ancient Constitution and the Feudal
Law,' Cambridge, 1957.
POLLOCK, FREDERICK, and F.W. MAITLAND, 'History of English
Law before the Time of Edward I,' 2 vols, Cambridge, 1898.
PORTER, DALE H., 'The Abolition of the Slave Trade in
England, 1784-1807,' New Haven, 1970.
POYNTER, J.R., 'Society and Pauperism: English Ideas on
Poor Relief, 1795-1834,' London, 1969.
RICHARDSON, HENRY G., and GEORGE O. SAYLES, 'Law and Legis-
lation from Aethelberht to Magna Carta,' Edinburgh, 1966.
ROBERTS, DAVID, Jeremy Bentham and the Victorian Adminis-
trative State, 'Victorian Studies,' II (1959), 193-210.
ROBERTS, DAVID, Tory Paternalism and Social Reform in
Early Victorian England, 'American Historical Review,'
LXIII (1958), 323-37.
ROBERTS, DAVID, 'Victorian Origins of the British Welfare
State,' New Haven, 1960.
ROSEVEARE, HENRY, 'The Treasury: The Evolution of a
British Institution,' New York, 1969.
THOMAS, P.D.G., 'The House of Commons in the Eighteenth
Century,' Oxford, 1971.
THOMPSON, E.P., 'The Making of the English Working Class,'
New York, 1963.
TWISS, HORACE, 'The Public and Private Life of Lord
Chancellor Eldon,' 3 vols, London, 1844.
VEITCH, G.S., 'The Genesis of Parliamentary Reform,'
London, 1913.

WADDELL, D., Charles Davenant (1656-1714) - A Biographical
Sketch, 'Economic History Review,' XI (1958), 279-88.
WAGNER, ANTHONY R., 'Heralds and Heraldry in the Middle
Ages,' 2nd edn, London, 1956.
WATSON, J. STEVEN, 'The Reign of George III, 1760-1815,'
Oxford, 1960.
WEBB, SIDNEY and BEATRICE WEBB, 'English Local Government
from the Revolution to the Municipal Corporations Act,'
8 vols, London, 1906-29.
WEINER, JOEL H., 'The War of the Unstamped,' Ithaca, 1969.
WILLIAMS, ORLO, 'Lamb's Friend the Census-Taker: Life
and Letters of John Rickman,' London, 1911.
WRIGLEY, E.A. (ed.) 'Nineteenth Century Society: Essays
in the Use of Quantitative Methods for the Study of Social
Data,' Cambridge, 1972.
WOODWARD, E.L., 'The Age of Reform, 1815-1870,' 2nd edn,
Oxford, 1962.

Index

STUDIES IN SOCIAL HISTORY

Editor: **HAROLD PERKIN**

Professor of Social History, University of Lancaster

Assistant Editor: **ERIC J. EVANS**

Lecturer in History, University of Lancaster